Toward the Final Solution

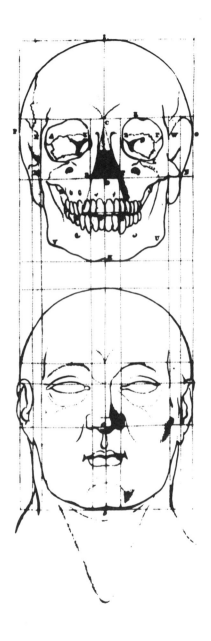

Toward the Final Solution

A HISTORY OF EUROPEAN RACISM

GEORGE L. MOSSE

THE UNIVERSITY OF WISCONSIN PRESS

The University of Wisconsin Press
114 North Murray Street
Madison, Wisconsin 53715

A hardcover edition of this book
is published by Howard Fertig, Inc.
It is here reprinted by arrangement.

10   9   8   7   6   5   4   3

Printed in the United States of America

Library of Congress Cataloging in Publication Data
Mosse, George L. (George Lachmann), 1918–
   Toward the final solution.
   Reprint. Originally published: New York:
H. Fertig, 1978.
   Includes index.
   1. Racism—Europe—History. 2. Antisemitism—Germany
—History. 3. Antisemitism—Austria—History. 4. Germany
—Ethnic relations. 5. Austria—Ethnic relations.
I. Title.
[HT1521.M63 1985]   305.8'094   84-40501
ISBN 0-299-10184-3 (pbk.)

Contents

Illustrations

Frontispiece. Skull and facial expression; the "average European"

Acknowledgments

The Jewish National and Hebrew University Library, Jerusalem, the Wiener Library, London, and the Bayrische Staatsbibliothek, Munich, provided most of the crucial primary and secondary material for this book. I am also grateful for help given by the Bibliothèque Nationale in Paris, The British Library in London and the University of Wisconsin Library. Peter Shellard provided the occasion for the writing of this work. Steven Uran assisted me in every aspect of this book and the editorial work of Ann Adelman and Howard Fertig helped give the text such clarity of expression as it might possess. Marilyn Baumgarten typed and retyped the book with exemplary patience. The dialogue with my students in the History of Racism course at the Hebrew University provided me with many new insights. To all these friends and colleagues I want to express my gratitude; they helped in making the writing of this book a gratifying experience, in spite of its tragic subject matter.

G.L.M.

Madison, 1977

Prologue: Affirmations and New Dimensions

". . . all ordered society puts the passions to sleep."
—Friedrich Nietzsche, *The Gay Science,*
Book 1, paragraph 4

THIS BOOK, first published in 1978, undertakes to trace the rise
of racism from its modern origins to Hitler's "final solution"
of the Jewish question. Racism as it developed in Western society was no mere articulation of prejudice, nor was it simply a metaphor for suppression; it was, rather, a fully blown system of thought,
an ideology like Conservatism, Liberalism, or Socialism, with its own
peculiar structure and mode of discourse. The Nazis' attempt to enforce the doctrines of racism collapsed with their loss of the Second
World War, and racism subsequently lost much of its power in Europe. It has had a somewhat longer life in the United States and in
other parts of the world where it had accompanied European imperialism, but even there it has declined in the decades following the
war and has become a political weapon to be used against one's enemies, rather than a powerful system of thought which could compete
with, and even triumph over, its rivals.

From the vantage point of today too little is said in this book about
imperial racism or about how racism spread to and became effective
in the United States. Yet because racism as a system of thought originated in and spread outward from Europe—whatever contribution
writers and thinkers in the United States or elsewhere made to the
theory, and in whatever manner the theory was adjusted to meet local
conditions—the understanding of European racism which this book
seeks to provide can be seen as applicable to other parts of the globe
as well.

Imperialism and racism, moreover, were never identical; their inter-relationship was dependent upon time and place. It was the particular European image of Africa or India at any given time which determined imperial attitudes and policies. During the eighteenth century, for example, Europeans could entertain enlightened and even utopian views of non-Europeans; the image of "darkest Africa," on the other hand, was a nineteenth-century invention, a symbol of geographical ignorance and supposed cultural superiority.[1] At first, the realization that different races existed did not lead to racism; instead the reaction might be curiosity about human types other than one's own or simply acceptance of them as a fact of nature — they were not necessarily reduced to stereotypes or regarded as lesser breeds. Nevertheless, as I hope to show, the fine line between the perception of the existence of racial differences and racism was only too easily bridged, as happened, for instance, when racism polluted the relationship between imperial masters and native populations.

In this book, however, as we move from the first to the second half of the nineteenth century, the focus narrows, to concentrate upon the Jews rather than upon blacks and colored peoples. We are examining the history of European racism, and while imperial racism was a part of this history, it was within Europe itself that racism was to achieve its goal and was able to express its true implications. The extermination, not of rebellious subjects or unruly elites, but of a whole people, represents the climax of racism — and no mistaken analogies to colonial wars or to colonial suppression must disguise this fact. The final solution of the Jewish question was no by-product of a mistaken policy; it was a program deliberately planned and efficiently executed, using the machinery of the modern state to devastating effect. The history of anti-Semitism, at first separate from the history of racism, which was concerned with blacks, comes to feed racist attitudes until racism and anti-Semitism can hardly be distinguished from each other. The history of racism in twentieth-century Europe cannot be written without taking full account of the development of anti-Semitism.

1. Philip D. Curtin, *The Image of Africa: British Ideas and Action, 1780–1850* (Madison, 1964), 9–10.

To find the origins of racism in the eighteenth century has filled many readers of this book with both wonder and consternation. The Enlightenment, after all, was supposed to have torn down the old superstitions which had denied men and women control over their lives. All men, regardless of religion, were endowed with critical minds—so the argument ran—while the universe, the destiny of man, and the ways in which men's lives were governed were no longer forbidden subjects, shrouded in mystery, but open to investigation and improvement. The self-cultivation of the human mind through the exercise of reason and the study of the classics was to create an efficient and beautiful society. The constant development of the mind's rational faculties would lead to a certain pragmatism and tolerance, and the study of the classics would refine aesthetic sensibilities.

The Enlightenment marked a crucial stage in the history of liberty, but to the history of racism, with which we are concerned, it made a different sort of contribution. For the Enlightenment believed in authority: not in the authority of Christianity or the authority conferred by tradition, but in the authority of the ancients and of the laws of nature, which were progressively revealed to the rational mind. These were authorities that left scope for the autonomy of man. But the emphasis upon rationality and clarity in the exploration of the laws of nature encouraged the classification of natural phenomena, including that relating to human beings. And the classics set a certain standard of human beauty which, as we shall see, lent itself to the creation of stereotypes. The Enlightenment tended to fit all human beings into the same mold—not only by its fondness for classification and its idealization of classical beauty, but also through its assumption that all of humankind shared its goals and that its moral order was part of the natural order and thus set for all time and place.

This was the underside of the Enlightenment that limited the "science of freedom."[2] The eighteenth century saw the development of new sciences, like anthropology or physiognomy (the study of the hu-

2. For the underside of the Enlightenment see Max Horkheimer and Theodor W. Adorno, *Dialektik der Aufklärung* (Amsterdam, 1974). For a positive appraisal of the Enlightenment see Peter Gay, *The Enlightenment: An Interpretation*, 2 vols. (New York, 1966 and 1969).

man face), concerned with classifying human beings, and the establishment of a stereotype of human beauty fashioned after classical
models as the measure of all human worth. In the conduct of life,
there was to be orderliness, as well; men were to control their sensual
natures through intellect. The moral order was reflected in the aesthetic
values which men had been taught to embrace: harmony and moderation, grace and quiet strength, as exemplified in the Venus and
Apollo of Greek sculpture. The contemplation of beauty, Friedrich
Schiller wrote in 1795, forms the bridge between the commands of
the law and human needs.[3] The result of such an aesthetic definition
of the moral order was a visual message, not theory hidden in weighty
books which most people could not read, but ideas and ideals which
could be readily apprehended, and were therefore attuned to the coming age of the masses. Men and women could see the beautiful and
the ugly stereotype, just as they could see the national flag or national monuments.

Racism was a visual ideology based upon stereotypes. That was
one of its main strengths. Racism classified men and women: this gave
it clarity and simplicity essential to success. But in addition racism,
as an emotion-laden ideology, took advantage of the reaction that
set in against the Enlightenment. Many factors came together in the
making of modern racism: the underside of the Enlightenment was
a crucial one and so were those movements like romanticism and modern nationalism which had their proper beginning in the age of the
French Revolution. Of course, bits and pieces of racism can be found
throughout the sixteenth and seventeenth centuries, though Christian belief that the unbaptized were living in a state of sin stopped
short of racism. To be sure, Jews were locked into ghettos as witnesses
to the fate of those who rejected Christ and the Church, but baptism, even enforced baptism, was supposed to end their Jewishness
and with it their vulnerability to persecution and discrimination. Thus,
for example, the Frankfurt schoolmaster Johann Jacob Schudt, writing in 1714, asserted that through conversion to Christianity Jews lost

---

3. Friedrich Schiller, *Über die ästhetische Erziehung des Menschen* (Stuttgart, 1965),
62, 61.

their peculiar odor, which had been imposed upon them as God's punishment.[4] Racism needed a secular base such as the Enlightenment or modern nationalism in order to overcome the implications of the Christian meaning of baptism and conversion, for the racially inferior must be locked into place and all escape routes closed. Eventually, as we shall see, Christianity came to be infected with racism, but this was Christianity on the defensive against an advancing secular age. While it is always possible to find certain continuities between a faraway past and the present, ideas dating from recent times often have more effect on men's minds. The actual perceptions of men and women, their attitudes toward life, must be taken into account in assessing the impact of any system of thought. A distant and largely unknown past will play a lesser role than the more immediate present or the influence of mythical ancestors who refine history through the collective imagination. The ideology of racism almost never refers itself back to any actual ancestors it might have had (for example, the persecution and expulsion of the Jews from medieval Spain), but instead transforms a mythological national past into a hypothetical past in order to appeal to those men and women displaced or frightened by modernity.

Racism presumed a social cohesion which nationalism or bourgeois society could provide, and it singled out those who were rejected by society as inherently different or dangerous. We shall look in some detail at how racism took advantage of nationalism as an immutable force in a chaotic world, but we shall also see how racism rushed to the support of respectability—those manners and morals which were thought to symbolize the cohesion and define the status of bourgeois society. Respectability both defined bourgeois society and protected the status quo in a society constantly endangered by the accelerating pace of social, economic, and cultural change. Respectability provided security through fixed social norms. However diverse it may have been in composition—from small merchants to the higher rungs of the civil service—the middle class used respectability as a weapon against the

---

4. Johann Jacob Schudt, *Jüdische Merkwürdigkeiten . . .* , I (Frankfurt-am-Main, 1715), 344.

so-called loose life of the aristocracy and the lower classes.[5] By the
end of the nineteenth century at the latest, however, respectability as
a way of life had spread throughout society: a state to which almost
everyone aspired.

The results of the alliance between racism and respectability are
analyzed fully in the body of the book, but one aspect of this alliance
—the association between racism and sexuality—deserves more extensive discussion than I was able to give it when the book was written. From the very beginning of racism in the eighteenth century, when
anthropologists accused blacks of inability to control their sexual
drives, to Adolf Hitler's description in *Mein Kampf* of Jewish boys
lurking at street corners, directing a flourishing traffic in prostitution
and white slavery, that association was immediate and direct. Racism
came to the aid of society's norms of behavior through attempting
to legitimize the distinction between normality and abnormality.

The stereotype of the outsider filled with lust was a staple of racism, part of the inversion of accepted values said to characterize black
or Jew who, at one and the same time, threatened society and by their
very existence confirmed its standards. To Jews and blacks, the prime
victims of racism, were joined others whose abnormal behavior put
them beyond the limits set by society. The insane, homosexuals, and
habitual criminals were seen as sharing the stigma of being unable
to control their passions, which ranged from sexual lust to murderous anger. All those who did not fit into the respectable patterns of
bourgeois society were lumped together, the "accursed race," as Marcel Proust called Jews and homosexuals.[6] The mental and physical
characteristics attributed to these outsiders reflected the fears of
society: restlessness, lust, and sloth, symbolized by a melancholy
"moveable physiognomy."[7] In the iconography of these nineteenth-
century stereotypes—whether of Jews, the insane, or other outcasts—

5. Isabel V. Hull, "The Bourgeoisie and Its Discontents: Reflections on 'Nationalism and Respectability'," *Journal of Contemporary History,* XVII (April 1982), 249;
see also George L. Mosse, *Nationalism and Sexuality: Respectability and Abnormal
Sexuality in Modern Europe* (New York, 1985).
6. Jean Recanati, *Profils Juifs de Marcel Proust* (Paris, 1979), 141.
7. Sander L. Gilman, *Seeing the Insane* (New York, 1982), 82.

exhaustion played a large part, as opposed to youthful vigor, which an expanding society needed and praised so highly. Jews and so-called sexual perverts were often pictured as fragile, close to death, the victims of premature old age. Jews on the nineteenth-century German stage or in Balzac's novels were almost always old men, and the philosopher Schopenhauer asserted that homosexuality was a function of old age—nature's way of preventing the old from conceiving children.[8] Oscar Wilde got it dead right when he satirized society's perception of the outsider: "Wicked people are always old and ugly."[9]

Self-control and public order were needed to counter private passions and public turmoil which would destroy the social fabric. The relationship between the sexes was determined by certain imperatives: the normal had to be clearly distinguished from the abnormal, and the roles assigned to every member of society, men and women, children and servants, must be clear and distinct. Society was based upon a sexual as well as a social and economic division of labor. This accepted order of things was clearly upset by the existence of homosexuals. And the accusation was made against Jews, in one of the most influential racist books, Otto Weininger's *Sex and Character* (1903), which we shall analyze later in greater detail,[10] that whatever their actual sexual practices, they possessed female rather than male characteristics. Racism supported this sexual division of labor as part of its commitment to support respectability. Toward the end of the nineteenth century racists proclaimed as an article of faith that ". . . the more feminine women are, and the more masculine men, the more intimate family life, the healthier society and the state."[11] Subsequently Hitler himself was to regard the division of labor between the sexes as a racial imperative: "It is one of the miracles of nature and providence," he told German women, "that a conflict be-

8. Alexandre Raviv, *Le Problème Juif aux Miroir du Roman Français l'Entre Deux Guerres* (Strassburg, 1968), 4; A. Schopenhauer, *Die Welt als Wille und Vorstellung, Sämtliche Werke,* ed. Arthur Hübscher, II (Wiesbaden, 1949), 648.

9. Quoted in Jeffrey Myers, *Homosexuality and Literature* (London, 1977), 24.
10. See pages 108–111.
11. C. Wilmans, *Die "Goldene Internationale" und die Notwendigkeit einer socialen Reformpartei* (Berlin, 1876), 195.

tween the sexes . . . is impossible as long as each fulfills the task set it by nature."[12]

Manliness stood for normality. Those who deviated from the norm were potential or actual outsiders who must be readily recognized and tightly controlled. Medical theory of the nineteenth century in dealing with human sexuality made an all-important contribution to what was considered normal and to the stereotyping of the outsider. Masturbation was considered the foundation of most vice, leading to a hideous deformation of the body and the exhaustion of the nerves. Moreover, it was a "secret vice" and therefore anti-social: a potential menace to state and society. Masturbation led to homosexuality, as the conventional medical wisdom had it: insanity and death were its consequence. Forensic medicine elaborated the homosexual stereotype in order to provide guidance to the courts which enforced the laws against sodomy. Thus Ambroise Tardieu at mid-century described the diseased and exhausted bodies of homosexuals, which gave them away. Even earlier, in Germany, at the end of the eighteenth century, Johann Valentin Müller had begun this medical tradition by describing for courts of law the so-called telltale traits of sexual perverts: reddened eyes, feebleness, fits of depression, and neglect of personal appearance.[13] Albert Moll, another famed physician, added for good measure that insanity was widespread among parents and kin of homosexuals.[14] The fear of modernity pervades such medical theories. At the start of the twentieth century Iwan Bloch, a celebrated sexologist, wrote that the "vibrations of modernity" led to homosexuality, while, as we shall see, anti-Semites and racists like Édouard Drumont claimed that Jews, exemplifying the rootlessness of modernity, were nervous people with a high rate of mental illness.[15]

That homosexuals could contaminate normal men was widely believed, sanctioned by a body of medical literature. Johann Valentin Müller was not alone in viewing the "disease" of unconventional sex-

12. Martin Klaus, *Mädchen in der Hitlerjugend* (Cologne, 1980), 169.
13. For a detailed account see Mosse, *op. cit.,* Chapter II.
14. Albert Moll, *Ärtzliche Ethik* (Stuttgart, 1902), 46.
15. Iwan Bloch, *Die Perversen* (Berlin, n.d.), 28; Édouard Drumont, *La France Juive,* I (Paris, 1944), 107.

uality as dangerous to the health of the state.[16] Medical theory gave scientific sanction to a subjective stereotype—a gift which racism would gratefully accept. Health was to be associated with the superior race which could control its sexual passions and which prized so-called manly behavior, while inferior races were considered sick and infectious.

Racism never closed the circle of vice around the Jews by adding homosexuality to the other immoral actions attributed to them, because Jewish family life was widely admired as an example of respectability. Even anti-Semites and racists had to acknowledge that Jewish life was centered upon the family, while at the same time they attacked Jews for undermining Gentile morality.[17] It was through evil but heterosexual drives that Jews were supposed to be a danger to society. To the accusation that Jews seduced blonde Christian girls was added the charge, popular from the end of the nineteenth century onward, that they trafficked in them as well. The accusation of white slavery fitted in well with conspiracy theories about the Jews. For racists it introduced a sexual version of the old blood libel or ritual murder calumny,[18] but in addition it provided an opportunity to accuse Jews of encouraging sexual excess and unrestrained passion. And eventually, the racist distinction made between the German and the Jewish bourgeoisie would solve the problem inherent in the assumption that the Jews whose own family life was intact were the enemies of the Aryan family, and would expel the Jewish family from respectable society.

The sexual dimension of racism was closely linked to both forensic medicine and the new medical specialty of sexology which got its start at the turn of the nineteenth and twentieth centuries. Medical theory devised generalizations about Jews as well as homosex-

16. Johann Valentin Müller, *Entwurf einer gerichtlichen Arzneiwissenschaft* (Frankfurt-am-Main, 1796), reprinted in *Der unterdrückte Sexus,* ed. Joachim S. Hohmann (Lollar, 1977), 136, 139.

17. See *Vorurteile gegen Minderheiten, die Anfänge des modernen Antisemitismus in Deutschland,* ed. Hans-Gert Oomen (Stuttgart, 1978), 62.

18. Edward J. Bristow, *Prostitution and Prejudice: The Jewish Fight against White Slavery 1870–1939* (Oxford, 1982), 4.

uals. Jean-Martin Charcot, the famed Paris psychiatrist and expert on hysteria, wrote in the 1880's that Jews showed a tendency toward insanity, neurasthenia, and nervousness. They were susceptible to such illnesses because of the inherent weakness of their nervous systems. The most famous sexologist of the time, Richard von Krafft-Ebing, attributed this loss of nerve to Jewish inbreeding. Such Jewish diseases, he tells us, lead to religious fanaticism and intensified sensuousness. Charcot and Krafft-Ebing thought that these weaknesses were tendencies which could be cured, while racists proclaimed that they were congenital, an integral part of the Jewish race.[19]

Racism sought to perpetuate medical notions which were based on prejudice rather than science, at a time when these were slowly changing. Sigmund Freud, for example, believed that the prevailing sexual morality made harsh demands upon men and women, and he sought to relax sexual restraints within the limits of the acceptable. Although Freud himself still believed in the evil consequences of masturbation and saw homosexuality as the result of inability to overcome childhood traumas, other medical men were abandoning such theories and moving toward a greater acceptance of deviant sexuality as congenital and therefore natural. But any relaxation of conventional morality was opposed by many men and women, and was apt to be branded as a Jewish conspiracy to undermine Gentile morality.

Racism, emphasizing the image of the outsider as unnatural and sick, made the most of the distinction between normality and abnormality. Racists were never tired of proclaiming that only the healthy and normal could be beautiful and could live in harmony with nature. An energetic and vigorous homosexual was unthinkable, and a beautiful Jew was regarded as a contradiction in terms (though the

19. Sander L. Gilman, "Jews and Mental Illness: Medical Metaphors, Anti-Semitism, and the Jewish Response," *Journal of the History of the Behavioral Sciences*, XX (April 1984), 153. These physicians also believed that women suffered fits of hysteria because their nervous systems were weaker than those of men. Hysteria was attributed not only to so-called sexual deviants, women, and the insane, but also to one's political enemies. Thus in France the clerical world was thought by its enemies prone to hysteria, in contrast to the representatives of rational and humane medical science. Jan Goldstein, "The Hysteria Diagnosis and the Politics of Anticlericalism in Late Nineteenth Century France," *The Journal of Modern History*, LIV (June 1982), 237–239.

beautiful Jewess continued to haunt the imagination).[20] The home of the outsider was the big city, which by the end of the nineteenth century had become a metaphor for the unnatural. Homosexuals practiced their vice there, and Jews were said to exercise control over prostitution and white slavery. Balzac had already written about the physical and moral degeneration which takes place in the rush and bustle of the city, where nothing is permanent and everything provisional. Parisians looked like living corpses, "people dreadful to behold";[21] and what Balzac the writer conjured up in his imagination physicians incorporated as part of the science of medicine.

Throughout the nineteenth century the healing power of nature was invoked against the degeneracy of the big city. Symbolizing the genuine and the immutable, nature served to reenforce human control over a world forever on the brink of chaos. Nationalism, racism, indeed all of society, sought to invoke closeness to nature: men and women felt a need to annex to themselves a piece of eternity in order to keep their bearings. Proust tells the story of how he thought a friend cured of his homosexuality after he spent a day riding, and then climbed a mountain and slept in the snow.[22] Here the healing power of nature had routed nervousness, while youthful energy had overcome exhaustion. Jews were generally accused of having no feeling for nature, and the portrayal of a Jew climbing a mountain or riding a horse is rare in European literature. Nature knows no vice, and in this context sexologists discussed among themselves whether or not homosexual animals existed.[23]

As the ideals of normality and abnormality were incorporated into the Nazi faith, along with the strengthening of racism the assault on

20. At Auschwitz Dr. Mengele carried out examinations on young Jews who seemed to meet society's standards of human beauty in order to find the physical blemish which racism said must exist. Miklos Nyiszli, *Auschwitz, a Doctor's Eyewitness Account* (New York, 1960), 175.
21. Honoré de Balzac, "Scènes de la Vie Parisienne," *La Comédie Humaine, Oeuvres Complètes de M. de Balsac,* IX (Paris, 1843), 236.
22. Marcel Proust, *A la Recherche du Temps Perdu,* vol. IV, *Sodome et Gomorrhe,* I (Paris, 1921), 276.
23. See the bibliography concerning homosexuality and animals in *Jahrbuch für Sexuelle Zwischenstufem,* II (1900), 126–155.

the sexually deviant as social outcasts was continued and reenforced. "He who is different," as the chief editorial writer of Heinrich Himmler's *Das Schwarze Corps* put it, "is unable to recognize the laws of nature."[24] In addition to the reaction to the social, economic, and political consequences of the First World War, which will loom large in these pages, there was also a reaction to the kind of life represented by Weimar Berlin, with its modern art, its avant-garde literary scene, its homosexual and lesbian bars. Clean-cut young men and modest, self-effacing young women seemed at a premium and, more often than not, so it seemed (however mistakenly), were to be found in the ranks of the political right. National Socialism, Hitler maintained, had put an end to Jewish cultural predominance by saving art from its embrace by homosexuals and "manly women"—here Hitler was lumping together the traditional outsiders: Jews, homosexuals, and women who overstepped the division established between the sexes. German art as the symbol of the German soul, he continued, was no longer to be a transitory experience, catering to the lower passions of man, but a reflection of the immutable natural and divine order.[25]

For those who were excluded from that order there was to be no accommodation in society. Heinrich Himmler, who believed that the German Reich contained some 2 million homosexuals infecting the nation, advocated the death penalty for homosexual acts. Here he used the fateful words "to snuff out life as if it had never existed." Himmler's ideal remedy was the drowning of homosexuals in swamps: the victim sinks of his own weight, and no human hand helps him die as nature rectifies her own mistake.[26] Symbol and reality coincide.

Yet not all homosexuals were lost, for most of them belonged to the Aryan race. When homosexuals were rounded up and delivered to concentration camps, they were made to lie with women, and if they reacted heterosexually, they were set free. Sexual deviance was considered a disease which could be cured, not only through such

24. *Auf Hieb und Stich. Stimmen zur Zeit am Wege einer Deutschen Zeitung,* ed. Günther D'Alquen (Berlin and Munich, 1937), 262.
25. Klaus, *op. cit.,* 169.
26. Heinz Heger, *Die Männer mit dem Rosa Winkel* (Hamburg, n.d.), 137. For Himmler's attitude toward homosexuality, see Mosse, *op. cit.,* Chapter VIII.

forced sexuality but also through social discipline and hard work. Here we see the effect of an ideal deeply rooted in society, which we will find again demonstrated in the questionnaire sent to insane asylums during the Nazi genocide, asking whether an inmate was able to work; if he was, he was fit for survival.[27] In his attitudes Himmler was repeating notions which had been a part of the medically propounded stereotype of the outsider.

While perhaps as many as 10,000 to 20,000 homosexuals may have died in the camps,[28] the extermination of them could never be pursued systematically because no reliable lists of homosexuals existed—they were denounced or seized according to subscription lists of suspect journals. Moreover, in practice even Himmler's SS did not rigorously enforce the death penalty for homosexuals within its own ranks, but often preferred to give these supposedly perverted comrades the benefit of the doubt. The Jews—the inferior race—were, of course, systematically killed, a process which is analyzed in this book as the climax of European racism. Since the book was first published it has been argued by some historians that no single comprehensive decision to kill the Jews was made, but that as the war shut off Jewish emigration from Germany and Europe, and the military situation made resettlement all but impossible, the wholesale destruction program developed out of a series of separate killing actions in 1941 and early 1942.[29] Yet the evidence that Hitler ordered the mass extermination of the Jews in the late spring or summer of 1941 is overwhelming, and so are the signs that this was his intention from the beginning —even if he could have driven the Jews out of Europe without resorting to mass murder, he would eventually have sought them out in order

27. See page 217.
28. There is a discussion of such figures, and an analysis of the number of homosexuals put in camps, in Ruediger Lautmann and Erhard Vismar, *Pink Triangle: The Social History of Anti-Homosexual Persecution in Nazi Germany*, a work which it is hoped will soon be published in the United States.
29. For one of the best discussions of this controversy and the evidence of Hitler's intentions, see Christopher R. Browning, "A Reply to Martin Broszat Regarding the Origins of the Final Solution," *Simon Wiesenthal Center Annual*, I (1984), 113–132; see also Shlomo Aronson, "Hitlers Judenpolitik, die Alliierten und die Juden," *Vierteljahrshefte für Zeitgeschichte*, XXXII (January 1984), 29–64.

to solve the Jewish question once and for all. Jews could not escape their fate through demonstrating the proper sexual attitudes or by devotion to so-called honest labor. The persecution of Jews always took precedence over that of homosexuals. In occupied Holland, for example, the local Dutch police were in charge of rounding up homosexuals, but the deportation of Jews was organized by the German SS. The attack on homosexuals was incidental there,[30] while Nazi anti-Jewish policy was pursued with all the energy the SS could muster, even against the resistance of local Dutch authorities.

Though homosexuals were not seen as a race, and though many of them were in fact Aryan, the attempt to destroy them is significant; it provides a new dimension to racism in power. Racism supported respectability as basic to society's existence: homosexuals were seen as contaminating and corrupting the Aryan race and, like the Jews, endangering its survival. The Jews, as we have seen, were also accused of employing abnormal sexual drives as one stratagem in the war between races, and it mattered little in the end whether heterosexuality or homosexuality was to be the weapon used to win the battle. The sexual dimension of racism contributed to the growth of stereotypes discussed in the second chapter of this book, and in addition to language and history, analyzed in the third chapter below, was another factor in widening the gap between peoples and races. It became part of the science of race through the medical profile of the outsider, and part of the mystery of race through society's irrational fears of sexual excess. Racism claimed a monopoly over those virtues society held dear and condemned as degenerate everything that ran counter to its standards. Sexuality played its part in those fantasies which made up the world of racism.

Jews and blacks were the principal outsiders who threatened the cohesion of society, the chief enemy who menaced the tribe, as we shall have ample occasion to discuss in the book, but beside them stood all those who differed from the accepted norms of society. It was the goal of the Nazis to rid society of all those who would en-

30. Peter Koenders, *Homoseksualiteit in Bezet Nederland* (The Hague, 1983), 109, 129.

danger its ideal of respectability and of others who did not fit in with the image it had of itself: youthful and virile, hard working, and healthy in body and mind. Thus the aged, the feeble, and the insane were sytematically killed through the process of euthanasia—a dress rehearsal for the final solution of the Jewish question, but also in its own way an effort to eliminate adults and children thought to drain the strength and destroy the material well-being of the race.[31] Whoever had forfeited his right to a place as an Aryan was to be killed; and the Jews—the arch-enemy—were to be first driven out of Germany and then slaughtered wherever they could be found. How racism prepared the way for the murderous practices of National Socialism this book seeks to tell.

31. See pages 216–220; and see also Eugen Kogon, Hermann Langbein, Adalbert Rückerl, et al., eds., *Nationalsozialistische Massentötung durch Giftgas* (Frankfurt-am-Main, 1984); Ernst Klee, *Euthanasie im NS-Staat* (Frankfurt-am-Main, 1984).

Introduction: The Meaning of Race

ANY BOOK concerned with the European experience of race
must start with the end and not with the beginning: 6 million Jews killed by the heirs of European civilization, by a
bureaucracy which took time out from efficiently running the state
to exterminate the Jews equally efficiently and impersonally. How
could this come to pass? The history of racism is basic to answering
this question, which seems closer to the center than to the fringes of
twentieth-century European history. It was the Nazis who perpetrated the deed, but men and women everywhere believed in the
distinction between races, whether white, yellow, or black, Aryan
or Jew. To some degree Englishmen, Frenchmen, Poles, as well as
Germans or Hungarians, used the word "race" in their daily lives
without thinking. This is so today as well, in spite of the holocaust,
although blacks rather than Jews are at this moment at the bottom
of the racial scale. Historically, Jews and blacks have always played
the outsider, the villain who threatens the tribe. Who knows but
that 6 million Jews might not have been joined by as many blacks
had these lived in the midst of the peoples of Europe. But Jews were
the prime victims of the European experience of race, and they were
to be exterminated root and branch. This was not true in theory or
practice for any of the other victims of European racism, neither for
the blacks nor for the gypsies, some of whom escaped as Aryans.

How was it possible for a country to attempt the deliberate extermination of a whole people? The history of racism provides sev-

eral clues. Racism annexed every important idea and movement in the nineteenth and twentieth centuries and promised to protect each against all adversaries. Scientific accomplishment, a Puritan attitude toward life—the triumphant middle-class morality, Christian religion, the ideal of beauty as symbolic of a better and healthier world were all integral facets of racism. Racism defended utopia against its enemies. Such noble ideals as freedom, equality, and tolerance would become reality only if the race were preserved and its enemies defeated. Racism promised all manner of blessings to diverse groups of men, and the mystique of nationalism, though most important, did not provide its sole appeal. Throughout our discussion, the very broadness of racist claims will engage our attention, together with its penetration into all regions and classes.

Racism in its various forms did not always follow the same inspirations or lead to the same results. There was a difference between the racism which rejected all scientific fact on behalf of a spiritual impulse, and that racism which attempted to pay some regard to scientific observation and to the influence of the environment. Even the Nazis eventually realized that racist ideas lacked a certain clarity. Race could, for example, be defined as chance variations manipulated through the environment, or as an organic substance that determined man's outward appearance and his soul, or as due to hereditary factors that could be improved. Moreover, some Europeans who believed in race classified Jews as whites or even Aryans, even if for the most part they were considered the enemy. A few defended blacks as not necessarily inferior, although the overwhelming number of racists put them lowest among men or held that they were hardly human at all.

In the midst of this diversity there were, nonetheless, vital areas of agreement. All racists held to a certain concept of beauty—white and classical—to middle-class virtues of work, of moderation and honor, and thought that these were exemplified through outward appearance. Most racists consequently endowed inferior races whether black or Jew with several identical properties such as lack of beauty, and charged them with the lack of those middle-class virtues, and finally with lack of any metaphysical depth. Here there was a good deal of clarity. Racism did not merely annex all movements and tastes of the age; despite differing conclusions, it also objectified them through strong and unambiguous symbols. Stereotypes provided both the essence of racism and the appeal of the movement. Racism gave everyone a designated place in the world, defining him as a person and, through a clear distinction between "good" and "evil" races, explaining the puzzling modern world in which he lived. Who could ask for more?

Yet the world of racist ideas initially bore no relationship to the existing world. Racism substituted myth for reality; and the world that it created, with its stereotypes, virtues, and vices, was a fairy-tale world, which dangled a utopia before the eyes of those who longed for a way out of the confusion of modernity and the rush of time. It made the sun stand still and it abolished change. All evil was blamed upon the restless inferior races, who lacked appreciation of a settled order of things. But on their own, none of these promises would have given racism its awesome success. People become disillusioned with a fairy tale whose happy end seems never to arrive, and with a mirage that must be chased endlessly; they turn to other promises and rival faiths. Traditional religion can satisfy human longings by promising a heaven after death. Racism, being a pseudo-religion, has to deliver its promises here and now. Surprisingly, racism did so even before it became the policy of a government, and that was its unrivaled strength. Racism transcended the ordinary utopia by turning myth into reality.

The world racism created was realized because racism willed it so, despite the fact that it lacked any basis in historical, social, or political reality. Such realities initially explain the world to us in retrospect. Racism reacted against social, economic, and political conditions, and refused to use these categories to explain the world. As its central explanation for the present and as its hope for the future, racism created myths which it subsequently attempted to bring into existence. Myth as reality is best explained by an extreme example. The Nazis created a department in their interior ministry concerned with unraveling the supposed Jewish world conspiracy. The bureaucracy acted as if such a conspiracy really existed, and so made it come true as a foundation of national policy. The myth had been turned into reality. But examples do not have to be so spectacular. As men began to be regarded as racial stereotypes, they themselves began to perceive themselves in this way. Bruno Bettelheim in his book *The Informed Heart* (1960), recalling his experience as a prisoner in the Dachau and Buchenwald camps, may have exaggerated the Nazi success in turning Jews in the concentration camps into the kind of stereotypes they thought them to be. But it is nonetheless true that Jews themselves, as we shall see, long before this had come to accept their unflattering stereotype and attempted to run away from it. Blacks experienced a similar trauma. Myth accepted as reality became the reality.

This horrifying fact is basic to all racism, regardless of its variations. The myth it put forward proved so blinding because it was based partly on legitimate anthropology and partly upon the obvious differences between the majority of Europeans and the Jewish and black minorities. Blacks did have a different color of skin and a different culture; and while Jews had the same skin color, they at first did have a different language, dress, and appearance. Culture clashes were essential to the success of racial myths, for throughout history the foreigner outside the tribe has never been truly welcome. Stereotyping and ideas generally about superior and inferior races tend to precede racism as official policy, whether at home or abroad. The concepts basic to racial theory come first—and with them the hostile attitudes, whether toward black or white. No one is born a "Sambo" or "Fagin," or for that matter a "clean-cut Englishman" or "Aryan German." The very depth of racism today, if only through the use of words and images which serve to perpetuate the world racism originally created, is additional proof that the myth has turned into reality.

This was no fairy tale ending in the triumph of virtue, but an orgy of blood that ended with the unmarked graves of more martyrs than Europe had ever known before. The story of racism is not pleasant to tell, and that is perhaps why it has been told so rarely in the fullness it deserves: not as the history of an aberration of European thought or as scattered moments of madness, but as an integral part of the European experience. It is a fact that most of our textbooks pay scarce attention to this phenomenon so central to modern times—perhaps because it is too painful for historians to concede that here myth became reality in the face of those supposedly provable facts which are still the staple of the historical profession. The holocaust, after all, gets short shrift even in respectable accounts of Nazi rule. Perhaps this book, incomplete as it is, can help to set the record straight. It will adhere to historical analysis and will not insert considerations of morality and justice that stand outside the preoccupations of history. In this case to understand is not to pardon. Indeed, it is simply a step toward contemplating evil which, neither unique nor banal, demonstrates how the longing of man for a happy and healthy world can be turned to an end never contemplated at the beginning, but nonetheless inherent within the particular myth. Writing this book has been like walking on a faulty rope bridge over an abyss; but perhaps the history which fills these pages will help to ensure that the bridge does not break once again. Millions have already fallen into the abyss that racism opened up before mankind some forty years ago. It would have been a source of great satisfaction if the end of racism in Europe could now be pronounced. But that is not possible, which is why we shall have a conclusion that does not conclude.

It is difficult to decide where in time to begin the history of racism. The term has been used ever since the Renaissance to denote a wide variety of meanings, including family traits and the characteristics of nations and animals. Furthermore, it was used to describe groups not necessarily based upon the principle of heredity. Certainly in sixteenth-century Spain racism existed in its modern sense, for there the concept of "purity of blood" was the justification for discrimination against anyone of Jewish ancestry. It could be argued that the Spanish *conversos* were the first victims of racial persecution in Europe. Yet the Spanish policy toward "Jewish Christians" faded with time and did not constitute a viable precedent for the rest of Europe.

European racism was grounded in those intellectual currents which made their mark in the eighteenth century in both western

and central Europe, namely, the new sciences of the Enlightenment
and the Pietistic revival of Christianity. Racism was not really a
product of one particular national or Christian development, but
a world view which represented a synthesis of the old and the
new—a secular religion attempting to annex all that mankind desired. Thus, the history of European racism must be seen as
originating in the eighteenth century, whatever antecedent elements
might be discovered in earlier times. It was in the eighteenth century
that the structure of racial thought was consolidated and determined for the next one and three-quarter centuries.

PART I

The Beginning

CHAPTER ONE

Eighteenth-Century Foundations

EIGHTEENTH-CENTURY Europe was the cradle of modern racism. The major cultural trends of that century vitally affected the foundations of racist thought. This was the age of Enlightenment, during which an intellectual élite attempted to substitute an emphasis upon man's inherent reason and virtue for the "ancient superstitions of the past." The Enlightenment was a revolution in aesthetic and intellectual tastes and conventions, but it found a specific focus in the revolt against Christianity. Christianity was regarded as synonymous with "ancient superstitions," and Voltaire's cry, "Écrasons l'infâme," was echoed by many other writers. The "enlightened" turned to the classics for inspiration and support in their revolt. But while they sharpened their critical minds on Greek and Roman models, Christianity proved to be alive and well for the mass of the population.

The eighteenth century was also a time of religious fervor and revival. Pietism on the continent of Europe and evangelism in England spanned the eighteenth century, running parallel to the Enlightenment. These movements stressed the need for an emotional Christian commitment, and displayed the yearning for true community in the notion of fellowship and a "religion of the heart." The tension between the Enlightenment and this underlying Christianity characterized much of the century during which modern racism was born and nurtured. European racism was fed by both trends, despite their conflict. The Enlightenment and the Pietistic and moralistic atmosphere would impress their stamp equally on racist thought.

The Enlightenment was also characterized by a radical attempt to define man's place in nature. Nature and the classics were thought vital for a new understanding of man's position in God's universe and were therefore taken as setting new standards of virtue and beauty. Thus from the outset of this sweeping inquiry into the nature of man and the universe, natural science and the moral and aesthetic ideals of the ancients joined hands. Indeed, these two crucial components were so bound together that it is impossible to separate the inquiries of the Enlightenment *philosophes* into nature from their examination of morality and human character.[1]

Science and aesthetics influenced one another reciprocally. In large measure, the scientific endeavor was directed toward a classification of the human races according to their place in nature and the effect of the environment. The beginning of the new science of anthropology during the second half of the century was based upon the attempt to determine man's exact place in nature through observation, measurements, and comparisons between groups of men and animals. Moreover, the quest for unity and harmony in the affairs of man and the cosmos led to belief in the unity of body and mind. This, in turn, was supposed to express itself in a tangible, physical way, which could be measured and observed. Both phrenology (reading the skull) and physiognomy (reading the face) had their origins in the last decade of the century.

But these observations, measurements, and comparisons that were basic to the new eighteenth-century sciences were combined with value judgments following aesthetic criteria derived from ancient Greece. The Enlightenment passion for the new sciences and the reliance upon the classics as authority were fused in this manner. Whatever the physical measurements or comparisons made, in the last resort the resemblance to ancient beauty and proportions determined the value of man. This continuous transition from science to aesthetics is a cardinal feature of modern racism. Human nature came to be defined in aesthetic terms, with significant stress on the outward physical signs of inner rationality and harmony.

Scientific classification was based upon the subjective ideals of the Enlightenment.

As it grew up, racism would also make contact with evangelism and pietism, which combined to form the second fundamental trend of the century. Here the need for an authentic and significant experience of God found an outlet in a Christianity marked by the call to give oneself to Christ. This was also bound up with the ideal of living a Christian life of love for one's neighbor as part of a renewed sense of community. Through printed tracts and preaching, an emotive atmosphere was created, very different from the rationalist Enlightenment of the intellectuals. From our point of view, this meant an emphasis upon the instincts, upon intuition, and upon the emotional life of the "inner man" which would eventually lead to racial judgments about man's soul. A longing for coherence, for community, and for an ideal in the face of a changing world was always to the forefront.

In short, racism had its foundations both in the Enlightenment and in the religious revival of the eighteenth century. It was a product of the preoccupation with a rational universe, nature, and aesthetics, as well as with the emphasis upon the eternal force of religious emotion and man's soul. It was part, too, of the drive to define man's place in nature and of the hope for an ordered, healthy, and happy world. Eventually, the racist outlook fused man's outward appearance with his place in nature and the proper functioning of his soul. Thus, religious emotion became integrated in racism as part of the "racial soul." Nevertheless, at first the Enlightenment concept of God and of the unity of human nature played a dominant role in the emergence of racism. We must therefore undertake a deeper examination of the Enlightenment before returning to the Pietistic contributions.

For all the Enlightenment's opposition to Christianity, it could not do without a God who pulled man, morality, and the universe together into one grand design. This God was said to be innate in man and nature: a deity revealed only through the order of nature and the behavior of man. The health and rationality of the world had to be guaranteed by a higher being who stood apart from the bustle and anxiety of daily life. Such deism, as it is often called, encouraged a quest for the unity between man and nature, and indeed between man and all that determined his life. The longing for such unity existed because for many contemporaries man seemed in danger of being atomized.

For the enlightened, understanding God's universe meant that man was an integral part of nature, a link in the unbroken "great chain of being." Ever since ancient times the unity of man, nature, and God had been defined as a hierarchy which, like a chain, stretched from heaven down to earth. This arrangement of all creatures of heaven and earth, the angels, stars, men, and beasts, assumed a cosmic order that passed from the highest to the lowest creature. It was a universe which was complete, and in which it only remained for man to discover and understand the links in the chain. Moreover, as the famed zoologist and botanist Georges Louis Leclerc de Buffon repeatedly asserted at mid-century, such an image also implied that there was no gap in nature. Therefore, man's task was to understand the relation between creatures linked without break in the cosmic order. Echoing this theme, an English poet wrote at that same time:

> [God's] parent hand,
> From the mute shell-fish gasping on the shore,
> To men, to angels, to celestial minds,
> Forever leads the generations on
> To higher scenes of being . . .[2]

The powerful myth of the "chain of being" explains why scientists were so preoccupied in finding the "missing link" of creation that joined man to animals in an unbroken chain of life. Indeed, the highest animal, usually thought to be the ape, reached out during the eighteenth century to the lowest kind of man, usually thought to be the black. Thus the idea of the chain was retained even when the existence of angels was denied and when God was thought of as innate in man and nature. The "chain of being" now began and ended on earth, and God worked not at the top of the chain as during the Middle Ages, but rather within every link of it. The *philosophes* might attack Christianity, but for most of them God's providence still ruled, establishing order and harmony.

Clearly, the belief in a cosmic unity also led to an emphasis upon unity within man himself: the unity of body and mind. To be sure, for the enlightened this seemed at times to mean exaltation of the flesh, and of earthly pleasures and beauty.[3] Nevertheless, this quest for unity also led to the belief that the "inner man" could be read through his outward appearance—a conviction that was to prove fatal in encouraging racism. It encouraged the passage from science to aesthetics in the pseudo-sciences of physiognomy and phrenology.

The anxieties that produced the quest for unity and authority had a still broader foundation. The world of the Enlightenment was a world without illusions, where man's critical mind reflected the supposedly clear and rational laws of the universe. The personal God who acted in mysterious ways retreated behind the unchanging laws of reason, which men could discover and classify. Some *philosophes* equated mathematics and thought, while others contrasted the lies of poetry to the truths of science. Voltaire's skeptical remark that some were led to admit no other God than the immensity of things was converted into praise by Enlightenment materialists.[4] The result of such an approach to the universe was that man himself tended to be viewed as a mechanical being within an equally depersonalized universe. The *philosophes* did not intend it that way, for their emphasis upon the critical mind was supposed to create a dialogue between men.[5] Yet their world seemed too sober and alienating, leaving man dependent only upon himself within a preordained system of rational laws.

Abstract cosmic laws opposed the ancient myths of personal demons and of a God who spoke to men through the burning bush; deism seemed to reduce God's universe to a measurable mathematical formula. This view of man and the universe could not satisfy many men and women in a time of rapid change. The French Revolution shook the political structure of Europe, at the same time that social and economic change challenged hallowed traditions. The very pace of time seemed to speed up with the improvement of communications and the faster rhythm of life in an industrializing world. Toward the year 1790, Goethe remarked that men hurried about absentmindedly, and bemoaned the lack of time for concentrated thought.[6] Indeed, the theoretical world view of the Enlightenment was accompanied by pragmatic changes which seemed to set men adrift. Politics itself was assuming an ever more abstract character as government in some parts of Europe was no longer personified by a king or prince but through the concept of the "nation" or the "people," or, as during the Terror in France, by the "Goddess of Reason" or the "Supreme Being." As a result, many people felt an anxiety and loneliness which this increasingly impersonal world could not abate; they longed for the safe anchor of ancient traditions, of a personal faith, and a universe that spoke to them through its myths and symbols.

Myths describe the various breakthroughs of the sacred into this world: interventions of the supernatural sacred stories which provide models for human rites and indeed all human activity.[7] However, these models do not remain abstract, but are personalized through symbols, whether by commemorative rites recalling a sacred story, or pictures and edifices which represent a sacred past and in a tangible way project it into the present. Nature itself could become symbolic of the sacred stories it witnessed—as in the holy mountain or the sacred brook. Myth and symbol created a sentient living world, which was not abstract but objectified through a ritual that people could act out or familiar artifacts that they could see or touch.

The myths and symbols which made abstract ideas of God and man concrete owed their vitality not to the Enlightenment but to the world of ritual and emotions that characterized pietism and evangelism. This other major trend of the century also sought the unity of man and of the universe, but it did so by stressing the prime importance of man's emotions rather than his reason. These emotions were induced by Christian piety and were expressed in a tangible form through common song, prayer, and life within a community of like-minded people. Such a Christianity was especially relevant in the disunited German-speaking lands where the Enlightenment had become a symbol of French domination. Through the concept of community and the longing for unity, pietism became concerned with the fatherland. In 1774, for example, the leading Pietist, Justus Möser, exclaimed: "He who does not love the fatherland which he can see, how can he love the heavenly Jerusalem which he does not see?"[8] The very emotional drive of pietism produced a need for tangible symbols which might stabilize the turbulent spirit. Thus, the inner fatherland of Christ was projected outward onto the national community.

It was not enough for Pietists to proclaim that the fatherland lay within man: myths and symbols were needed to personalize it and thus to give it reality. Toward the end of the eighteenth century in most of Europe such symbols as the flag, the holy flame, and the national hymn emerged to exemplify new nations. These national symbols were accompanied by an urge to personalize the world within a Romantic universe opposed to the arid system building of the Enlightenment. Nature was thought to symbolize the emotions of man; plants and animals exemplified various legends and myths. Thus a world of myth and symbol was created within which racial thought was to take root.

The abstract was made concrete through the correspondence between the "inner realm" of the soul and the "outer realm" of the tangible world. Here the Enlightenment and pietism intertwined: the results of the new sciences were adopted, and so was the ideal of classical beauty. These were thought symbolic of a properly working soul—rooted not in rational comprehension but in the emotional world of Christianity and patriotism.

The world of myth and symbol was closely related to nature and history, and both were thought to embody permanent forces which could not be changed by man. Nature was seen as the immediate work of God. It moved in regular cycles corresponding to the seasons and was orderly, being integrated into the grand design of God's universe. God could direct nature from the pinnacle of the "chain of being" and be innately present in all its manifestations. But nature itself was infused with romantic and emotional meaning, symbolizing rootedness and vitality, and serving to discipline man's passions without abolishing them. Thus, nature symbolized man's most genuine emotions as opposed to man-made rules or systems. Nature therefore became a force which was "genuine" and whose rhythms served to unify all that lived within it. The result was a glorification of the peasant and an increasing suspicion of urban life. The idea that there had to be a correspondence between the emotions of man and nature was basic to most Pietistic and Romantic literature.

History lay outside human determination, and was seen as part of a divine plan; indeed, history determined the course of man and nature. It was another organic force, the objectification of destiny through time. As the Romantic poet Novalis put it at the beginning of the nineteenth century: "Nothing perishes which history sanctified."[9] In this way, nature and history embodied the eternal and genuine forces of the universe. (The historical dimension itself is discussed in a later chapter, for in the eighteenth century both the Enlightenment and the religious revival emphasized nature rather than history in their search for truth.) To be "genuine" was to be close to nature, and in opposition to a disorganized modernity which had broken away from God's organic plan for the world. Here Pietistic romanticism and the Enlightenment again linked up, since both exalted the primitive as genuine. For the *philosophes* in the first half of the eighteenth century, the primitive seemed pure, as yet uncontaminated by Christianity and superstition; for the Pietists, the primitive lived a life close to nature.

The secularized paradise which Rousseau's *Émile* and Defoe's tale of Robinson Crusoe presented fascinated men already familiar with the Arcadias of earlier ages. Primitivism here had a naïveté which saw man as "virtuous, tender and moral."[10] The "noble savage" of travelers' accounts also served as a critique of contemporary society, for he lived as one among equals and in a society where everyone had sustenance. Sometimes, a "native" was taken to France in order to voice the criticism of a child of nature sitting in judgment upon European civilization. In one case this involved a condemnation of the inequality and poverty in Paris, together with a word of censure about the presence of courtesans. Primitive innocence spoke the truth about contemporary society that others dared not voice.[11]

Most information about primitive peoples derived from travel literature and from the numerous voyages into strange lands popular during the seventeenth century. The first of the most famous accounts by Hakluyt, Purchas, Hulsius, and de Bry appeared between 1590 and 1610. In the seventeenth century travel literature tended to be a part of the biblical story. This softened the new encounter between Europe and the extra-European world by assimilating it into the drama of salvation. The natives were living symbols of the account of creation in Genesis or identified with the famous lost tribes of Israel. However, as this literature continued into the eighteenth century, the sacred analogies played less of a role, and the encounter with pagans became more immediate and shocking.[12]

Idealization of the primitive soon made way for a greater hostility. Tales of travel still constituted an important body of source material which enabled anthropologists to pursue their classifications. The fascination of the noble savage for men like Swift, Pope, or Rousseau, who bent the exotic elements of travelers' tales to their own critical purposes, was not to last. Soon the notion of European superiority and intellectual dominance asserted itself and charming naïveté was regarded as atavism, a reversion from modern to uncivilized man. The image of the primitive as a lower stage of the great chain of being was contrasted with the progress of higher creatures.

Primitivism in the eighteenth century was applied to natives in those faraway countries with which Europe was making its first contacts. The European peasant, the shepherd, and those living close to nature at home were thought examples of genuineness and superiority residing higher on the chain; but natives abroad who lived close to nature were soon stigmatized as barbaric. Especially in the second half of the eighteenth century, the primitive mind became the foil of reason. Bernard Fontenelle, for example, believed that the primitive mind was atavistic and childish, to be compared only to peasant dolts or fibbing children. John Locke regarded the primitive mind as capable of grasping only simple and concrete matters.[13] This was an important assertion, for it was generally agreed that the human mind as it developed from a lower to a higher state passed from the concrete to the abstract. The primitive mind, it was believed, had stuck at an earlier stage of development. Natives were regarded now not so much as noble savages but as children who had to be educated and ruled.

The image of the feckless black, lazy and undisciplined, arose on all sides in the eighteenth century. It was an image that was destined to last: the black as a delightful but undisciplined child would become transformed into the dangerous infant, anarchist, or *sans culotte* of the French Revolution.

Soon, therefore, this concept of primitivism clashed with the Enlightenment ideal of moderation and order. The *philosophes* had challenged tradition and believed passionately in the critical mind, but they also felt a need for authority, perhaps all the greater because of their challenge to old truths. The laws of nature were one such authority; the classics another. Both symbolized law and order. Restraint of passion, moderation, and tranquility were the messages which the eighteenth-century classical revival spread abroad.

The classical ideal of beauty contained all of these elements as well as the longing for unity. In turn, such beauty corresponded to the order of nature guided by natural laws. The eighteenth-century gardens and parks made nature conform to this theory, and the example of Greek sculpture applied the same ideals to man himself. Harmony and proportion (the Greek ideal) must suffuse the whole figure and could not be confined to any one part of it. J. J. Winckelmann's *History of Ancient Art* (*Geschichte der Kunst des Altertums*, 1764), a work of enormous influence, defined beauty as noble simplicity and quiet grandeur: "As the depth of the ocean always remains calm however much the surface may be agitated, so does the expression in the figures of the Greeks reveal a great and composed soul in the midst of passions."[14] For Winckelmann and many subsequent writers, such a soul was exemplified by the statue of Laocoon being strangled by two serpents, who remains tranquil despite the most extreme suffering.

Beauty meant order and tranquility; it thus revealed an unchanging, genuine world of health and happiness beneath the chaos of the age. Greek beauty provided the ideal-type, which set the aesthetic criteria to which man must relate himself. Beauty symbolized the uncorrupted world; it put men in touch with God and nature. This was no longer the primitivism of the noble savage, but rather a concept of beauty which had been given to the world by a highly sophisticated people and which depended upon abstractions like unity and grandeur.

The ideal of beauty bridged the gap between the rationalism and system building of the new age and the emotional, spiritual impulse that searched for symbols in order to overcome man's feeling of atomization and confusion. Classical beauty symbolized the perfect human form within which a true soul would be bound to reside. For the *philosophes*, too, these classical laws of beauty were in fact as much natural laws as those governing nature or morality. This explains why contemporary natural scientists also praised moderation and why some classified man not according to the principles of science but according to aesthetic criteria. Beauty and ugliness became as much principles of human classification as material factors of measurement, climate, and the environment. Christian Meiners in his influential *Outline of the History of Mankind* (*Grundriss der Geschichte der Menschheit*, 1785) classified humanity according to color and geography, and then added: "One of the chief characteristics of tribes and peoples is the beauty or ugliness of the whole body or of the face." [15] However, these characteristics were not inherent qualities of the racial soul, but a result of the climate in which such tribes lived. In 1784, one of the founders of modern anthropology, Johann Friedrich Blumenbach, praised the beautiful, symmetrical face, but maintained that the faces of nations are determined by the climate within which each lives—the more moderate the climate, the more beautiful the face. [16] This proved to be a bizarre if portentous application of the ideal of moderation.

Within the environmental approach, aesthetic criteria came to the fore. Not yet regarded as inherent and unchanging, they were nevertheless already present as an ideal-type to which racial classification must correspond. This ideal-type also implied certain ways of behaving that once more stressed moderation. Meiners, for example, inveighed against gluttony, shamelessness, and lust—vices which he felt went hand in hand with irritability, egoism, and lack of compassion. Meiners saw the "Mongol race" in this light, while the superior "Caucasians" were courageous, lovers of freedom, compassionate and moderate.[17] Not surprisingly, others shared his attitude toward moderation. In this area, again, the Enlightenment and the popular religious movements of the century came together.

The new moral concerns were largely a product of the evangelical and Pietistic movements, but also of the shock which the French Revolution sent through Europe. Some men actually regarded the Revolution as a punishment for the loose life of the nobility. Here the stress on a morality based upon moderation and restraint clearly corresponded to the Enlightenment ideal of beauty and order.

Earlier ages had found the non-European ugly and sometimes viewed the Negro as a man-beast.[18] But there had been no common standard of judgment upon lesser peoples, no common ideal to which the superior race was supposed to conform. From the eighteenth century onwards, however, the ideal-type and counter-type would not vary much for the next century and a half, nor would it matter fundamentally whether the inferior race was black or Jewish. The ideal-type symbolized by a classical beauty and proper morals determined attitudes toward all men.

The foundations of racism were strengthened by two additional factors—the growing contact between white and black, and the introduction into Europe of the Jews as a newly emancipated minority. As a result of travel, knowledge about Africa and the West Indies had increased; moreover, a number of blacks had lived in England for some time. Jews, of course, had always lived in Europe, but since the sixteenth century they had been herded into ghettos and separated from the rest of the population. Indeed, the Jewish "nation" (as it was commonly and revealingly called), with its different dress, customs, religion, and language, was the only sizable group of a foreign people in Christian Europe. But toward the turn of the nineteenth century, thanks to the Enlightenment and the

French Revolution, many ghetto walls fell and Jews entered into European life, while at the same time the contact with blacks became more frequent.

The growing intensity of contact with other peoples was what mattered. Those strangers who were rare in Europe and whose home was barely known were regarded with benign curiosity. Thus, a Chinese partook of the character of a sage—an image popularized by the Jesuits. Chinese in Europe were a novelty, much honored wherever they went. Moreover, they benefitted from the Chinese vogue in the mid-eighteenth century: Chinese gardens, Chinese porcelain, even mock Chinese villages. The Chinese seemed to complement and extend the rococo and baroque world of illusion. The "noble savage" had also for a period fulfilled this function, but familiarity and greater contact bred contempt and fear of ever present Negroes and Jews. Eventually, the Chinese too were drawn into the racist picture. Comte Joseph Arthur de Gobineau, one of the most famous racial theoreticians of the mid-nineteenth century, was to set the tone for a hostile view of the yellow races, but by that time there had been a vastly extended contact between Europe and the Orient.[19] Thus, it is untrue that sentiments about black inferiority could have existed without contact with blacks, or that anti-Jewish feelings could have persisted even where there was no knowledge of Jews. The reverse was actually the case. People needed to see the frightening stranger, so supposedly different from themselves, with their own eyes.

There was, for example, a direct connection between the ways Englishmen regarded their blacks at home and abroad in the Empire.[20] The number of blacks in London increased during the eighteenth century, and the fears about intermarriage and violence at home reflected the vision of blacks in Africa or the West Indies. They were regarded less as exotic than as objects for education and discipline. Attempts were made to inculcate in them the proper morality and to imbue them with the gospel of work. If, at times, the English at home reduced the black to the level of an ignorant beast and even held some as slaves,[21] the view of the slave as a chattel in Africa or the West Indies was modified by efforts at their conversion

to Christianity. Nevertheless, there were clear signs of a crystaliza-
tion of racial feeling, and the fear that English blood might be
tainted through intermarriage became increasingly widespread.

Similar views of the Negro prevailed among anthropologists con-
versant with travel reports. Thus Blumenbach, writing from Germany, accused Negroes of extremism, lack of a sense of proportion,
and lack of culture. But he still believed that the Negro, like
everyone else, was created in the image of God and therefore should
not be treated brutally.[22] Christian missionaries shared such compassion. The racial attitude toward the black was not yet clear-cut,
though he consistently ranked low whenever men were classified.

The Jews were either ignored by anthropologists during most of
the eighteenth century or considered part of the Caucasian race,
and still believed capable of assimilation into European life. Even a
champion of their emancipation such as Wilhelm Christian Dohm
thought that Jews were Asiatic by origin. But in 1781 Dohm declared that Jews were capable of enlightenment and should be assimilated.[23] Ideas of cosmopolitanism, equality, and toleration operated for the Jew as they could not for the Negro; after all, the
Jew was white. Typically for the age, Johann Kaspar Lavater, in
classifying human faces toward the end of the eighteenth century,
gave the Jews aquiline noses and pointed chins; even so, he admitted that he did not know how to classify them properly, and in the
end gave up.[24] Indeed, only after the mid-nineteenth century was
racism applied to Jews with any consistency.

No one seemed to feel such ambiguity toward blacks. Blacks,
unlike Jews, had a fixed lowly position in the "great chain of being." No longer were they the noble savages "with virtue fraught."[25]
More often they were considered close to the animal world. It was
thought no coincidence that the gorilla had its home in Africa
side by side with the black; travelers had popularized the notion that
there must be a close relationship between apes and blacks. Anthropologists chimed in, especially when aesthetic judgments came to the
fore. Peter Camper, writing in 1792, was not the only anthropologist
to compare the skulls of apes and Negroes. But here the "great chain
of being" also intruded: was the black the "missing link" between

animal and man? The chain must be kept complete. If there was a gap, lower creatures must be promoted one step in order to fill the void. Thus, for example, apes might become the lowest type of man, so providing the "missing link": "Inferior orders in succession rise to fill the void below." [26]

The English anthropologist Edward Tyson had posited the Pygmies as this link in 1699. He criticized the ancients for seeing Pygmies as human when in fact they were more akin to animals. Significantly Tyson, a physician and a fellow of the Royal Society, based his arguments on classical mythology. [27] The concept of the man-beast had never vanished from Europe. It was widely believed that apes were, in fact, not a totally different species but a lower species of man, who refused to speak in order not to become slaves. [28] For Tyson, Pygmies were apes because of their flat noses and their small stature. This latter point was repeated by others as proof of the animal nature of these blacks, even when such scholars as Camper and Buffon attempted to demonstrate that apes were a different species from man. But in spite of basic differences between man and ape, Camper still believed the Negro to be closer to monkeys than the rest of the human race. [29] He cited as his reason the Negro's appearance, as well as skull measurements, but in reality the aesthetic criterion was paramount, as it was for Tyson. Most anthropologists equated small stature with racial inferiority: "Size is the characteristic of Caucasian nobility," wrote Christian Meiners. [30] Nose shape was also a determinant for the black, whose flat nose was taken, once again, as proving closeness to the animal world, while the so-called hooked Jewish nose likewise became an outward sign of the absence of inward grace.

The reconstruction of the "chain of being" was an exercise in which many eighteenth-century anthropologists joined. Thus, Meiners posited a hierarchy from the lowliest creatures, through apes, through the legendary "Negro of the forest," to "Hottentots," "Bush-Negroes," and aborigines, and further to the yellow races and Slavs, until he arrived at the white race which was the master of the world. That he believed in the inevitable decline of the superior race through miscegenation makes him, in fact, a forerunner of Gobineau. [31] Al-

ways the outward beauty of form was adduced as one of the most
important ways of classifying the species within the hierarchy of the
universe.

Characteristically, as these examples show, diverse notions were
combined in such classifications: the natural order, ancient mythology, travelers' tales, and aesthetic prejudice. At the same time, the
cosmopolitanism of the Enlightenment and its pull toward environmental theories of human behavior tended to counteract idealist and
Romantic prejudice. Man was a part of nature, and the laws of nature themselves must produce the observable differences between
groups of men. If, as Locke thought, all ideas were acquired and
not inherited, racial differences were chance variations. Because
nature, man, and indeed all the world are formed in the image of
God, and are pregnant with possibilities, the Negro could not be
doomed or regarded as inferior. Blumenbach was not the only early
anthropologist who stated such a belief, for Lamarck and Buffon
also lent their weight to this view.

Despite the ambivalence of these scientists, and because of the
equally strong pull toward subjective judgments of permanent
superiority and inferiority, for a time science and aesthetic presuppositions existed side by side. The world of ideal-types, of myth and
symbol, was given its dynamic through concepts basically opposed
to the Enlightenment: pietism, evangelism, and pre-romanticism.
The link between the Enlightenment and such a world view was
forged by anthropologists who in their racial classifications would
pass from science to art.

CHAPTER TWO

From Science to Art: The Birth of Stereotypes

NTHROPOLOGY originated out of a curiosity about faraway countries and their inhabitants. This in turn led to questions about man's origins, the beginnings of human culture, language, and religion. The classification of the races of mankind was from the start one of the principal preoccupations of anthropologists, and a means of coming to grips with newly discovered and startling varieties of the human species. To this very day anthropology in most nations means—besides the study of customs and behavior—the classification of races and peoples.[1] Debates about classification centered upon the question of whether the environment might to some extent influence the creation and development of a race, or whether most of its characteristics were inherited. These are vital considerations, for such factors determine how deep and wide is the gap that separates different races: whether inherent and therefore permanent, or environmental and thus subject to change.

In the past, exotic peoples had been considered a part of the sacred biblical drama. But by the eighteenth century, the savage was severed from his supposed biblical descent and became an object of secular study. Nevertheless, the emphasis upon description unclouded by biblical prejudice as the basis for classification was accompanied by standards which departed from the principles of empirical observation. In spite of the growth of a secular historical consciousness, nonscientific judgments were made upon the historical evolution of a race, and the problem of primitivism, as we have seen, was widely discussed in terms of racial roots. But the most ominous standard which was applied to racial classification during the eighteenth century was based upon aesthetic preferences that were necessarily highly subjective. The new emphasis on classical beauty set the tone. It led to a stereotype which would never leave racism from that day to this.

Material and environmental factors continued to be stressed and invoked in opposition to aesthetic principles of classification. J. B. Antoine de Lamarck (1744–1829) became the most important advocate of this point of view, and "Lamarckism" remained the designation for an environmentalism said to determine the nature and mutation of each species. Lamarck in his *Zoological Philosophy* (*Philosophie Zoologique*, 1809) held that any species could maintain its continuity of form as long as the environment was constant, and that while such constancy prevailed, acquired characteristics could be inherited. Thus, if the giraffe had a stretched neck because otherwise it could not obtain food, then the offspring would also have extended necks. This situation would change when the environment changed—if, for instance, instead of growing on trees, their food started to grow on the ground.[2] Thus no race was eternally locked into its present characteristics.

Lamarck was also one of the most thorough materialists of his time, believing that while living bodies did have a soul, it was made up of electricity, heat, and nervous fluid. He held that "in all acts of intelligence, the nervous fluid is the only active factor,"[3] and moreover that intelligence, like the body, developed through exercise. Races were chance variations, determined by material factors; no inherent superiority could exist within Lamarck's scheme of classification. Idleness, carelessness, and lack of success were not racial qualities (although others attributed these precise characteristics to the Negro) but rather the result of the habit of submitting to authority from early youth.

The themes of freedom, equality, and the possibility of change run throughout Lamarck's works. Man could understand himself and his universe, for he was capable of having clear and distinct ideas which, in typical Enlightenment fashion, corresponded to the laws of God's creation. There was nothing "inward," spiritual, or mystical about Lamarck's concept of race. It stood within the Enlightenment, based upon reason and a critical mind that attempted to reject preconceived judgments. Oddly enough, through this effort Lamarck arrived at a crude materialism and a questionable theory of heredity. Some of Lamarck's famous contemporaries did not follow his materialism, but instead began to introduce spiritual factors into their scheme of racial classification. The future was to belong to their subjective science—to the reflection of contemporary prejudices and hopes within a supposedly scientific definition of race.

Georges Louis Leclerc de Buffon (1707–1788) in his famous *Natural History of Man* (*Histoire Naturelle de l'Homme*, 1778) also put forward environmental theories. Yet his environmentalism and materialism were watered down, and subjective aesthetic influences made themselves felt even if they were not yet predominant. He was convinced that climate, food, manners, and customs determined race. The Negro's skin was black because of the heat of the tropical climate, and it would change if the climate became colder. But unlike Lamarck, Buffon felt himself compelled to step outside a discussion of material forces, however ambivalently. "Our existence is organization of matter with spirit," he wrote.[4] On the one hand, he argued that physical appearance denotes character; thus the Negroes of Senegal who were well proportioned were also a good and talented people. On the other hand, such judgments still rested upon a tenuous environmentalism, for Buffon like Lamarck equated the spiritual realm with the action of nerves. Though he was concerned with ideas of beauty and physical appearance, races were, for Buffon, mere chance variations.

Buffon and Lamarck represent a tradition of the Enlightenment which prevailed in the second half of the eighteenth century. Not only do we find a greater materialism in some of these thinkers, but also a strong belief in observation and experimentation. Together with this trend, a more emotional and spiritual way of looking at the world made an increasing impact upon such scientists. The emotionalism of the Pietistic and evangelical revivals slowly displaced the Enlightenment throughout much of society, not necessarily as a renewal of religious faith but as a need to encompass the emotional and spiritual side of man's nature. At the start of the nineteenth century, a time of "storm and stress" (as the Germans called it) was ruffling the steady devotion of the Enlightenment to reason. Buffon felt the winds of change when he put spiritual factors side by side with scientific materialism.

Carl von Linné (1707–1778), the Swedish naturalist, also paired observation and description with subjective judgments. As one of the most influential pioneers of racial classification, he reflected that urge toward subjectivity in the ranking of race which was to be the trend of the future. Linné regarded the white race as inventive, full of ingenuity, orderly, and governed by laws. For him this was the superior race as it reflected middle-class values. By contrast the Negroes were endowed with all the negative qualities which made them a convenient foil for the superior race: they were regarded as lazy, devious, and unable to govern themselves. They were feckless *sans culottes*, and such they would remain in racial thought, in contrast to the image of the orderly, clean, and industrious European.[5]

These racial judgments substituted the values of middle-class morality for environmentalism, social assessments thus replacing scientific ones. The aesthetic importance of proper outward appearance would summarize the virtues of law and order which Linné prized; yet Linné also kept environmental factors intact, and assigned no hereditary cause to human variations. Between environmentalism and such subjective criteria of racial classification lay obvious contradictions. These may have been derived from his strong belief in the common origin of all races—a belief that militated against an unduly wide gap between them. Linné conceived of races as mere chance variations. Thus materialism existed side by side with social and aesthetic prejudice in his outlook.[6]

Johann Friedrich Blumenbach (1752–1840), who is considered one of the founders of modern anthropology, also believed in the unity of the human race. Moreover, Blumenbach stressed environmental factors such as climate to explain variations in color and form. He seems to have denied the conclusiveness of racial characteristics; he was unable, for example, to find a single distinctive bodily characteristic among blacks which could not be found in many other races. Blumenbach wrote in 1775 that all Negroes are "more or less different from one another . . . and through all sorts of graduations run imperceptibly into the appearances of men of other kinds up to the most pleasing conformation."[7]

The "pleasing conformation" points to an aesthetic criterion of classification in conflict with ideas of equality and racial flux. Blumenbach believed that there were national characteristics which determined facial structure, and he ascribed these variations to climate or food. For all that, in Blumenbach's scientific writings the word "beauty" began to be prominent. The symmetric face was said to be the most beautiful because it approximated the "divine" works of Greek art, and such a face, according to Blumenbach, was more likely to occur in moderate climes than in extreme temperatures.[8] This concept of beauty implied the ideal of moderation and order which Linné too stressed so heavily. Greek sculpture defined the proper anatomical proportions. The absence of nervousness and passion was also a part of the "quiet greatness," which appealed so much to a century fraught with political and social upheaval. Beauty was synonymous with a settled, happy, and healthy middle-class world without violent upheavals—and a world attainable solely by white Europeans. No one could claim that Negroes had faces which reflected the Greek aesthetic ideal.

The equality Blumenbach gave to the Negro with one hand he took away with the other. In 1775 he was still largely an environmentalist, but by 1789 he had allowed science to take second place to aesthetic judgment. However, Blumenbach was not yet an advocate of any peculiarly national racial superiority. He held that the beautiful white race stretched from western Europe to the Caspian Sea and the Ganges, as well as to Finland and northern Africa. Indeed, he thought that the Georgians in Russia had the most pleasing proportions of all.[9]

Blumenbach cited Peter Camper, the Dutch anatomist, whose most important books on human anthropology were published in the years 1792 and 1793. Camper, unlike Blumenbach, made only a short bow to scientific classification before taking off into aesthetic heights. With his works the ideal-type moved to the foreground and was only loosely connected to scientific observation. Camper's lasting influence was no doubt the result of his exaltation of the "physically beautiful" through the so-called scientific method of cranial comparisons and facial measurements (see Plate 1). His contemporary Johann Kaspar Lavater had already shed any real claim to science in inventing physiognomy, the "science of reading the human face." Lavater's *Essai sur la Physiognomie*, which appeared in 1781, antedated Camper. Yet in our argument it is all important to show the progression from a scientist like Blumenbach to a pseudo-scientist like Camper and eventually to Lavater who merely advocated training in visual intuition. It must be clear, therefore, that within the eighteenth century we have in microcosm a development that will recur repeatedly throughout the history of racism.

Camper was trained as a painter, not a scientist. His aim was not merely to enrich the new science of anthropology, but to instruct young artists and sculptors in natural history and the love of antiquity. Indeed, Camper won the gold medal of the Amsterdam School of Art in 1770.[10] This background is significant—and not for Camper alone, since many future theoreticians of race were to be painters and writers rather than scientists.

Camper's most important "discovery" was that of the "facial angle," which could be measured through comparison of the heads of Kalmucks and Negroes with those of Europeans. These, in turn, he compared with the head of a monkey. Camper first measured the angle from the upper lip to the forehead, and horizontally across the face. He then measured the angles between these two lines. If the vertical line formed a 100-degree angle with the horizontal, this was the ideal-type: Winckelmann's Greek "beau idéal," as he called it.[11] But such perfection does not exist in fact. To account for a margin of variation, he posited that any angle 70 degrees or less corresponded to the Negro, and that this figure was closer to the lines of apes and dogs than to men. Europeans would measure around 97 degrees, which is closer to the ideal-type of Greek sculpture (see Plate 2).[12]

Anthropologists accepted the "facial angle" as a scientific measurement. But in so doing, they also accepted a standard of beauty as a criterion of racial classification. Camper attempted to overcome his own prejudices, but with little success. He believed that beauty depended on national custom, so that what Negroes saw as beautiful might be ugly to Europeans.[13] Indeed, Winckelmann had made the same point. Not only does beauty seem relative here, but Camper also made much of climate and food as producing the European ideal-type. However, this environmentalism was not central to his argument (as it was to Lamarck, for example). Emphasis was always upon the ideal of Greek beauty as Winckelmann had described it. Thus he believed that not only were skull measurements telling, but one could rank heads by their profile according to levels of beauty. Moreover, in describing beauty he abandoned his earlier assertion that Negroes have their own aesthetic standards, and therefore left no doubt about the superiority of the European ideal-type. Classical beauty had become a general principle valid for all times.

Why, asked Camper, is a tall person so much more beautiful than a small one, thus repeating the prejudice that had surfaced in the animalization of Pygmies seen as the "missing link"? For Camper, ancient proportions and stature were beautiful because they avoided all imperfection. Such beauty was close to that genuine nature which represented God's final truth. The beautiful face and the beautiful body are at one with beautiful nature, and Winckelmann himself had written that beauty must represent a totality. For Camper this unity also included man's soul. The outward appearance represents inward grace. And here moderation is once again stressed. The example, already cited by Winckelmann, is the tranquil statue of the strangling Laocoon.[14] The aesthetic had swamped the scientific, though there was still an effort at empirical proof through measurements.

With all this emphasis upon the ideal-type, Camper was not concerned with any one nation within Europe, and in this he was still a man of the Enlightenment. Nor did he let historical development play a role, although it was already beginning to be important in the minds of some of his contemporaries. Moreover, Camper did not know what to make of the Jews who were, after all, Europeans. He believed that they had their own characteristics, such as distinctive curvature of the nose, citing typically enough the contemporary American painter Benjamin West as his authority.[15] But for all Camper's subjectivity, the concept of the superior race encompassed all Europeans and was not yet regarded as a national monopoly.

The emphasis upon outward appearance was greatly aided by physiognomy. Attempts to explain the character of an individual man by observing his face, limbs, and gestures go back at least to the sixteenth century. At that time, features like kinky hair or hooked nose were already thought to be signs of an evil disposition, even though they were ascribed to the accidents of change of air or to illness.[16] But it was in publishing his *Essai sur la Physiognomie* in 1781 that Lavater (1741–1801) became the true father of the new science of physiognomy. Although a committed Protestant theologian, Lavater was still a man of the Enlightenment. He was a close friend of Goethe, who aided him in editing and publishing his physiognomic findings. Lavater had no racism in mind when he wrote about the importance of knowing men by reading their faces. He supported the French Revolution, which broke out several years after he had founded his new "science." Indeed, Lavater was no reactionary, either in religion, where he tended toward a peculiar spiritualized view of Christianity, or in his politics. To be sure, he seems to have held that the Jews slandered Jesus, but this hostility was hardly racial. He admired Moses Mendelssohn, the famous Jewish philosopher and champion of Jewish emancipation, and believed that this wise Jew must be ready to accept Christianity.[17] And about blacks he had very little to say. Yet in the end his pseudo-science of physiognomy proved a powerful weapon against those people who were different. Lavater also held classical ideas of beauty according to which he classified and ranked the human species. But for this no scientific studies were required, only visual ability and taste.

The importance of the emphasis upon the visual for racial

thought cannot be overestimated. Unlike Camper, Lavater was not a painter, but for him "the art of painting" was "mother and daughter" of physiognomy.[18] An early editor of Lavater's work put it well: the true language of physiognomy is painting, because it speaks through images and speaks equally to the eye and to the spirit.[19]

How was one to go about observing a face? Lavater wrote: Trust your first quick impression, for it is worth more than what is usually called observation.[20] One can judge the whole man by observing the exterior intuitively, for it is in total harmony with a man's soul. The external is nothing but a continuation of the internal, and vice versa. All those concerned with human classification believed this, but few stated it with such refreshing clarity. What did one look for as constituents of a beautiful face and therefore a beautiful soul? For Lavater the homogeneity of body and face, the uniformity of outline, the dimensions of the figure, and "honesty" in the forehead and brow. In short, his standards were those that had informed Greek sculpture.[21] But Lavater was even more specific about the face. He emphasized the necessary uniformity of the three main divisions of a beautiful face—forehead, nose, and chin; horizontal forehead (i.e., corresponding to Camper's 100-degree angle), with nearly horizontal thick eyebrows. Moreover, it was preferable to have blue eyes, a broad nose nearly parallel but a little bent back, a round chin, and short brown hair.[22]

No proof is provided for such a concept of beauty, except the example of the ancients (and here again Winckelmann influenced the ideal-type). Beauty for Lavater was what attracts us at first glance, but this always meant a uniformity underneath which lay variety, a complete harmony without one unbalanced member or part.[23] The Greeks had been more beautiful than those people he observed during his lifetime, and though Greeks were not Christians, yet he held that God in His inscrutable manner had wanted it this way. But if contemporaries would become true Christians, then Greek beauty might even be enhanced through humility and love.[24] Clearly, the impact of classical beauty threatened to disorient the Christian theologian.

Lavater did try to classify national physiognomies, arguing that there must be such a thing as national character among Moors and Englishmen, Italians and French. But he confessed that he had little skill in defining such distinctions. For example, he recognized the Germans by their teeth and laughter, the French by their noses; but his efforts became bogged down in futility. With evident relief he returned to universal ideals, for in Lavater they and not national characteristics were crucial. All men, he wrote, were modeled by nature according to one basic form, which varied in a multitude of ways.[25] Yet for all these remnants of Enlightenment universalism in Lavater, there was still the contrast between the noble soul, the Greek God, and the ugly face, the ugly body, and the criminal. One wrong facial line would destroy beauty and, given the identity of inward and outward, become a sign of evil. Lavater exclaimed: How many crimes could be prevented if men could only read vice in the face.[26] He would have denied Lessing's rhetorical question in *Nathan the Wise* (1779): "Do faces not resemble one another?"[27] Indeed, Lavater loathed Lessing and this play which, he contended, favored the Jew while making Christians rogues and knaves. (Lavater's intolerance was the outcome of his missionary fervor, not a sign of racism.)[28]

With Lavater we confront the stereotype divorced from scientific proof and embedded in irrationality. Lavater had many contemporary and learned imitators, the most important of whom was the Neapolitan Jean Baptiste Porta. In 1805 Porta developed his speculative theory of physiognomy, not only following Lavater, but also based on the notion that the resemblance of a human face to that of a beast indicates the degree to which the individual's character will be endowed with the main traits of that animal. Men might not only look like sheep, oxen, or lions, but also share their predominant instincts.[29] Physiognomy thus put some people in direct touch with the animal world, just as Camper had compared the skulls of blacks and apes. Such animal analogies would become the staple of racial thought.

Among Lavater's more famous contemporaries, his theory impressed not only Goethe but also the much younger Sir Walter

Scott. Scott's novels abound with physiognomist interpretations. Scott read all sorts of judgments into the countenances of his characters: honesty and resolution, gentleness and goodness; Rowena, the heroine of *Ivanhoe*, had the fair complexion which "physiognomists" considered led to a mild, timid, and gentle disposition.[30] Clearly, such ideas were not just spread by learned treatise but had almost immediately made their way into popular literature.

Franz Joseph Gall's (1758–1828) phrenology added a pseudo-scientific dimension to the reading of faces. Gall's basic notion was that character could be read through the configuration of the head. Phrenology rested on three principles: that the brain was the organ of the mind; that the brain was composed of a variety of organs, each of which had a specific function; and, finally, that the brain shaped the skull (see Plate 3).[31] These were the basic ideas propounded by Gall in 1796, when he contended that the various functions of the brain could be read and judged by the shape of the human skull.

Like Lavater, Gall was very precise as to the meaning of the head's features. A forehead that was especially arched denoted aptitude for metaphysical speculation, for example; but if the skull was arched toward the rear, that connoted love of fame. The base of the brain was considered the seat of all animal and vital forces. Criminals, it was said, were apt to have a brain large at the base and at the side where, for Gall, the lower impulses and propensities resided.[32] Thus, there were outward signs of inward predispositions. Yet Gall rejected any idea that there might be "national skulls"; he refused to classify races of men, and concentrated instead on individual heads, each showing its own variations within the general principles he laid down. In addition, Gall was not hostile to blacks. He specifically rejected the idea put forward by some of his contemporaries that the Negroid skull was particularly narrow and thus contained less brain than that of the white European.[33]

For all these reservations, phrenology was soon enlisted in the cause of racial classification. Anders Retzius (1796–1860) in Sweden made phrenological measurements more useful because more precise. He devised a simple formula to express the ratio of the

length to the width of the head (the cephalic index). Long and
narrow heads he called dolichocephalic, broad ones brachycephal-
ic,[34] terms which entered the language of race, where long and narrow heads were thought to be both especially beautiful and a mark
of the superior European.

But there were those who sought to change some features of
phrenology in the cause of a racism that Gall had always rejected.
For example, Carl Gustav Carus, writing in Germany in the mid-
nineteenth century, acknowledged Gall's pioneering efforts in reading the skull, while himself attempting to give phrenology an
idealistic, intuitive foundation. In his *Symbolism of the Human
Form* (*Symbolik der Menschlichen Gestalt*, 1853), he stated that
just as one assessed an architectural column in its totality (by its
base, height, and strength), so too the proportions of the whole
human body must be measured. Not the skull alone, but the entire
skeleton of man would tell the tale.[35] The posture of Greek
sculpture was, once again, taken as superior to all others, and
he judged the human face according to Porta's animal analogies.
But Carus soon abandoned this pseudo-science for Romantic irrationalism. He posited an analogy between superior and inferior
peoples and the relationship of the sun to the earth. There were
"day-people" like the Europeans, night people like the Negroes,
and twilight people such as the Asiatics and the American Indians.
It followed that blond coloring derived from the sun was a sign of
superiority, together with blue eyes which reflected the sky. The
excellence symbolized by coloring was borne out by measurements
and principles of physiognomy.[36]

The mixture between romanticism and the new sciences was to
have a promising future. As a professor of anatomy and a Romantic
painter, Carus himself exemplified this promise. He was a racist for
whom the superior people were also the superior race. The world
was hierarchical, Carus maintained; therefore, humanity must be
structured in an ascending order, with the "day-people" at its head,
for their beauty was a direct gift from God. The Aryan stereotype is
completed here by adding color to structure and form.[37]

Carus also wrote about the hooked nose as a Jewish characteristic, but without removing the Jew from the company of "day-people."[38] The "Jewish nose," which was to play such an important role in characterizing the Jewish stereotype, dates from the eighteenth century when it was described by Johann Schudt of Frankfurt in his *Jewish Peculiarities* (*Jüdische Merkwürdigkeiten*, 1711). Winckelmann described it in 1764 and contrasted it with the symmetry of the Greek nose. But the idea of the Jewish nose entered popular consciousness also from another, perhaps even more effective direction, as a result of the many broadsides and cartoons in 1753 and 1754 that were published around the attempt to emancipate the Jews in England. The "Jew Bill," as this measure for emancipation in 1753 was popularly called, pushed the Jew into the center of attention. Though passed and then immediately repealed by Parliament under popular pressure, it was the first serious attempt to emancipate the Jews in Europe. Before that time, Jews in England had been portrayed realistically; but now, to give one example, caricaturists who knew perfectly well what the Jewish banker Samson Gideon really looked like gave him a nose he did not possess in real life. At the same time, where earlier Jewish peddlers had been depicted much as they really were, now they were shown as dirty, with big noses and malignant eyes. Hogarth in 1754 popularized this image of the Jew; he was followed by Rowlandson, Gillray, and Cruikshank (see Plate 4).[39]

The nose is, in effect, the most prominent member of the face, and singling it out should not surprise us. Lavater had a whole theory of noses that depended upon their shape. Turned-up noses designated a choleric man, snub noses meant prudence and discretion, and noses turned downward meant heartlessness.[40] The phrenologists took up this classification, positing Roman, Greek, Jewish, snub, and "celestial" noses. Roman and Greek noses indicated the conqueror, the man of refinement of taste; but the Jewish nose designated a wary and suspicious character.[41]

Phrenology itself—widely if intermittently popular during the nineteenth century, especially in England, France, and the United States—lent its weight to the doctrine of race. The more benevolent skulls were found among Englishmen or Frenchmen (as the case might be), while Africa and her inhabitants exhibited moral and intellectual desolation through their skull formations.[42] Especially as phrenology took over physiognomy, it tended to support these racial stereotypes. It was in this sense, for example, that the Nazis eventually took it up. Thus a popular Berlin periodical declared in 1935: "Faces are like a book; phrenology can read their lines." The Nazis mixed up Lavater and Gall, but what mattered was that "nature has written our fate and individuality upon our face."[43] Here the nose was most important, and after it the forehead, with its length, its peaks and valleys. A nose that sprang out of a face was said to denote courage; a pale nose the hidden force of personality. The Jewish nose is missing from this discussion, but it is well known how big a role it played in the Nazi stereotype of the Jews.[44]

A stereotype was thus put forward within which aesthetics dominated science, while environmental factors played relatively little part. Yet the Enlightenment factor of scientific observation and environmentalism remained, serving as proof for aesthetic and moral judgments closer to the emotionalism of the Romantic movement. This was not always so—for example, it was not true of Lavater's intuition, nor of the racial theory of Immanuel Kant. Because Kant ignored environmental factors, he could formulate propositions about the human species which were to have great impact. For it was he who clearly stated the immutability and permanence of race. *The Different Races of Mankind (Von den Verschiedenen Rassen der Menschen*, 1775) asserted that those animals who maintain their purity despite migrations from one region to another, or despite the temptation to mix with others, may be called a race, and that the same applies to human beings: "Thus whites and Negroes are not two different kinds of species but nevertheless two different races."[45]

Kant thus distinguished sharply between species and race. He argued that species which seem to develop as a result of local climatic peculiarities are merely chance variations, and he went to great lengths to prove that God created all men for all the earth, and that they were free to live anywhere. If races have their specific homes (such as Africa for blacks), it is because of geographical factors that pushed them into a region. Kant put forward four main races (white, Negro, Mongol or Kalmuck, and Hindu), but of these he considered the white and Negro to be the basic races (*Grundrassen*) because of the clear differences in personality and character.[46] Though Kant emphasized the common origin of all men, to avoid attacking the biblical account of creation, he nevertheless formulated a concept of race which would remain constant. Racial make-up becomes an unchanging substance and the foundation of all physical appearance and human development, including intelligence.

Races said to be independent of external influence cannot change through evolution. "Race Unchanged Through Thousands of Years," a Nazi headline would proclaim, in line with this tradition (see Plate 5). How can a stereotype ever change? This is an important point, for racism has usually been thought of as an integral part of social Darwinism. To be sure, the race struggles against its enemies and attempts to keep itself pure in order to survive; but unlike Darwin's survival of the fittest, it does not change during this struggle. A race cannot evolve, for it must persist as it was created; it stands outside time.

The emerging stereotype did indeed have deep roots. For example, the ideal of personal beauty in English letters of the thirteenth and fourteenth centuries seems to anticipate Winckelmann's much later standard. The figure prized in medieval romances corresponded to Greek statuary, physiognomy was important, and a "skin of dazzling whiteness" exemplified true beauty. Such beauty symbolized goodness, while blackness, small stature, and an ill-proportioned body meant ugliness and evil. Walter Clyde Curry writing in 1916 believed that these medieval English examples were duplicated in medieval Italy, Germany, and France.[47] Thus the revival of classicism in the eighteenth century may have corresponded to a deep and rather constant stream of European ideals of beauty and ugliness. Perhaps this is one reason why the ancients seemed so relevant. But we are also confronted with an ideal human type which stood outside historical change as something lasting and constant over a long period of history.

Racial classification annexed symbols which, in a world of rapid change and anxiety, denoted permanence and restfulness. Science believed in change, but aesthetics did not, and racism cannot be understood without the factor of timelessness. There was a preoccupation with origins rather than with change, for these determined the qualities of the race. No doubt, the preoccupation with history which became increasingly important as the eighteenth century drew to a close directed attention to the importance of the origins and early years of peoples and nations. Although for Johann Gottfried von Herder (1744–1803) historical continuity and not race counted, his enormously influential works did popularize theories of origins and beginnings which were eagerly annexed by those who divided humanity into races.

Herder emphasized the youth of a people as the time of spontaneity and genuine national expression. Legends, sagas, and fairy tales represented the eternal heritage of a people, far removed from the scientific and modern emphasis of the present. The songs of a people in its youth, so Herder tells us, reflect a genuine and sentient world.[48] Thus the *Volksgeist* is expressed through mythologies, songs, and fables. Such an impetus to go back to the origins also informs Rousseau's enormously popular *Confessions* (1782): the sentiment of nature must prevail among peoples and do away with the foolish civil institutions which history has produced.

Returning to the origins meant grappling with the origin of races, for as they began so will they continue. Kant and the majority of those concerned with racial classification held fast to the story of Genesis, which proclaimed the common origin of all mankind. It was only after the flood that Shem, Ham, and Japhet founded separate nations. Some writers from the sixteenth century onward had felt that God's curse upon Ham or upon his son Canaan was entirely sufficient to account for the blackness of the Negro and his inferior status.[49] At any rate, Chapters 10 and 11 of Genesis could be interpreted as an explanation of racial difference even if all mankind had a common father. These monogenists, as they were called, could still believe in inferior and superior races; but somehow they had to reconcile this with the fact that God had created all men—a point Blumenbach was fond of citing, though, as we have seen, it did not keep him from making aesthetic and moral judgments about whites and Negroes.

Once the classifications had been made and value judgments fastened onto them, it made some sense to ignore Genesis and to separate the races from their very beginning. Christoph Meiners, for example, bolstered his belief in European racial superiority by holding that races were created separately, each with eternal and inherited characteristics.[50] Such a belief in separate origins was called polygenism. Polygenists believed that while the white race was descended from Adam, the black races must have been created by events separate from the biblical story of creation. For monogenists, race could be considered chance variations; for polygenists, differences were bound to be absolute.

Polygenesis was opposed to religious orthodoxy, and for that reason it attracted *philosophes* like Voltaire. Moreover, the classification of species from animal through man gave fuel to polygenism, so that anthropologists like Camper purported to show that Negroes were closer to apes than to Europeans. As late as 1831 a multi-volume work was published in which orang-outans were classified as human and integrated into the "chain of being."[51] But though monogenism and polygenism grew up side by side in the eighteenth century, polygenesis was relatively unimportant until the second half of the nineteenth century when it was resurrected by anthropologists like Paul Broca in France. Nevertheless, it was almost immediately drowned by the Darwinian concept of evolution. Darwin believed that there had been one creation in which all existing species were implicit but not yet present, evolving later according to a great original plan. This was a non-biblical monogenism, which had great scientific appeal.[52]

Above all, polygenism excited the attention of travelers and explorers but left very little mark upon European racial thought itself. Why confront the Bible and later Darwinian science when such a confrontation was irrelevant to arguments about racial permanence or superiority? Monogenesis and polygenesis were less important as dividing lines between races than was a growing national consciousness, which surged forward during the second part of the eighteenth century and all but buried the cosmopolitanism of the Enlightenment. Modern nationalism was built upon a common history, shared language, and shared emotions, all of which restricted human vision to one's own native community. The *Homo Europeus* about which the eighteenth-century anthropologists wrote would become the German, Slavic, or French race.

It was not really until the mid-nineteenth century that racism and nationalism began to fuse. Only by that time was the ideal human stereotype complete. For while from the eighteenth century onward the stature and proportions of body and face were set, as yet the coloration was missing. It was supplied in the mid-nineteenth century, notably by Carl Gustav Carus, when the Aryan—blond and blue-eyed, built like Winckelmann's Greek statues—finally stood ready to face the world and to do battle. Yet in reality the foundations for a closer union of racism and nationalism had been laid long before. To the development of anthropology, physiognomy, and phrenology in the eighteenth century must be added the newly stimulated interests in history and linguistics at the end of the eighteenth and beginning of the nineteenth centuries. The awakening national consciousness in many parts of Europe embraced history and linguistics, so that in the event it proved easy to integrate these with the stereotypes which anthropologists, phrenologists, and physiognomists had already put forward.

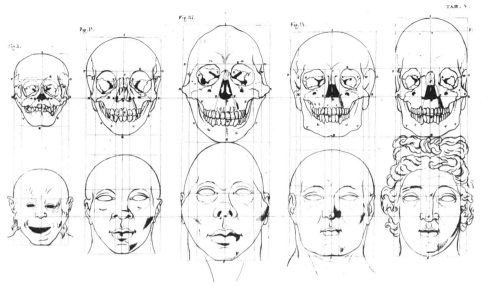

1. The progression of skulls and facial expressions—from monkey, through black, to the average European, and thence to the Greek ideal-type. From Peter Camper, *Dissertation sur les Variétés Naturelles* . . . (Paris and The Hague, 1791), plate V.

2. The "facial angle." From Robert Knox, *The Races of Men* (London, 1862), p. 404.

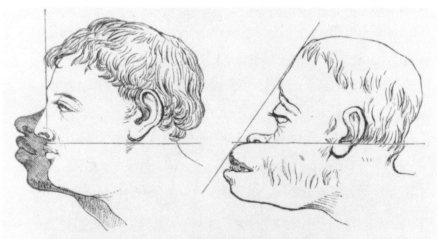

[*Profile of Negro, European, and Oran Outan.*]

3. Lavater and Gall's phrenologically mapped head, giving the locations of the diverse parts of the brain and their meaning. From *Physiognomie et Phrénologie,* ed. A. Ysabeau (Paris, 1810), p. 271.

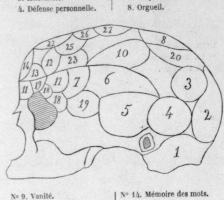

N° 1. Propagation.
   2. Amour de la progéniture
   3. Affectivité.
   4. Défense personnelle.

N° 5. Meurtre.
   6. Ruse.
   7. Propriété.
   8. Orgueil.

N° 9. Vanité.
  10. Circonspection.
  11. Mémoire des faits.
  12.   — des lieux.
  13.   — des personnes.

N° 14. Mémoire des mots.
  15. Philologie.
  16. Peinture.
  17. Musique.
  18. Mathématiques.

4. The Jewish stereotype, as satirized by Thomas Rowlandson in "A Jewish Dandy." From Eduard Fuchs, *Die Juden in der Karikatur* (Munich, 1921).

Raſſe

unverändert durch Jahrtauſende

Es hat lange gedauert, bis der Menſch, der forſchend Himmel und Erde durchdrang, endlich zu ſich ſelber gelangte. Das Wiſſen um Raſſe und Vererbung iſt eine ſpäte Erkenntnis, aber ſie wird entſcheidend in Weltanſchauung und Leben ganzer Völker eingreifen.

Kulturen ſind verſchwunden, Völker ſind vergangen, aber ihr Antlitz iſt geblieben

Antiker und moderner Grieche. Noch in vorgeſchichtlichen Zeiten gelangten auf langſamem Koloniſationszuge indogermaniſche Stämme in die Gebiete des heutigen Griechenland. Dieſe Landſchaften waren vorher keineswegs menſchenleer, ſondern beſaßen ſchon eine andere Bevölkerung von weniger heller Hautfarbe und geringerer Körpergröße. Die einwandernden nordiſchen Stämme verſchmelzen dann ſpäter mit dieſen Elementen, wodurch der gegenwärtige Volkstypus geſchaffen wurde. Aber der klaſſiſche griechiſche Typus, wie er uns in den alten Bildwerken entgegentritt, kommt auch heute noch vereinzelt immer wieder vor

Das ägyptiſche Geſicht:
Der Pharao in der altägyptiſchen Darſtellung und ein Sultan aus dem Norden des ehemaligen Deutſch-Oſtafrika. Ein Typ, wie er uns von altägyptiſchen Denkmälern her vertraut iſt, hat ſich in vielen Vertretern der Bewohner des oberen Niltals und der amuſierenden Gebiete erhalten. Links: Eine Reliefdarſtellung des Pharao Seti I. aus dem Tempel von Abydos; rechts: Mbima-Sultan Kiſſioreho aus Moceve im Norden Deutſch-Oſtafrika.

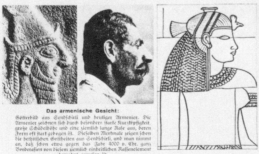

Das armeniſche Geſicht:
Götterbild aus Sendſchirli und heutiger Armenier. Die Armenier zeichnen ſich durch beſonders ſtarke Kurzköpfigkeit, große Schädelhöhe und eine ziemlich lange Naſe aus, deren Form oft ſtark gebogen iſt. Dieſelben Merkmale zeigen ſich bei den hethitiſchen Gottheiten aus Sendſchirli, und man nimmt an, daß ſchon etwa gegen das Jahr 4000 v. Chr. ganz Vorderaſien von dieſem ziemlich einheitlichen Raſſenelement bewohnt geweſen iſt.

Das nubiſche Antlitz:
Alte nubiſche Gottheit und moderne Nubierin. Südlich an Ägypten anſchließend breitet ſich oberhalb der erſten Nilkatarakte das Land Nubien aus, das ſchon in den älteſten geſchichtlichen Zeiten von Völkern mit rötlicher Hautfarbe bewohnt wurde, den Kuſchiten. Außerdem aber lebte in dem "elenden Kuſch", wie die Ägypter das Land verächtlich bezeichneten, eine negeriſche Bevölkerung, deren Raſſenmerkmale ſich von denen der Kuſchiten miſchten

Aufn.: Weltbilderdienst

5. "Race Unchanged Through Thousands of Years," comparing ancient and modern Aryan faces. From a Nazi newspaper, *Märkischer Adler* (June 7, 1936), Wiener Library, Tel Aviv.

HOUSTON STEWART CHAMBERLAIN †

Am 9. Januar 1926, um die Mittagsstunde, starb einer der bedeutendsten geistigen Wegbereiter des kommenden dritten Deutschen Reiches. Houston Stewart Chamberlain, der Schwiegersohn Richard Wagners, zu Bayreuth, wo er, der geborene Engländer, seit vielen Jahren seine deutsche Heimat gefunden hatte.

*

Chamberlain war am 9. September 1855 zu Portsmouth als Sohn des Admirals William Charles Chamberlain geboren. Er studierte, vorgebildet auf dem kaiserlichen Lyzeum zu Versailles, seit 1879 in Genf Naturwissenschaften, widmete sich aber daneben, besonders seit 1885, wo er in Dresden lebte, kunsthistorischen, musikalischen und philosophischen Studien. 1899 siedelte er nach Wien über.

Seit Jahren datierten schon damals seine engen Beziehungen zu dem Kulturkreis, der um Richard Wagner entstand, und aus ihnen erwuchs eine große Anzahl tief gehaltvoller Werke, die für unsere Zeit ebenso grundlegend sind wie für die kommenden Geschlechter. Unter ihnen seien besonders erwähnt:

„Das Drama Richard Wagners" (Leipzig 1892), die reich mit Bildern geschmückte Biographie „Richard Wagner" (München 1896), „Die ersten zwanzig Jahre der Bayreuther Bühnenfestspiele" (Bayreuth 1896). Ihnen folgte das große geschichtsphilosophische Werk „Das neunzehnte Jahrhundert", von dem der erste Band „Die Grundlagen des zwanzigsten Jahrhunderts" 1899 in München erschienen. Von seinen zahlreichen Werken müssen außerdem noch Erwähnung finden seine Arbeiten über Goethe und Immanuel Kant; ferner „Arische Weltanschauung", „Worte Christi" und aus seiner letzten Schaffensperiode, seiner Leidenszeit, „Lebenswege meines Denkens" und „Mensch und Gott".

Chamberlain gehört zu den vielen Ausländern, auf die das deutsche Wesen wie eine magische Anziehungskraft wirkte. Das mag wohl im tiefsten Grund seine Abstammung erklären; sein Vater stand als Kapitän in der britischen Marine, allein seine Großmutter war eine geborene Deutsche. Das Blut der nordischen Rasse schlägt in dem Enkel endlich in einem überzeugten Bekenntnis zum Deutschtum wieder siegreich durch; seine Lehr- und Wanderjahre mit ihrer fast chaotischen Vielgestaltigkeit an Eindrücken können dem eigentlich Heimatlosen die Sehnsucht nach dem ruhenden Pol in der Erscheinungen Flucht erst stillen, als er im Geist von Bayreuth die Erfüllung seines artverwandten Strebens fand. Aus dem Bayreuther Kulturkreis, dessen Mittelpunkt Wagner war, ist neben vielen anderen Großen als einer der bedeutendsten Chamberlain hervorgegangen. Seine ganze Entwicklung ist ohne die Bayreuther Gedanken nicht vorstellbar. Bei aller Reichhaltigkeit, Vielgestaltigkeit seines Wissens bedeutet Bayreuth gerade

die Synthese, die Zusammenfassung der Einzelarbeiten zu einem organischen Ganzen, das in ähnlich gewaltigem Umfang am Beispiel Goethes gemessen, nur wenigen anderen gelungen ist.

Die entscheidende Wendung im Leben dieses Denkers trat ein, als er in den denkwürdigen Tagen des Kriegsausbruches 1870 deutschen Boden betrat.

„Hier ist nur das zu betonen", berichtet er, „der Einfluß, den diese Erlebnisse auf das Gemüt des Vierzehnjährigen ausüben mußten, indem ihm . . . ein heroisches Deutschland vor Augen stand, sich aufrichtend in der unüberwindlichen Kraft seines Rechtes und seiner reisigen Mannschaften, angeführt von unsterblichen Helden: Wahrlich, ein großartiger Auftakt zu meiner Einführung in die Welt des Deutschgedankens!"

Und 1876 schreibt er:

„Je mehr ich andere Nationen kennen lerne, desto mehr liebe ich Deutschland und die Deutschen. Mein Glaube, daß die ganze Zukunft Europas, d. h. der Zivilisation der Welt Deutschland in Händen liegt, ist zur Sicherheit geworden. Das Leben der Deutschen ist ein ganz anderes als das von anderen Menschen."

Dann kommt Bayreuth, das er selbst als die „Sonne seines Lebens" bezeichnet. Er erlebt 1882 die Festspiele. So fand er, an der Schwelle seines

Die letzte Aufnahme des Verblichenen

vierten Jahrzehnts stehend, sein Vaterland in Deutschland, seine Heimat in Bayreuth, sein Vorbild aber in Wagner.

„Richard Wagner schenkte mir den archimedischen Ankerpunkt im Raume, er schenkte meinen Augen das gestaltende Licht, meinem Herzen die treibende Wärme."

*

Chamberlains Lebensarbeit ist so groß, so umfassend und vielgestaltig, daß in einer kurzen Skizze nur andeutungsweise auf das Bedeutendste eingegangen werden kann. Um sein großes Werk, die „Grundlagen" allein ist eine Literatur entstanden, die dem Umfang der Goethe- und Wagnerliteratur wenig nachstehen dürfte. Sie bilden mit dem Kernpunkt seines Schaffens, sowohl als politisches wie auch als kulturelles und ethisches Werk. In Wien entstanden, gaben sie der damals sich entwickelnden großdeutschen Bewegung und damit allen verwandten späteren Richtungen, die sich von jener seitdem ableiten, das feste wissenschaftliche Fundament. Selbst wieder im Bayreuther Kulturkreis verankert, eröffneten die Grundlagen einen Rückblick und Ausblick über das gesamte Leben der Zeit vom Gesichtswinkel der Rassenfrage aus. Seine weiteren Schriften fügen sich organisch in dieses Gefüge grundsätzlicher Weltanschauung in wunderbarer Fülle ein. Er hat mit ihnen allen dem deutschen Volk die geistigen Waffen geschmiedet und geschärft, die es in seinem letzten Lebenskampf so notwendig wie noch nie braucht. Mit Seherblick durchdrang der Geist dieses Mannes die letzten Tiefen der Zusammenhänge deutschen Wachsens und Blühens, deutscher Not und Anfechtung. Seine Erkenntnisse sind Gemeingut aller erwachenden Deutschen geworden, bis zu einem Grade, daß man von einer Ineinssetzung seines jahrelangen theoretischen Schaffens mit dem Tageskampf der völkischen Erneuerung sprechen muß.

Der Nationalsozialismus, diese Kern des erwachenden Deutschlands, war dem großen Denker ein Symbol der Zukunft unseres Volkes, zu dem er sich trotz der Schwere der Zeit und trotz der Schwere seines körperlichen Leidens, in rückhaltloser Zuversicht und zuversichtlicher Hoffnung bekannte. Und in den schwersten Stunden der jungen Bewegung hat er sich mit größtem Bekenntnismut für sie ausgesprochen.

Unsere Pflicht wird es sein, das geistige Erbe des großen völkischen Denkers zu hüten, zu seiner Verbreitung beizutragen, bis sie allen deutschen Volksgenossen zum Gemeingut geworden sind; denn dies wird die größte Stärkung und der stärkste Ansporn im Kampf um Deutschlands Sein oder Nichtsein werden.

DEVTSCHLAND

7. Nazi propaganda against racial mixing, superimposing a Jewish stereotype on an Aryan woman. From *Antisemitismus der Welt in Wort und Bild,* ed. Robert Korber and Theodor Pugel (Berlin, 1935), p. 229.

8. "Victims of the Jews!" The famous "ritual murder" number of *Der Stürmer,* withdrawn by Julius Streicher almost immediately as the Nazis did not want to spoil their "respectable" image at that point. From *Der Stürmer,* Sondernummer I (May 1934), front page.

Judenopfer

Durch die Jahrtausende vergoß der Jud, geheimem Ritus folgend, Menschenblut
Der Teufel sitzt uns heute noch im Nacken, es liegt an Euch die Teufelsbrut zu packen

9. "The Eternal Wandering Jew"—colored woodcut by Gustav Doré (1852). Generations of Europeans were raised on the "Doré Bible." From Eduard Fuchs, *Die Juden in der Karikatur* (Munich, 1921).

10. Title page of a popular French edition of the *Protocols of the Elders of Zion* (Paris, 1934). The picture itself can be found in many earlier editions as well. From the Wiener Library, Tel Aviv.

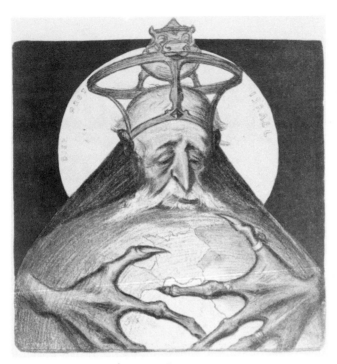

11. One of the most famous caricatures of the House of Rothschild, created by C. Léandre, a minor French painter, in 1898. It was taken over by most anti-Semitic movements, and was also used to illustrate some of the editions of the *Protocols of the Elders of Zion*. Notice that the halo is a coin. From Eduard Fuchs, *Die Juden in der Karikatur* (Munich, 1921).

12. Front page of *In Plain German: A Weekly for Law and Justice* (1920), the racist newspaper published and written by Hitler's political mentor, Dietrich Eckart: The subhead reads: "From Hungary's Days of Horror," and the text beneath Belá Kûn's picture: "Look, just look! You don't have to do any more than that to realize what threatens us." The stereotype is used, once more, to characterize the Jewish-Bolshevik conspiracy.

1ʳᵉ Année. — N° 1.   Paris et Départements, le Numéro: 10 Centimes.   Lundi 17 juillet 1893.

LA LIBRE PAROLE

ILLUSTRÉE

La France aux Français

| RÉDACTION 14, boulevard Montmartre | Directeur : ÉDOUARD DRUMONT | ADMINISTRATION 14, boulevard Montmartre |

LA SÉCHERESSE

Elle devient sèche, cette vieille terre De France :
Elle a encore soif de sang et de larmes.
Il faudra l'arroser incessamment.

13. Front page of the first issue of Édouard Drumont's *La Libre Parole* (*Free Speech*), July 17, 1893. The text under the drawing reads: "This ancient land of France is getting dry: it is thirsty again for blood and tears; it must be watered constantly." The crown on the head of the Jewish figure is a reminder of Alphonse de Toussenel's pamphlet, *The Jews, Kings of the Age* (1845), directed against the House of Rothschild. From Eduard Fuchs, *Die Juden in der Karikatur* (Munich, 1921).

14. A British Fascist pamphlet which lampoons the Public Order Act of January 1, 1937, outlawing public demonstrations and the wearing of uniforms. The pamphlet also characterizes the young man who leads this illegal procession into London's predominantly Jewish East End as "a fine example of the type of young man growing up in the British Union of Fascists and National Socialists." From an undated pamphlet in the Wiener Library, Tel Aviv.

15. Cover of *Degenerate Music: An Accounting* by Hans Severus Ziegler (director of the German National Theater, Weimar), published in 1938 on the occasion of the Exhibition of Degenerate Music at Düsseldorf. The "invasion by brutal jazz rhythms of the Germanic world of music" illustrated by the cover represents supposed Jewish-black degeneracy. From the Yad Vashem Library, Jerusalem.

CHAPTER THREE

Nation, Language, and History

T HE REVIVAL of historical consciousness that took place in the eighteenth century was of fundamental importance for the growth of the racial ideal. It posited laws of organic development which were also transferred to anthropology and linguistics. The journey of a people through time was regarded as crucial, separating one from another. For Lamarck and Buffon, historical development had been conditioned by environmental factors such as climate and geography. For them the differences between peoples were merely chance variations. But now a deeper gulf was carved between men and nations. It was not merely the fact of a people's distinctive history that was involved here. Men like Herder believed that a people's history was not man-made but followed a divine plan. History became national myth.

The Pietistic background of the eighteenth century as opposed to the Enlightenment becomes important here. It was more widespread and at the same time it penetrated deeper into the popular consciousness. Pietism restored the personal bonds which the Enlightenment tended to dissolve in its concern with abstract principles. The "galloping Christians" (as the Evangelicals were often called) felt a personal relationship to Christ, which they expressed through prayer and a life that constituted the outward sign of inward rebirth. Pietistic brotherhoods, conventicles, or even the daily worship within the home, brought people together as a true community of shared commitment and a felt rebirth.

Such a view of life tended to push aside the outward world and to concentrate upon the rhythm of a personal, shared piety. But the Pietistic universe was not static, for the relationship between God and His creation was dynamic, involving daily struggle and rebirth. This struggle and rebirth strove toward an ever more perfect union of men with God and of men among themselves. God forms and extends creation from within man; and such striving, while primarily inward, must also push outward into the world. It is at this point that the ideal of the fatherland becomes important.[1]

As we saw earlier, the fatherland—especially in Germany—was regarded as a product of man's inner striving toward unity within the divine plan. In 1766 the Pietistic author Justus Möser wrote of the continuity of history, in which there were no breaks because God would not suddenly change course. History fulfilled a divine plan, and the vehicle for such fulfillment was the fatherland. Here the Pietistic ideal of community acquired a new dimension. Pietists always wanted to live within a true community, to be loved and to give love, a desire which determined their ideal of peoplehood. The fatherland must be a community filled with friendship and enthusiasm.[2] For a patriot like Lavater, an heir of pietism, this longing for community was decisive.[3]

Herder, writing in Germany, vitally influenced the disunited peoples of Europe who longed for national unity. For him, the nature of a people was expressed through the *Volksgeist*—the unchanging spirit of a people refined through history. What gives unity to the life and culture of a people is the persistence of the original juices which are its basic strength. Herder likened history to a tree. Root and tree are analogous to the relationship of God and creation. They are the principles which govern a people and its changing historical shapes.[4] In this organic approach, change and continuity exist as parallel layers of the "tree of life." The continuity derives from the roots, which exemplify the *Volksgeist* and whose ever-flowing juices a people must conserve through the changes of history.

The *Volksgeist* revealed itself to Herder through the mythologies, songs, and sagas of a people. These go back to the origins of a people, and if conserved will rejuvenate their spirit. Herder did not deny the modern world, for he could not very well go counter to the divine plan which regulates the course of history. Nevertheless, there is an ambivalence in his attitude. For example, he praised the progress that had been made in matters of morality, behavior, and culture during modern times, but cautioned against condemning earlier ages. Every stage of historical development has its divine purpose. However, the roots of a people represent an unspoiled genuineness of feeling, spontaneity, and force.

Whatever the details of Herder's philosophy, he accorded each separate people a separate *Volksgeist*, which was expressed through its culture and thereby encompassed the whole community. At times the inner spirit seemed to produce an ideal-type which never varied within the organic historical development. The Germans, he wrote in 1787, had provided a wall against barbarian penetration and had thus conquered, protected, and fertilized a great part of Europe. Their warrior community and tribal character were the foundations for Europe's freedom, culture, and security. Long resistance against the Romans had strengthened their character. The Germans possessed a heroic spirit and strength of body, with "their big, strong and beautiful figure, their terribly blue eyes . . . filled with the spirit of moderation and loyalty." [5] Herder also was an admirer of Winckelmann and his Greek ideal-type, yet he was still a man of the Enlightenment and certainly no racist, though it is easy to see how his *Volksgeist* could be used to describe innate qualities of race.

Herder explicitly rejected racial classification. He thought that there is no real biological link between peoples, but only cultural and linguistic bonds—"A monkey is not your brother, but a Negro is, and you should not rob and oppress him." He made similar remarks about the Slavs against whom the Germans sinned grievously, and he hoped that the Jews would soon be fully assimilated throughout Europe. In no other continent, Herder tells us, had peoples mixed so much as in Europe. [6] He gave the impression that the urge toward totality, toward unity, accommodated different peoples within a shared culture like the branches of a tree.

Nevertheless, Herder was instrumental in awakening national

consciousness in central and eastern Europe. Growth, vitality, and originality were all characteristic of the national community and expressed through the national language. A shared language, according to Herder, was the basic factor which in the dim past had brought the community together. Language exemplified the spontaneity of the *Volksgeist*; it was the "juice of life" of a people. The German language was pure, a stepsister of that most perfect of languages—Greek.[7] Thus German legends, sagas, and ancient poetry concretized the spirit which derived from the roots of the Volk. Culture was defined as centering on the national language and the traditional national literature. Again, Herder did not mean to denigrate non-Germanic peoples, whose literature he also praised highly. Cultural contacts between nations were important and no nation should force its culture upon another. For instance, he condemned the efforts of Austria's Emperor Joseph II to spread the German language in his domains. The principle "Equal but separate" defines Herder's approach to a world of nations.

Herder was in some sense a cosmopolitan, not only because of the influence on him of the Enlightenment but also because of his Christianity, which saw human diversity as part of a divine plan. He was a democrat who hated despots, and an optimist who thought universal peace was possible. His ideal of national consciousness through that literature which the people themselves had produced was bound to democratize nationalism. But this, in turn, created a still deeper chasm between the different peoples. The nation was not symbolized by the ruler who could unite many different people under his banner, or confined to people who happened to live in a certain territory. Rather, the nation was a community separated from others by its own inner spirit, as expressed through its language and its culture. The stimulus afforded by Herder's thought was vital to the national awakening during the nineteenth century not only of Germans, but also of Czechs, Magyars, and Poles, to give but a few examples.[8]

At first, such modern nationalism was tolerant. Thus, when Germans celebrated the anniversary of victory over Napoleon at the Battle of Leipzig, in 1815, Jews attended services of thanksgiving

together with Protestants and Catholics, singing patriotic songs side
by side with Christians.[9] One has the feeling that the elation over
national liberation cemented a community of which Herder would
have approved (he had been dead twelve years). But even by 1815,
signs that racial classification would intrude upon national consciousness and that language would become a means to explore
racial roots already existed. Nor would the ideal-type be forgotten.
Tolerance would have no place here; only a thin line separates
struggles for national liberation and ideas of national dominance.

Herder's emphasis upon language as the expression of a shared
past was common to a whole generation of philologists by the end
of the eighteenth and the beginning of the nineteenth centuries.
These philologists conceptrated upon the search for linguistic origins in an attempt to unveil the roots of race. They concluded that
Sanskrit had been the basis of all Western languages and that it had
been imported into Europe from Asia by the migration of Aryan
peoples. And it is here that the ominous term "Aryan" makes its
first appearance.

This linguistic root was intimately connected with the current
Romantic worship of India, praised for her mystery religions and
for the grandeur and durability of her monuments. Egypt was
thought to have been a colony of India, and by the eighteenth century pyramids had come into fashion not only as ornaments for
gardens, but also as tombs, perceived by many as "mysteries in
granite"—as Théophile Gautier was to call them later.[10] Moreover,
pyramidal forms were used to give greater dimensions to the classical and Greek architectural forms. Certainly, there is a connection
between the cult of things Egyptian (and hence also Indian) and the
supposed Aryan origins of language. For those peoples who had
produced this language and emigrated into Europe shared the
durability and the grandeur which this part of Asia and the Near
East exemplified for so many Romantics.

The most celebrated expert on India of the eighteenth century, Sir
William Jones, in his lectures to the Asia Society of Calcutta
(1784–94), refused to deal with the common origins of West and
East. Nevertheless, Jones claimed that there was a connection be-

tween Egypt, India, Greece, and Italy long before these nations had settled within their respective territories. He proved this interrelationship through a comparison of the gods that had ruled over all these peoples in heathen times. But he refused to decide "which was the original and which was the copy." Moreover, Jones was skeptical about the use of language in order to find roots or common denominators. For all that, he admired Asia and felt that Sanskrit was more perfect than Greek and Latin. He believed that Europe and Asia were different, for reason and taste were the prerogatives of Europeans, while Asians soared to the loftier heights of imagination.[11]

Sir William Jones saw shared traits between India and Europe, but no common origins. He held that Greece and Rome shared these traits in a special manner—not an unusual thought for someone steeped in classical culture and at the same time filled with admiration for India. Some of Jones's contemporaries, for example, thought that Ulysses had come from India. It was Friedrich Schlegel who in 1808 put forward a full-blown theory of Aryan origins traced through linguistics. His *Concerning the Language and Wisdom of the Indians* (*Über die Sprache und Weisheit der Inder*) used those very word comparisons between Sanskrit and other languages which Sir William Jones had deplored.

Schlegel asserted that German, Greek, and Latin had a common root in Sanskrit. English was included in this family, but Slavonic, for example, was explicitly excluded. Classical grammar was said to be especially close to Sanskrit. In order to prove this contention, Schlegel went beyond his linguistic comparisons to posit a feeling, an affinity, between these languages, which was based upon the "inner character" of letters.[12]

If some scientific method informed word comparisons, here we are wandering in the pastures of Romantic emotions. Suppose the inner man was important and the external world was always internalized, why should this not also apply to grammar? If there were deep affinities between Indian wisdom and that of the Germans and Greeks, then common linguistic roots would surely reflect them. More significantly, Schlegel called the languages deriving from Indian roots "organic languages," living seeds of growth and vitality. But languages thought to derive from the Chinese, like Slavonic, American-Indian, or Japanese, Schlegel branded as atomized and lacking in depth. Indeed, languages without Indian sources of inspiration formed for him a random community, "blown together by the wind," and liable to be pulled asunder at any moment.[13]

Language therefore typified community: the Germans, ancients, and Indians formed a true organic community; others did not. The Aryan peoples thus shared common roots, and a great number of them had left India for northern Europe. They did so not out of any necessity, but because of "some sort of miraculous concept of the high dignity and splendor of the North," which Schlegel believed was verified through the content of Indian sagas.[14] In this way Schlegel set down the maxims of an Aryan superiority exemplified by linguistic roots and reaffirmed through the Aryan migration to the wondrous European north. Though he never stated such a superiority explicitly, it is inherent in his theory of noble and ignoble languages.

Scholarship was used to support highly subjective judgments about the excellence of Indian origins. Christian Lassen (1800–1876), a pupil of August Wilhelm Schlegel (Friedrich's brother) and his successor as a professor at the University of Bonn, was more popular among later racists than any other Indian scholar because of his monumental learning. From Lassen's hefty four-volume *Indian Antiquities* (*Indische Altertumskunde*, 1858–62) they culled statements to the effect that those who originated in India possessed the highest and most perfect genius, and alone enjoyed true harmony of soul. Lassen wrote that India combined the deep imagination which Hegel had already ascribed to her, with sharp reason as exemplified in the construction of her grammar. There were peoples who lacked this balance, especially the Semites (including both Jews and Arabs), who were playthings of their own selfish will. Neither Jews nor Arabs, he exclaimed, possessed epic poems in which the ego of the poet vanished before the concerns of the community.[15] Literature was once more offered as proof for a subjective attitude dividing the races from one another.

Lassen no longer feared to make racial judgments. India's Aryan origins set the noble Indo-Germanic people against the ignoble Semites. Admiration for India had become a means of racial identification, and linguistics was crucial in making this judgment. Language symbolized the common journey of a people through time; therefore the Aryans, who gave the superior nations of Europe their language, were endowed with all the ideals Europeans were supposed to hold high—honor, nobility, courage, and an aesthetically pleasing appearance. They were said to be a rural people, a virile peasant race. Friedrich Max Müller (1823–1900) teaching at Oxford held that the original meaning of the word "Aryan" was "tillers of the soil." For this reason, in 1864, he included the Slavs among the Aryan people, for they had remained peasants.[16]

Long before Müller, the concept of Aryan origins through language had captured the imagination of many Europeans. In France Jules Michelet, the historian, looked to India as the mother of French culture; and in 1831 a French Catholic journal wrote about the "natural revelation" which came from that continent.[17] Adolphe Pictet, writing in France between 1859 and 1863, affirmed that the Aryan race did once exist in India, but that through many waves of migration it had settled over almost all of Europe and parts of Asia. Whenever people spoke an Aryan dialect this was undoubtedly the decisive element in the make-up of such a race. Pictet's classification and comparison of the many languages spoken among "our Aryan family" was widely regarded as laying the groundwork for reconstructing the world of the ancient Aryans.

Pictet painted the life of the Aryan ancestors as a terrestial paradise. He saw them as young and vigorous peasant farmers, who in faraway India had developed free political institutions and maintained a solid family life. He added that the Aryans as a race were destined by providence to dominate the globe at some future date.[18] For Pictet, Müller, and many other philologists, this paradise was in sharp contrast with that modernity in whose midst the present Aryans had to live.

Both German and French scholars collaborated in forging the Aryan myth. At mid-century, Comte Arthur de Gobineau, most famous of all, made full use of these linguistic theories and the Aryan entered European history as racial myth. The quest for Aryan origins would continue; already by mid-century some looked to the north, to Scandinavia, rather than to Asia for racial roots. Eventually, Heinrich Himmler would attempt unsuccessfully to finance an expedition to Tibet in 1937–38 which, in addition to geographical and anthropological exploration, was also supposed to pursue linguistic investigations. Other young Nazis would travel to Lapland or Sweden to seek their Aryan ancestors.[19]

It was Friedrich Max Müller who best summed up the racial consequences of Indomania. Müller brusquely rejected the relevance of anthropology to race. In 1854, he gave a lecture accusing those who measured skulls and bones of failing to agree among themselves how many races there were, and therefore falling back upon a belief in the unity of the species and chance variations. It was quite true, as we saw, that anthropologists could not agree about the number of races, but it was not accurate to accuse them of failing to make racial divisions stick. Nevertheless, such strictures enabled Müller to claim that linguistics was the "science" which established the existence and nature of the Aryan family of people: "it is language that makes man." Language, he claimed, is surely closer to the essence of man than his skin or his color, his skull or his hair.[20] This was an extreme rejection of ideal-types—one that would have little actual effect but that demonstrated a single-minded devotion to linguistic Aryan roots.

Yet rejection of the ideal-type by denying outward and bodily conformity did not mean chaos. Instead, Müller believed that certain virtues sprang from Aryan origins and were continued by those who had migrated to Europe. Independence and self-reliance were two Aryan qualities which must have developed during the migration from one continent to another. These qualities in turn were associated with a life close to the soil, always considered the reservoir of Aryan strength. The peoples who brought numerous varieties of Aryan speech to Europe continued the virtues that had characterized the original Aryans and developed them further through the "irresistible impulse" that had started the great migration. The Aryans of ancient India were still alive, Müller asserted, for their "thought still runs in our thoughts, as their blood may run in our veins." There was a "great Aryan brotherhood" and, once more, it encompassed the glories of Greece and Rome.[21]

By the time Müller wrote, emphasis on language as a crucial element of nationality had long been established. Müller was partly correct when he wrote that common blood without common language leaves men strangers and that language formed the essence of any community. Many of the nationalities in the Austrian Empire had in fact developed their national consciousness in the struggle against eighteenth-century attempts to impose German upon them as the official language of the government, and the language disputes during the last decades of the nineteenth century would once more demonstrate the identity of language and national feeling.

The rising intolerance of nationalism was often directed toward showing that those who did not share the common Aryan roots could not handle the native tongue. For example, influential anti-Jewish works of the early nineteenth century, such as Sessa's *Our Visitors* (*Unser Verkehr*, 1816), made much of the supposed inability of assimilated Jews to speak German properly. Indeed, it became usual in anti-Semitic works for Jews to speak a mixture of German and Yiddish, a "jargon" from which not even a Rothschild could escape. The linguistic abilities of African Negroes were treated with similar contempt: language was made a test for their ability to integrate into English and for that matter French society.[22] Thus, language became one of the pillars of nationality and a means to stigmatize strangers.

Despite its crucial importance, language was only one element in the definition of national origins and character. The word "Aryan" attained general currency, but it was not unchallenged. The term "Caucasian" became equally important, derived not from linguistics but from anthropology. Friedrich Blumenbach introduced this word in 1795 to describe white Europeans in general, for he believed that the slopes of the Caucasus were the original home of the most beautiful European species. Blumenbach's scientific proof for such a contention was that the Georgian skull was archetypical, other types departing from it in various degrees. The Mongolian and the Negro were furthest from this true beauty.[23] The term "Caucasian" restricted the European-wide *Homo sapiens* of Linné, but it was broader than the "Aryan," which took in only a fraction of the Caucasians.

Eventually for some even the term "Aryan" included too many people and was too cosmopolitan. Gustaf Kossinna in his *German Prehistory* (*Die Deutsche Vorgeschichte*, 1911) attempted to detach the Germanic heritage from both the Indians and the ancients. The Germans were said to have been superior to the Romans (not to mention Asians), and this was supported by an analysis of artifacts from the stone, bronze, and iron ages. Thus the vision became still more restricted. Not *Homo sapiens*, not Caucasians, nor Aryans, but only Germans were a superior people. Kossinna's work was later to be continued by Alfred Rosenberg during the Third Reich in an attempt to control all prehistorical research and to use it to prove the racial superiority of Aryan Germans.[24] Heinrich Himmler, who also claimed competence in this field through the *Ahnenerbe* (ancestral heritage), an institution within the SS, ranged wider afield in order to find the cradle of the German race; but he too restricted Aryan roots to the Germans and the Dutch (who as "lower Germans" were thought to be of the same race). Racism by its very nature tended on the one hand to become ever more narrowly defined, and on the other to pose a synthesis of all the qualities a true people must possess.

The terms "people," "nation," and "race" tended at times to become identical during the second half of the nineteenth century, despite Herder's earlier efforts to keep them apart. To be sure, toward the end of the nineteenth century some Germans attempted to circumvent the chauvinism inherent in such belief by maintaining that the Volk was merely a stepping stone toward a common humanity. First, man had to be a part of his Volk; as such he could then proudly join the wider fellowship of all men of good will. But this trend of Volkish thought was isolated and, in the main, embraced by Jews like Gustav Landauer and Martin Buber.[25] These men wanted to guard their membership in the German nation without giving up ideals of a common humanity that had served to free Jews from their ghetto past and might yet rid them of their stereotype. Even when believing in peoplehood, nation, and race, it was possible to deplore ideas of superiority and posit a world made up of separate races who respected each other. But the contracting tendencies of race and the growing exclusiveness brought with them an increasing emphasis upon ideals of superiority and domination.

It should not surprise us that the Indians themselves were soon excluded from the Aryan race which had left their shores for the mysterious north. Adolf Hitler, for example, believed that Indians must be ruled by white men, and was therefore hostile to the movement for Indian national liberation. His low estimate of the Hindus was shared by others like Alfred Rosenberg. For Rosenberg the light-colored Aryans had conquered the black and brown Hindus in the first place, and after their emigration had left an inferior people behind.[26]

The narrowing vision was combined with the effort to grasp the people or race as a totality. Linguistics and the subjective judgments of anthropologists had been conceived as a way into the essential characteristics of race. After all, Herder had made language a symbol of the culture of a people; and once its roots had been discovered, the mainstream of national consciousness formed a synthesis of language, anthropology, geography, and history. Scholars and popularizers were concerned with all of national culture.

Heinrich Riehl in his *Land and People* (*Land und Leute*, 1853) pleaded for a "natural history" of the Volk which should include everything about a people as it lives and has its being.[27] His book ranges from the formation of villages and towns, to the geography and demography of the German people, ending with a discussion of politics and the Church. What holds all these facets together are the ancient customs of the people, which saw their true effectiveness during the "splendid Middle Ages." Riehl founded the pseudo-science of "Heimatkunde" in central Europe—a term that does not merely mean civics but studying one's "native country," encompassing a unity symbolized through the persistence of immemorial customs. Custom sanctified through history, here taking the place of language, becomes the integrative force of the race.

Whether in Protestant northern Germany or Catholic southern Germany, such ideas became institutionalized in education from the first decades of the nineteenth century onward, and spread among all the awakening nations of Europe. History books used in German schools attest to their efficiency. Some books, like that by August Hermann Niemayer written in 1796, stressed the spiritual community of the people linked through a common language; others saw in the lasting influence of German prehistory the road to national consciousness. Here especially the praise of Germanic ideas was combined with emphasis upon Christianity. The Germans, not the Jews, became the chosen people and the vessel of salvation.[28] Tacitus's laudatory description of the ancient Germans was linked to the New Testament, and both were presented as a vast advance over the Old Testament of the Jews. The journey of the people through history was a sacred drama, in which they symbolized not only the unity of life and nature but salvation itself. At the beginning of the nineteenth century, the brothers Grimm in their preoccupation with fairy tales had already written: "The eternal, invisible, toward which every noble spirit must strive, is revealed in its purest and most distinct in the totality, that is, in the idea of a Volk."[29]

The Volk was the vessel of faith. In this way the Volk was exalted as a separate unit, charged with the custody of the Holy Grail (the mythical chalice in which Christ's blood had been gathered at the crucifixion), and within which each member fulfilled a sacred function. Superiority was established within a cosmic framework, to which linguistics and history contributed the proof. We have earlier discussed the ideal-type of anthropology that came to represent the outward appearance of the new chosen people. All these factors worked hand in hand to produce an identity of racial and national superiority. But such a superiority was also a search for roots, and therefore its final proof had to be historical. The roots determine the firmness of the tree.

National historiography had made great strides since Herder. The emphasis on the origins of one people also served to distinguish it from all other peoples. Books like Tacitus's *Germania* (A.D. 98), rediscovered in the sixteenth century, were now used as witness for the virtues practiced by Germanic ancestors. Tacitus's account of the ancient Germans stressed precisely those qualities of their life which the philologists had identified among the Aryan forefathers. The ancient Germans kept themselves pure and did not mix with other tribes; they did not live in cities and barely tolerated any kind of cohesive settlement. These Germans were self-reliant, courageous, and loyal; they were incapable of lying and cheating, wearing their heart on their sleeve, as it were. The Germans showed the same characteristics which Müller had attributed to India's Aryans who migrated into the European north.

This theme persisted. For example, in 1870, William Stubbs, bishop of Oxford, wrote in the introduction to his *Select Charters and Other Illustrations of English Constitutional History* that the Anglo-Saxon forefathers shared the primeval German pride of purity of extraction, and honored their women and family ties. Migration here did not create individuality but a sense of order and reliance upon the community. The common Teutonic heritage, the bishop continued, set England on the road to a strong and steady development of freedom exemplified by the *Magna Carta* and parliamentary government. Excerpts from Tacitus's *Germania* were included in Stubbs's collection, which was one of the standard books for the teaching of English constitutional history until well after the Second World War. Once again, primeval purity of extraction and love of freedom were fused together; true freedom therefore was in the custody of the Teutonic race.

The French could hardly be expected to agree. On their behalf the historian Numa Denis Fustel de Coulanges (1830–1889) made an identical plea, only here the French monopolized the Teutonic heritage. Fustel de Coulanges believed that the Teutonic Franks were destined to fight the Germans in order to civilize them. However, such a theory of internecine warfare among Teutons proved clumsy, and Fustel came instead to propagate the notion of a Celtic race as the ancestor of the French. Celts displaced the Teutons in French racial thought, though the mission to civilize Germans was not abandoned.[30] Statues of the Celtic hero Vercingetorix were erected at Clermont-Ferrand and elsewhere, just as the Germans celebrated their ancient hero, Arminius the Cheruskan, in drama, poetry, and monuments.[31] For all their supposed differences, German and Celt had certain traits in common.

The conviction grew that the ancient Germans and Celts were free men, who in their primeval tribal institutions practiced a rough and ready kind of equality; their kings or nobles used persuasion rather than force. Müller had also stressed freedom as a part of the Aryan world of self-reliance. Historians in Germany, England, and France investigated the past in order to find the origins of free institutions which might serve to explain the abiding love of freedom ascribed to their respective peoples. The rise of modern nationalism entailed a competition as to which of the peoples of Europe had a greater love of freedom. This element of modern nationalism is often overlooked, unjustly, since the community which formed the nation was supposed to make the individual free. The national community was based upon shared emotions, language, and history, and not upon force. Moreover, in central and eastern Europe, nationalism between roughly 1815 and 1870 was embattled against the reaction that wanted to suppress it. National liberation meant an emphasis upon national freedom. Certainly, until such nationalities achieved unity, both outward liberty and freedom within the national community were deemed essential. For England and France, each long unified, the task was to root ideas of freedom more firmly, relying on the past as a weapon against the corrupt present. The image of the free man on his free acres, whether in India or in Germany's Teutoburger Forest, appealed to many. So did the supposedly free ancient tribal institutions which Germans, Englishmen, and the French now discovered in their past.

Those who did not share these roots were inferior precisely because they did not know freedom and therefore wanted to enslave the world. This was a major accusation against the Jews. The urge toward acquiring power over others was thought inherent in their lack of spirituality. Voltaire had already put the case graphically: the Jews either had to conquer everybody or be hated by the whole human race.[32] The Negroes, in turn, could not know true freedom because they were thought incapable of forming a true community in the first place. If the Jews longed only for domination, the blacks lived in chaos, as Gobineau emphasized. Thus, Jews and Negroes could never become viable nations, and this was thought to be an innate fault of each race.

The developing ideal of a national community had left behind Herder's cosmopolitanism.[33] Between human communities a deep gulf had been created, which was based not on equality but on Aryan domination. The subjective factors of history, language, and national salvation provided a fertile soil for the doctrine of race. From the beginning, that doctrine had passed from science to myth, and at the same time attempted to account for the total human being, both his inner nature and outward appearance. Nationalism added his roots in history, language, and the native landscape, and traced the Aryan virtues from the past to the present. This edifice was not yet completely erected by the mid-nineteenth century, but the scaffolding existed. Comte Arthur de Gobineau seemed to many of his contemporaries destined to complete the edifice. He would prove not so much the father of racist ideology as its synthesizer at a peculiarly apt moment in European history, when the revolutions of 1848 and their consequences were shaking the continent.

CHAPTER FOUR

From Gobineau to de Lapouge

OMTE Arthur de Gobineau (1816–1882) was not an original
thinker, but a synthesizer who drew on anthropology, linguistics, and history in order to construct a fully furnished
intellectual edifice where race explained everything in the past,
present, and future—whether triumphs, such as the Renaissance, or
the decadence symbolized by the France in which he lived. His
Essay on the Inequality of Human Races (*Essai sur l'Inégalité des
Races Humaines*, 1853–55) spelled out his racism in awesome detail and was based upon the best scholarship then available, as well
as upon his own observations made during extensive travels.

But it was a personal and psychological obsession which gave
him that outlook upon the world his racism was meant to explain.
He was exceptionally proud of the antiquity and supposedly noble
lineage of the Gobineau family. In reality, Gobineau's branch of
that family was not noble at all, for after the death of an uncle,
Arthur Gobineau had adopted a title to which he had no proper
claim. But he had always praised the nobility as necessary for the
establishment of true freedom and virtue in this world. Chivalry,
honor, and an aristocratic ideal of freedom as exemplified in ancient Teutonic tribal organization made up his particular utopia.
The France to which he referred in his writings was a mythical nation of aristocrats and peasants, where local relationships determined the polity, giving it a stability lacking in the real world. This
point of view was in itself unoriginal. It had long since informed

French conservatism, and had already occupied those concerned with national origins.

Through this perspective, Gobineau grasped dangers of the modern age which others had overlooked. This was not only an age of centralization but also one of confrontation. Newly risen Caesars and the mob faced each other, he thought, and in the process crushed all those forces that protected freedom and virtue. The *Essay* was written when this nightmare seemed to have come true: Napoleon III had carried out a *coup d'état* in 1851, and his dictatorial régime had been ratified by a vote of the people. Conservatives deplored centralization, but Gobineau saw the future as the age of the masses, giving a new dimension to his fears and to his attempts to explain them.

What had gone wrong? Gobineau reached out into the past in order to understand the present. He believed that the world was dominated by a series of civilizations. These civilizations, he held, could not be influenced by the environment because many different civilizations can co-exist in a single geographical region. Moreover, the rise and fall of civilizations was not the result of any chance variation but instead determined by a single cause: "The basic organization and character of all civilizations are equal to the traits and spirit of the dominant race."[1] Gobineau had found the one single cause which unlocked the door to the understanding of past, present, and future.

Gobineau classified races as his predecessors had done. Three basic races—yellow, black, and white—existed in the world and had produced their own civilizations. To understand the role which each race had played or was still playing in world history, its social structure and culture must be carefully analyzed. Gobineau was never concerned with skull measurements or facial angles. Instead, he reasoned partly from his own observations, partly from his wide reading, and partly from his considerable knowledge of linguistics. But observation and learning were buried under the analogies to the present which ran throughout the *Essay* and which gave each race its place in the present age.

The social and cultural effects of his three basic races led

Gobineau to take these out of their native landscape and instead to transfer their characteristics to a part of the French social structure. This gave a direct relevance to these races and served to explain conditions at home rather than in faraway places. Gobineau's importance lies not only in making race the key to world history, but also in the notion that observing foreign races helped to explain domestic frustrations: France herself was a microcosm of racial perils. Environmentalism was rejected, for the attitudes of yellow or black races could be found on one's own doorstep.

The yellow race, he believed, was materialistic, pedantic, and taken up with "a steady but uncreative drive towards material prosperity."[2] It lacked imagination and its language was incapable of expressing metaphysical thoughts, a point Friedrich Schlegel had already made about the Chinese language. The yellow race was destined to fulfill itself through commerce and trade. This race had all those characteristics which Gobineau fastened upon the bourgeoisie, whom he blamed for having destroyed the true France, based upon regionalism, nobility, and peasantry. Clearly, the yellow race possessed none of the virtues that characterized true nobility, and so was analogous to the French bourgeoisie.

The blacks also fitted into the scheme of contemporary politics. Gobineau gave them the characteristics by now traditional in racial thought: little intelligence, but overdeveloped senses which endowed them with a crude and terrifying power. The blacks were a mob on the loose, the masses that Gobineau envisaged in action during the French Revolution and in his own lifetime, eternal *sans culottes* who had collaborated with the middle classes to destroy the aristocratic France for which he yearned.

The white race represented the ideal of France, for it embodied the virtues of the nobility—love of freedom, honor, and spirituality. Again, Gobineau reverted to linguistic proof: the white race were Aryans, "innately" superior through those qualities they exemplified and the other two races lacked. Origins were crucial here, as they are in all racial thought. The Aryans, who first provided India with her élite and then formed the Teutonic heritage, stood opposed to the materialism and sensuousness of yellows or blacks. Freedom and honor worked in tandem to produce a nobility that ruled not by force but rather through its incontestable virtue. But, alas, the ideals of the white race no longer corresponded to the present state of affairs. Centralization and rule by force had taken the place of aristocratic example. The bourgeoisie had corrupted the nobility, and the people had been abandoned to false leadership.

Why had this happened? No race could stay pure, according to Gobineau, for it was bound to mix with inferior races and thus to degenerate. "The word degenerate applied to a people means . . . that this people no longer has the same intrinsic value as it had before, because it no longer has the same blood in its veins."[3] How did this degeneration of the white race occur? Gobineau believed that the yellow race had been the original inhabitants of Europe, and that these "Finns" populated all Europe, forming its lowest element. The Aryans were subsequently superimposed upon this population and eventually began to mix with it. Such miscegenation was destroying the white race. But was there still hope? Gobineau believed in the rise and fall of civilizations. The Aryan had created this civilization and inevitably miscegenation meant its fall. "The sad knowledge is not death," Gobineau concludes in his *Essay*, "it is the certitude that we arrive there degenerated; and perhaps that fear, reserved for our descendants, would leave us cold if we did not feel, with secret horror, that the hands of destiny are already upon us."[4]

The drama of the rise and fall of civilizations is a racial drama in which the white race is the pawn. Gobineau noted that the white race was becoming more like the yellow peoples in its materialism and more like the blacks as a mob that must be ruled by force. Such inferior races were in any case bound to dominate the next stage of history. He condemned slavery and was unhappy with the use made of the *Essay* in the American Confederacy (where his pessimistic conclusions were deleted). As for the Jews, in spite of Palestine—the "miserable corner of the earth" which had been their home—they were a race that had succeeded in everything it did, a free, strong, intelligent people of peasants and warriors that had produced more men of learning than merchants. The ancient

Jews demonstrated that the value of race was independent of all the material conditions of environment. But like all races the Jews had declined through miscegenation, mixing increasingly with peoples tainted heavily by black elements.[5] The Jews shared the fate of the Aryans.

There is no warrant for considering Gobineau anti-Semitic. At the end of the century, as we shall see, his ideas were turned against the Jews and he was used to demonstrate the lasting superiority of Germans, but that was not his intention. Gobineau was no prophet of German unity; he felt that the small states between the rivers Rhine and Elbe exemplified the regionalism he thought so important. The nation he despised most was England, which seemed to him the most bourgeois of all states. Thus, he advocated neither the use of force (which in any case would have been counter to what he considered true nobility) nor Germanism or anti-Semitism. He was, in fact, resigned to the fate of the white race, however sadly and with whatever frustrations.

Yet Gobineau's pessimism about the fate of the white race did not last his lifetime. *The Renaissance*, published in 1877, expressed his hope that the disaster might yet be averted. For that reason, perhaps, this proved the most immediately popular of all his writings, in spite of its abstruse content and form. *The Renaissance* was a "philosophical drama," which pictured an élite confronting a decadent Italy. Such heroes as Savonarola, Cesare Borgia, or Pope Julius II had risen above their age through their visions of national unity, creativity, and power. Their enemies were the forces which Gobineau had always feared: the masses who rob and plunder or follow false leadership, and the bourgeoisie, small-minded, selfish, and mean. None of the Renaissance élite could triumph over these forces of evil; but they did provide an example for the future, through their vision and ideals, which might yet save the white race. Moreover, since the heroes of this drama took their inspiration from Roman virtues and Greek beauty, the continuing appeal of the ancients could still act as a barrier against racial corruption. Eventually, Gobineau was to be followed by Germans like Ludwig

Woltmann, who in *The Germans and the Renaissance in Italy* (*Die Deutschen und die Italienische Renaissance*, 1905) ascribed the creativity, virtue, and classical revival of the age to the Aryan race.

During the last years of his life, Gobineau formed a close friendship with Richard Wagner which served to popularize his works and to save them from the threat of oblivion. Wagner had read Gobineau and found himself confirmed in his own racism. His widow Cosima Wagner and her friends at Bayreuth took up and spread Gobineau's message. A member of the Bayreuth circle, Ludwig Scheemann, dedicated his life to popularizing and translating Gobineau into German, and was supported by the Bayreuth circle both financially and morally. Eventually, in 1894, Scheemann founded a Gobineau Society.[6] Gobineau was now firmly connected with Wagner in the public mind. The Society was successful in infiltrating rightist groups in Germany which gave Gobineau's racism a still broader base. Above all, the Pan-German League took up Gobineau's thought, and this was important not only because it was a powerful political movement, but also because school-teachers made up much of its membership. Finally, during the First World War several thousand copies of *The Renaissance* were distributed by the Gobineau Society to front-line soldiers.[7]

Bayreuth and the Pan-Germans perverted Gobineau's message; or rather, they adapted it to German requirements. Black and yellow races played little part in the fantasies of a nation which until the end of the nineteenth century had no intimate colonial contact with either people. The acquisition of colonies in Africa in 1884 and the occupation of a base in China (1897) came too late to influence the development of racism in Germany. But the Jews who were present throughout Germany and in the ghettos at her eastern border had become the target of racism long before Wagner himself held them responsible for national degeneration. The Pan-Germans also blamed the Jews for the nation's degeneracy, through their supposed opposition to militarism and expansionism.[8] Thus, Gobineau's condemnation of the black and yellow races was turned against the Jew. It was here that Gobineau got his undeserved reputation as an anti-Semite. But Bayreuth and the Pan-Germans also relied on Gobineau for proof of a specific German racial superiority. He had awakened "the primeval Germanic spirit which was rocked in the cradle of Asia," as the *Bayreuther Blätter* put it. The *Essay* was not only described as a "mighty and scientific weapon in the hands of anti-Semites"[9] but also as proving the Aryan superiority of Germans.

Indirectly, Gobineau himself was responsible for this distortion by putting forward a racism filled with analogies to his own times. Others were then able to bend or extend such analogies. The important point, never lost, was the superiority of the Aryan, to whom all true nobility, honor, and freedom were due. The Aryan had appropriated all the virtues of the world, and all its culture; and there could be nothing left for those who did not share in this wondrous blood. His theories about the inevitability of racial mixing, on the other hand, could be easily discarded or ignored.

For several reasons, Gobineau found a home in the German rather than in the French right. The French right was Catholic, and therefore not without ambivalence toward racial theories which, for example, denied the efficacy of baptism for converts. The Action Française—founded in 1899 and destined to be the most powerful French rightist movement—ignored Gobineau in spite of its own virulent anti-Semitism. This anti-Semitism rested upon the belief that Catholicism was the historical faith of the nation, and that whoever did not share this faith was undermining France. Moreover, the Action Française emphasized ties to the soil and the small property holder, while regarding Jews as symbolic of a restless and menacing capitalism. To be sure, at times the anti-Jewish feeling within the movement is difficult to distinguish from racism; but even so, Gobineau played no role here. After France's defeat by Germany in 1871, the nation was the focus of political attention, and Gobineau was attacked by Maurice Barrès, a powerful figure of the right, for supporting a cosmopolitan nobility rather than national unity.

Gobineau was rediscovered in France only in the 1930's, partly through the efforts of his grandson Clement Serpaille, and partly through the intellectual coterie centered on a radical right-wing journal, *Je Suis Partout*. There, in 1933, Pierre-Antoine Costeau presented the count as the forerunner of Fascist thought, while one year later the *Nouvelle Revue Française* published a special number devoted largely to Gobineau's literary heritage.[10] Even for the small group of French Fascists, Gobineau remained at best a marginal figure. He had no genuine role to play in the French right, for all its anti-Semitism and fascism. It was on the other side of the Rhine that his real influence was felt.

Nevertheless, we can trace some of Gobineau's ideas in the Swiss botanist Alphonse de Candolle (1806–1893) and in his pupil Comte Georges Vacher de Lapouge (1854–1936), a librarian and lawyer who, second to Gobineau, became the most important racial thinker in France. Unlike Gobineau, Candolle and de Lapouge attempted to base themselves on so-called scientific facts. Vacher de Lapouge wrote under the shadow of Darwin, and that in itself gave his racism a pseudo-scientific tone absent from Gobineau's writings. These men were subjective in their attitudes, but both represented a difference in style that made them acceptable in France as scientists rather than as prophets of a new racist religion.

Candolle, like Gobineau, also wrote about black, white, and yellow races. For him, too, decadence was inevitable. The whites were doomed, but the blacks, who were more adaptable, might be successful. Indeed, Candolle departed drastically from Gobineau by discussing environmental factors such as the exhaustion of natural resources which, in his opinion, would lead to demographic suicide. However, he also regarded the Negroes as uncultured, and the Chinese as vulgar and immoral. In his writings only the Jews emerged as a cultured people who had rejected the use of force and thus avoided the brutal and atavistic instincts common to many Christians. At times, oddly enough, the Jews were considered the climax of the white race. Lapouge was not to continue this tradition.[11]

Vacher de Lapouge shared with Gobineau an apocalyptical view of the future. He held that the nation's life force had been exhausted as a result of the degeneration of the race and the dominance of a plutocracy. De Lapouge's *The Aryan and His Social Role* (*L'Aryen, Son Rôle Social*, 1899) equated the superior race with the *Homo*

Europeus, and here, as with Gobineau, the nation was relegated to a minor role. For one thing, de Lapouge believed that the Aryan had conquered not merely Europe but the entire world, including America. Yet he left room for national variations in the Aryan race by asserting that some nations possessed more and others less of the Aryan's intrinsic qualities.

These qualities had, at one time, all been present among the Greeks, and de Lapouge shared in full measure the universal admiration for the Greek genius, never surpassed in its harmony. Among the Greeks, the Spartans were the purest, a race of heroes endowed with iron will but also with moral virtues and intellectual ability. They had descended from the primeval Aryans who were close to nature, a race of fishermen, hunters, and shepherds. For de Lapouge, the Aryan origins were identical with those which linguists had apparently discovered.[12] The myth of the Aryan peasant as the father of the race was thus strengthened. Unlike Gobineau, de Lapouge turned not to language but once again to skull measurements: the long narrow skulls, dolichocephalic, and blond coloring of Aryans played an important role in his thought. We are told that the Greeks, drunk with sun, believed that all their heroes were blond. De Lapouge also believed that the Aryan could be recognized by reading his face, and Lavater's physiognomy was not forgotten.[13] In this way de Lapouge synthesized several trends in racial thought.

The Aryan now faced the challenge of survival, for de Lapouge was influenced by Darwin's theory of natural selection and of the survival of the fittest. The Aryan, he believed, was adaptable; his nature destined him to be a peasant, but he could become any kind of worker and, indeed, was the only reliable worker in modern society. Ignorant of the concept of leisure, unlike the inferior races, the Aryan's whole attitude symbolized the gospel of work. Once again a middle-class ideal became part and parcel of the definition of Aryans, who presumably derived their strength from a primitive rural age. Moreover, the Aryan was an individualist, but one able to put all his services at the disposal of the commonweal. This was of special importance for de Lapouge because for him the Darwinian

struggle of one against all had been transformed into a struggle
between human groups. The factory had replaced the shop, and the
army individual combat. Unlike Gobineau, de Lapouge included
the modern world in his racial scheme because he was a social Darwinist, for whom the world advanced through natural selection determined by the struggle for existence.[14]

Who was the racial enemy? In his view, the inferior races such as
the yellow race and the Jews were without scruples and had no
sense of values, being wholly commercial. The bourgeoisie in de
Lapouge's racial analogy seems the enemy once more, but here a
distinction is made which is a staple of racist thought: Aryan commercial society lives by honest work. The Aryans care about the
values with which they speculate; but the Jew loves speculation for
its own sake. This fateful distinction between the Aryan and the
Jewish bourgeoisie is thus found in France as well as in Germany—
the Aryan middle class can only survive by destroying the Jewish
bourgeoisie.

De Lapouge defined the Jew as at once enemy and rival, doubly
dangerous because of his own consciousness of race. But he felt that
Jews could not win the contest with Aryans, for as an inferior race
they had no spirituality, were unable to fight, and lacked all political instinct. The world could not be conquered merely through
economic power; the Aryans had shown how it must be done instead—through strength, will, honor, and morality.[15] This being
so, the conspicuous mood of pessimism about the future of the only
race fit to rule strikes us as inconsistent. Surely for de Lapouge the
end would not come through the revolution of the inferior races,
since the Aryans ruled (like Gobineau's nobility) not by oppression,
but rather by their example and by a moral superiority which compelled others to follow.

There is a dichotomy here between de Lapouge's belief that the
French race was exhausted and his advocacy of a racial war between Aryans and the inferior race. The Aryan, he tells us, had not
only high principles but also adaptability. However, in France, a
mold clearly had settled upon the tree of race. But this virus could
yet be defeated. De Lapouge's racial pessimism was not fatalistic;

instead, it sought to remedy the situation. Several parasites on the tree of the French Aryan race were especially pernicious, in his opinion. Firstly, Catholicism had sapped the vitality of the race through its stress upon resignation in the face of Jewish domination. Like his contemporary Édouard Drumont, he accused the Church of giving up the fight against Jews.[16] As a result, de Lapouge praised Protestantism as encouraging action, honest labor, and strength of will. Beyond this, he thought that Protestantism rather than Catholicism could serve to dissolve the Jewish race by encouraging assimilation. Here de Lapouge was not really pro-Jewish; he believed that assimilated Jews would lose their racial will and thus their power to survive as well.

Secondly, the physical degeneration through which the Aryan lost his strength and beauty must also be eliminated, together with the hereditary evils it portended. In his *Social Choices* (*Les Sélections Sociales*, 1896), de Lapouge argued that racial mixing was a sure way to contaminate the race and must be prohibited. Further, those individuals who had engaged in it or were its product must be eliminated—the solution being euthanasia.[17] Thirdly, a still more immediate sign of degeneration was the urbanism and plutocracy that was based upon Jewish greed and domination. Apparently, when all was said and done, the Aryan genius for honest work could not compete against a "Judaized" economic system.

One other proposed remedy for racial degeneration is worth mentioning. In the *Social Choices* de Lapouge praised a socialist society, holding that only such a society could take the coercive measures necessary to prevent infertile marriages and to impose upon women a regular cycle of births. Even Spartan infanticide might be possible under such a rational régime.[18] The problem of the undoubted decline of the French population during the nineteenth century was much discussed at the time, and de Lapouge saw in this decline a sign of Aryan sterility.

The prominent English eugenicist Karl Pearson at the beginning of the twentieth century also believed that socialism could most easily dictate eugenics: policies which assured that the race's offspring would be free from hereditary sickness and signs of degeneration.

Moreover, a healthy race would not be menaced by a decline in fertility.[19] De Lapouge and other theoreticians of race, in turn, were thus not so far removed from the contemporary Fabian Socialists, particularly Sidney and Beatrice Webb, who felt that the deterioration of the Anglo-Saxon race through a decline in fertility was a danger to socialism. For this meant that the one race which was best fitted to build socialism would be overrun by mongrels.[20] Socialism and eugenics were not inherently conflicting concepts, and neither occasionally were socialism and race.

De Lapouge's influence in France far exceeded Gobineau's because he succeeded in integrating Darwinism and racism. Indeed, he was the first Frenchman to do so, but his son's later claims that such racism had exclusively French roots was absurd.[21] For one thing, de Lapouge limited his effectiveness in a Catholic country through his advocacy of Protestantism. Admittedly in 1940, after the defeat of France, a commission was set up with the approval of Pierre Laval to study how the *Social Choices* could be put into practice. No doubt the subsequent commission for the study of racial biology (1942) and the Anthropological (racial) Institute founded the same year were also influenced by the heritage of the elder de Lapouge; but all these efforts were stillborn.[22]

Oddly enough, apart from Darwin himself, English racial ideas had little impact upon de Lapouge. Yet it was from England that a fresh impetus was to come, not only in the novel concepts of selection and survival but also through the eugenics movement.

PART II

The Penetration

CHAPTER FIVE

Britain Lends a Hand

BOTH IN HIS metahistory and in the ideal of race as an explanation for contemporary problems, Gobineau indicated the direction which racism was to take. The stereotypes were embodied within a total view of the world, and were ostensibly based upon the most recent scholarship and the widest experience. Although Gobineau's influence was spread mainly by the Wagner circle, his ideas corresponded to those of others who had never read his work.

Typical of this trend set by Gobineau was the use of the word "metapolitics." The German conservative Constantin Franz wrote to Richard Wagner in 1878: "To be genuinely German, politics must soar to metapolitics. The latter is to commonplace pedestrian politics as metaphysics is to physics." [1] Metapolitics views the political process as arising from the subconscious of the Volk or race. Politics is thus transformed into a secular religion, which seeks the salvation of the Volk through the defeat of its enemies. Metapolitics was common currency among the Wagner circle at Bayreuth, where enthusiasm was apt to be confused with profundity. But in a more general way, the rise of new disciplines like the "psychology of peoples" (*Völkerpsychologie*) in the 1860's shows on another level the attempt to grasp the world through a *Volksgeist* that was conceived as all-encompassing—the binding spirit of the community. [2] Yet the advances of science and technology seemed to call for a religion of reason and progress; metapolitics must be joined to a scientific method. Racism, with its innate tendency to pass from science to subjectivity, was ideally suited to fulfill this need.

These ideas were widely dispersed throughout Europe. While the German-speaking lands and France were crucial laboratories of racial thought, England did not stand aside. Not only did the English make their own important contributions to racism through Darwinism and the eugenics movement; they also reflected the usual preoccupation with anthropology, history, and linguistics.

The search for Germanic roots proved important here as well. By the end of the eighteenth century, the English concern with Anglo-Saxon origins was already widespread. The revival of ancient ballads by Thomas Percy in his *Reliques* (1765), as well as the vogue for historical novels such as Sir Walter Scott's *Ivanhoe*, emphasized Saxon freedom and honesty. By mid-nineteenth century many Englishmen had placed their nation within the Anglo-Saxon heritage. The Anglo-Saxons themselves were regarded as part of the Teutonic tribes who had fathered the strongest and most creative European nations.[3]

This revived national pride was not necessarily intolerant of others. For example, Sir Walter Scott extolled Saxon virtue when locked in battle against the Normans, but he was tolerant and respectful of Jews and other strangers who had not set out to conquer the realm. Ideas concerning national origins received their racial flavor above all in the second half of the nineteenth century, when virtues like honesty, loyalty, and love of freedom were thought to be inherent solely in the Anglo-Saxon part of the Teutonic heritage. Geography, the actual setting of the nation so important for Thomas Percy and Sir Walter Scott, was now of small account; Englishmen exemplified the qualities of the race wherever they went, and especially in the United States of America as colonized by Englishmen. In 1882, the English historian Edward A. Freeman on a visit to America told his audiences that the Anglo-Saxon nations were bound together by "ties of blood and speech and memory" which existed despite political separation. For Freeman, as for other English historians, the descendants of the Saxons were the only true members of the Teutonic race. Freeman claimed Arminius, who had defeated the Roman legions in the Teutoburger Forest, as an English ancestor, while the rival Germans built a monument to Hermann (as they called him) in order to honor a Germanic hero.[4] The Teutonic tribal association, the Comitatus, was claimed by both nations as their own, as was Tacitus's Germania. History as racial myth spanned the stormy channel which divided England from Europe. Englishmen monopolized this Teutonic heritage as an explanation of their love for freedom, excluding others from its blessings even if, like the Germans, they looked to the identical past for inspiration.

In England, however, anthropology and the stereotypes discussed earlier also found a home. England had its own Gobineau: Robert Knox (1798–1862), the famous Scottish anatomist. Knox was a contemporary of Gobineau; unlike the Frenchman, he is remembered today not for his racial views but for an episode early in his life which ruined his academic prospects and embittered him. As professor of surgery and anatomy in Edinburgh, Knox became involved in the spectacular accusations leveled against Burke and Hare—that they had snatched dead bodies for the purposes of anatomical research. From 1830, when this incident took place, until 1856, when he joined the London Cancer Hospital, Knox believed with some reason that every man's hand was against him, preventing him from obtaining the employment he seemed to deserve, for contemporaries agreed that he was the most brilliant lecturer in anatomy they had known. The Ethnographical Society of London found him a valued member, and the Anthropological Society of Paris conferred a corresponding membership upon him.

These honors were accorded because of Knox's research into race, whose findings he carried through public lectures into most British cities. The topic was the *Races of Men*, the title of his most famous book (1850). Quite independent of Gobineau's *Essay* but in the precise year of its publication, Knox stated that "Race is everything, civilization depends on it." Each race has its own form of civilization, as it has its own language, arts, and science. There is no such thing as a European civilization.[5]

Knox's classification of races did not posit one superior Aryan race, but rather two superior races. For him, the Saxons—tall, powerful, athletic—were "the strongest, as a race, on the face of the earth."[6] It should not surprise us that Knox adopted Camper's ideal of the facial angle and the idea of perfection as symbolized by the Greeks. In Knox's view, the Saxons represented this ideal-type, and they also had a proper attitude toward the soil, believing it to be the property of the community. Yet Knox felt that they lacked one quality necessary for true superiority: the aptitude for abstract reasoning.

Here Knox's thought was both original and unique. For him the Slavonic races might be ugly in appearance, but they possessed a superb rationalism and faculty for transcendental thought which the Saxons lacked. Furthermore, they displayed a special ability for art and music. Knox did admit some southern Germans into this Slavonic circle, but not the English contemporaries who persecuted him. As usual, the Greeks exemplified perfection and thus were seen as a racial mixture of Saxon and Slav, combining depth of thought and sensibility with true beauty. This was the one time when racial admixture (among the two most superior races) seemed to result in a height never reached before or since.

But what of Gobineau's yellow and black races? The blacks, according to Knox, lacked the "grand qualities which distinguish man from animal," namely, the generalizing power of pure reason; the desire to know the unknown; the love of perfectability; and the ability to observe new phenomena. He was convinced that there was no hope of civilizing them. Indeed, their psychological and physical inferiority predestined them to slavery (cf. Plate 2). For Knox, the nonwhite races were so inferior that they lacked even the unflattering qualities—unruliness and the commercial spirit—which Gobineau had attributed to them. Here they were closer to the inchoate nature of animals.[7]

Like Gobineau, Knox had his *sans culottes* enemies, but the Jews and not the blacks played this role. Knox's Jews were ugly ("dark, tawny, yellow coloured persons, with jet black hair and eyes seemingly coloured"),[8] and even a superficially beautiful Jewish face could not withstand close scrutiny for want of proportion. The perfect type of man discovered by the sculptors of ancient Greece had found its foil. This stereotype was not unique, but Knox went further than most in denying the Jews any quality man might hold dear: the Jew was no craftsman, no tiller of the soil, he had no ingenuity or inventive power, and no love of art, literature, music, peace, or war. In fact, the Jew had no occupation at all, but like the gypsy, lived by cunning alone.[9]

Here Knox revealed his social commitments. Unlike Gobineau, the frustrated nobleman, he had no quarrel with bourgeois life. The Saxon was superior to other races in love of labor, love of order, punctuality in business, neatness, and cleanliness. This Aryan bourgeoisie he then contrasted to the Jewish middle class, and the qualities which Gobineau had projected upon the yellow race were now fastened solely upon the Jew. He was the distorted image of the bourgeoisie—cunning, scheming, and usurious. This fateful distinction between the Aryan and the Jewish bourgeoisie appeared earlier in de Lapouge and will continue to reappear constantly. Indeed, it was to become a general principle of racism on the continent. The annexation of middle-class morality by racism had prepared the way, for that class exemplified Aryan virtues, while the Jew who lacked such virtues symbolized the perversion of the middle class. (The Nazis would similarly support and praise the Aryan bourgeoisie while eliminating the Jewish middle classes.)

That such an image of the Jew could be spread in England as well as on the continent reveals something of the depth of racial thought at mid-century. Knox's contention of the permanence and immutability of race was basic to his attitudes. He held that variety meant degeneracy, and that race must encompass all aspects of life and thought. To prove his point, he drew upon both anatomy and anthropology, and also made much use of physiognomy. His random observations from London streets loom large. The all-encompassing emphasis upon race meant that all wars were race wars, though he hoped that they could be avoided.[10] Writing before the influence of Darwin had been felt, for Knox the superior race was not yet committed to fight for its survival against inferior races. It would somehow survive in any case.

Knox was not very original. Shortly before him, Benjamin Disraeli had already proclaimed that "all is race, there is no other truth." The racial stereotype had made deep inroads, and Disraeli's noble Jew, Sidonia, might well be taken as revenge for Dickens's ignoble Fagin.[11] Whereas Knox, Disraeli, and Dickens, each in his own way, were concerned with the Jew, the mainstream of English racism centered upon the black. In England, both internally and because of the Empire, contact with blacks was intimate and constant; on the continent, where no such regular contact existed, the highly visible Jews took the place of blacks as the "foils" of race.

James Hunt (1833–1869), founding president of the Anthropological Society and an admirer of Knox, put the Negro to the forefront of his concern. For Hunt, too, racial differences were absolute, encompassing physical appearance, religion, art, and morals. Hunt's older contemporary, Thomas Carlyle, had in the 1850's supported black slavery but had left the door open to the industrious, self-denying Negro who could buy his freedom.[12] By the 1860's, however, Hunt denied that racial qualities could be transcended, contending that racial classification represented a judgment upon every aspect of man and society. The importance of Hunt lies not so much in his racial theories as in his justification for them. As the first president and guiding spirit of the London Anthropological Society, he sought to set the tone in 1863 by basing racism upon what he called "good reliable facts."[13] All so-called prejudices must be rejected.

Hunt listed three prejudices in particular which had worked against science: religious mania, the obsession with the rights of man, and the belief in equality. To these culprits Hunt added the works of J. C. Prichard, an anthropologist whose books were among the most influential at the time. Prichard believed that mixed races were superior to pure races, and Hunt used the words of Robert Knox to castigate such a "misdirection of the English mind as to all the great questions of race."[14] Clearly for Hunt, following in Knox's footsteps, praise of mixed races belonged in the category of anti-rational and anti-scientific prejudice. Writing after Darwin, Hunt asserted that the existence of a well-selected hereditary aristocracy was more in accordance with nature's laws than those "glittering trivialities respecting human rights."[15] By this he did not mean the English aristocracy of his day, but rather one that would be properly selected according to its inherited qualities.

When Hunt called upon the Anthropological Society to "apply our science," he exhorted men to work against racial mixing and for the natural selection of a ruling class. That, then, was his vision of the purpose of exact science, in spite of his own warning that not all the results were complete.[16] His statements were dogmatic. Hunt, in common with most racists, worshipped the scientific method even while admitting the incompleteness of the data available. Science and subjectivity were forever married in his mind.

Hunt's view of the Negro's place in nature did not differ from that of Knox in that he believed that the black advanced no further in intellect than an intelligent European boy fourteen years of age. Once more the Negro was seen as a creature of extremes—a *sans culotte* who knew no law. Hunt's evidence for such assertions derived from travelers' reports and was partly supplied by his French colleague, the anthropologist François Pruner. Yet Hunt opposed treating Negroes like slaves. These men of the nineteenth century were by and large unwilling to draw such logical conclusions from their racial thought. Hunt believed that Negroes were part of the human race, but inveighed against monogenists who in consequence of their doctrine advocated the basic equality of all races.[17]

So-called scientists like Hunt wanted to be abreast of modernity, and that meant opposing the discredited institution of slavery (in spite of praise for the American Confederacy) and indeed any undue oppression of the inferior race. Their answer was paternalism —a view shared by most European racists as well. Nazi doctrine, inasmuch as it advocated a race war to the finish, was to come from the fringes, not the center, of European racism. English racial thinkers were normative in their paternalism, which attempted to keep the inferior race in its place. Thus Hunt at times would even advocate leaving the natives alone in their primitive state without European influence or interference. Their natural situation provided "a freedom to suit their capacities," he thought. At other times, echo-

ing Gobineau, he stressed that the savages would be amply re-
venged by the degeneracy and extinction of their conquerors.[18]

The most important and original English contribution to racist
thought was made through Darwinism. Charles Darwin himself
was no racist, but ideas like "natural selection" and "survival of the
fittest" were eagerly adopted by racial theoreticians. The necessity
of struggle seemed to be built into Darwinism, and it added a new
scientific dimension to the combat between superior and inferior
races. Darwin's own theory of survival and selection was complex,
and depended upon environmentalism rather than upon heredity.
But racism simplified Darwin, took the "good reliable facts" which
he described, and applied them to the struggle for survival and
selection of the fittest race.

Darwin sometimes wrote in a way that could be easily misinter-
preted as encouraging racial ideas. Thus he eventually substituted
the phrase "favoured races" for "survival of the fittest." Moreover,
he defined the measure of successful survival by the number of
progeny an animal could produce. Such a scientific hypothesis when
applied to men could be taken to mean that fertility determined
racial survival.[19] This idea was especially relevant at a time when
some nations—for instance, France—were concerned about their
falling birth rate. The production of healthy progeny became a racial obsession. Darwinism not only encouraged visions of race war;
it also led in more immediate terms to the founding of racial
eugenics.

The doctrines of natural selection and of the survival of the fittest
were easily used as guidelines for racial classification. What Darwin
had called the extinction of less improved forms might also be
applied to inferior races. Those who applied Darwinism to social
problems proclaimed that the survival of the fittest, together with
the right of the healthy and strong, established the principle by
which the lives of men and states must be governed.

When applied to races and men, Darwinism underwent another
immediate change of great significance. Darwin himself had believed that natural selection and the variation of species was due to
the environment and to the changes which took place within it. He

stated that variety arose from "the indirect and direct action of the conditions of life and from use and disuse."[20] Later, Darwinists changed this environmentalism to an emphasis upon heredity. Francis Galton, in 1872, insisted on the generational continuity of germ plasm which is found in our reproductive cells. Karl Pearson said that "the greatest truth that we have learned since Darwin" was the idea that the chief source of variation lies in the heterogeneity of germ plasm, of which the individual is the bearer and not the creator, and which is not substantially modified by either his life or his environment.[21] Such truths, though not meant to be racist, turned Darwinism in a direction that racists could use. These rules of heredity were supposedly derived from the Darwinian idea of natural selection and survival which Pearson attempted to prove statistically.

Darwinism was thus brought into line with the ever present notion that man inherited his characteristics. Indeed, new research which seemed to affirm the importance of heredity meant emphasizing the inherent qualities of racial stock. This was a reaffirmation of Kant's position and was opposed to any environmentalism. Toward the end of the nineteenth century, the German anthropologist Eugen Fischer and the zoologist August Weismann proved to their satisfaction the primacy of heredity. Fischer as a result of his research on the natives of Samoa, and Weismann, by applying anthropological research to Germans, discovered the immutability of sex cells. However, it was Sir Francis Galton (1822–1911) who came to dominate research into heredity both in England and on the continent.

Galton can well be regarded as the founder of eugenics. He came to the science of heredity from a preoccupation with evolution, and as a passionately devoted follower of Darwin. Galton was fascinated by statistics and measurement. He sought to express Darwin's theories quantitatively and thus to determine the qualities needed to survive. "Speaking for myself," he said, "if I had to classify persons according to worth, I should consider each of them under the three heads of physique, ability and character."[22] The assessment of such worth must be placed upon statistical foundations. Just how this could be done was explained in Galton's most influential book, *Hereditary Genius* (1869).

Galton listed thirteen kinds of natural ability, then ranked men accordingly, from the judges of England to the wrestlers of the north country. Three natural, inherited abilities were especially important to raise men from mediocrity: intellect, zeal, and devotion to work. His book paid special attention to marriages, and argued that all social and moral help must be extended to those couples that might bear exceptional children. The "civic worth" of the progeny should preoccupy national policy. Galton changed the practical consequences which should be drawn from his classification several times during his long life; but, by and large, he held that the birth rate of the unfit should be checked and that of the fit encouraged through early marriage.

Eugenic worth therefore determined the quality of the race. Like most eugenicists Galton used the word "race" loosely, to denote a group linked by some sort of kinship and heredity. Such a definition was not exclusive—those who shared the qualities Galton thought desirable could join. For example, he advocated selective immigration into England, and here he thought both Huguenots and Jews fit to apply. Yet in spite of the greater openness of the concept as Galton and most other eugenicists conceived it, they did divide mankind into races replete with the usual virtues and stereotypes. Natural selection could still be used to improve the race that practiced it. This meant the application of eugenics and the assessment of people according to the standards he set forth, even though these might not be confined to one single race.

For Galton, the key to racial health was that healthy parents would have healthy children. Children can inherit a tendency toward genius, but insanity is also hereditary. Galton looked forward, at the end of his life, to a time when eugenic certificates would be issued. These might ask personal questions about the bridegroom's athletic and academic distinctions, his character as reflected by the positions of trust he had held, and, last but not least, his parents' history and associations. But this was a dream. The Francis Galton Laboratory for National Eugenics (founded in 1904) was supposed to investigate the relationship of inheritance to environment, or, as Galton put it, the relationship of nature to nurture. Karl Pearson (1857–1936) was to work in the confines of the Galton Laboratory, calculating that environmental factors do not have the sixth part of the intensity of the hereditary influence of a single parent.[23]

The qualities praised as superior were once more those prized by the middle classes, indeed those traditional in racism itself: physical prowess, intelligence, hard work, and character. Physical prowess was put first by Galton, because it was most easily measured.[24] He was concerned with improving the British race rather than any other, and he extended Darwinism until it made an alliance with those basic forces that had informed the history of racism. The emphasis upon inherent human qualities transmitted from generation to generation, upon the physical and mental qualities the middle classes prized, was combined with the struggle to survive. The proper inbred qualities of nature were decisive in this struggle. All this was put forward in the name of science. Eugenics societies were formed to spread knowledge of the laws of heredity in order to improve the race.

The eugenics movement was not confined to England. Galton, and subsequently Karl Pearson too, were studied and reprinted in Germany as well. The *Journal for Racial and Social Biology* (*Archiv für Rassen und Gesellschaftsbiologie*), founded in 1904, followed closely the activities of Galton's Eugenics Education Society and the results achieved by the Galton Laboratory. There was a great deal of cross-fertilization between the two nations.

By the time of Galton's death in 1911, journals concerned with eugenics had been established in many European nations. The doctrine of heredity as applied to a race had attained scientific respectability and had entered the universities. Eugenics made racial hygiene respectable, though breeding schemes also continued to be advocated. Admittedly, those who suggested such schemes came from the fringes rather than from the center of racial thought. For example, Willibald Hentschel, a former disciple of Darwin, became well known in Germany through his book *Varuna* (1907), named after an ancient Indian god. Invoking the memory of ancient

Aryans, he advocated the establishment of isolated settlements where a better and purer race could be bred. After the First World War a youth movement called the *Artamanen*, after a supposedly ancient Aryan and Indian word meaning the truth (once again invented by Hentschel), attempted to work on the land and to "cleanse their blood."[25] Heinrich Himmler had been a member of the *Artamanen* before he tried to take up such schemes in practice during the Third Reich. His *"Lebensborn"* experiment, which was destined to help improve the race, will be dealt with in detail later.[26]

At this point, racial hygiene as an adjunct to the "mysticism of race" (especially in Germany), and racial hygiene as a part of the eugenics movement which used the tools of science in order to control the inheritance of a race, must be distinguished. Eventually both would fuse, as when in 1934 Karl Pearson praised Adolf Hitler's racial policy as an attempt to regenerate the German people.[27] But the seventy-seven-year-old Pearson was hardly the level-headed man who had continued Galton's labors. At the end of his life he craved to see eugenics become national policy before it was too late. The mainstream of eugenics and of racial hygiene did not lead directly into Nazi policy, though it indirectly helped to make it possible. It is surely significant that not only the aged Pearson but also German scholars like Alfred Ploetz and Eugen Fischer, who while thinking in racial categories were not specifically anti-Semitic before 1933, could so easily become supporters of Nazi racism thereafter. The heady prospect of a nation willing to make its race fit to survive wiped out any blemishes this process might entail. It is important now to look closer at the eugenics movement and its interaction with racial anthropology, a mixture which after the close of the nineteenth century was to become known as "racial and social biology."

CHAPTER SIX

The Science of Race

A S RACISM moved into the twentieth century, it carried with it the heritage of the nineteenth century which was expressed in two traditions: the mystical idea of race, which extended the ever present subjectivity of racial thought until it left any pretense of science behind; and that tradition which sought scientific and academic respectability for racial classification. James Hunt's "reliable facts" must concern us here, as well as those who based their racism upon an actual scientific method, however tawdry. Because such men attempted to found their work on demonstrable proofs, whether biological, zoological, or statistical, they tended to adopt an ambivalent attitude toward racism as a doctrine of aggression or superiority, while nevertheless accepting racial categories and stereotypes. This, in fact, was the mainstream of racism: the fusion of anthropology, eugenics, and social thought. These traditional concepts were now linked to Darwinism, and so led to a racist preoccupation with heredity and eugenics as vital for the survival of the fittest. Germans called such Darwinian racism "racial and social biology" because of the emphasis that had to be placed upon the proper hereditary factors.

"Racial and social biology" was a doctrine of heredity and survival based upon racial eugenics. But anthropology also became involved, drawing conclusions from racial classification as well as from natural selection and heredity. Those who thought in racial categories had always attempted to preserve relevance to the present, and Gobineau's own theories were now termed "social anthropology."[1] Galton too was annexed by anthropologists, just as he himself had used anthropological observations on his many travels as subject matter for eugenic measurements and statistics. The sweeping analyses of man and society which this racial thought attempted are illustrated by the foreword to the newly founded *Journal for Racial and Social Biology* in Germany (1904), which stated that individual life ends but race forms the continuous unity of life. Referring to Darwin, the journal asserted that the survival of the race was connected to racial heredity and racial hygiene, and that the concept of race was basic to any social doctrine, national economy, law, administration, history, or moral philosophy.[2] The idea of race had always served as an explanation of the present and as a hope for the future; but here it was systematized into a general science of society, though, as we shall see, without aggressive intent.

A new tone of urgency informed racial biology. This seems to have stemmed from the confrontation with an accelerated urbanism and population growth in both western and central Europe. If ideas of natural selection and heredity were not translated into practice, many thought a catastrophe might result. Karl Pearson, whom the Germans admired so much and whose works they reprinted so frequently, asserted that the principle of natural selection could no longer be applied solely to individuals, but must instead be discussed within a national context. The community was important, and moral conduct was what tended to strengthen it. At times, Pearson claimed, it was perhaps moral to kill a member of a hostile tribe, but it was always a crime to kill a member of one's own tribe. Conversely, an indifference to eugenics implied murder of one's kin, and was therefore responsible for the degeneration of the nation.[3]

Such a definition of community did not necessarily imply that the fit were inherently members of the superior race and the unfit inherently members of an inferior race. Certainly for Pearson, racial health was not so simply distributed. Any race could improve itself through the application of eugenics. He admired Nazi racial policy in his old age because it seemed a large-scale attempt to breed the fit (though one which Pearson thought might yet fail); but he himself praised what he called socialism. "Socialism" to him meant the evolution of the national community through struggle. A strong social instinct would be developed in this way, and rewards given for the efficiency and magnitude of socially valuable work. Pearson opposed class war, emphasizing instead a gradual evolution led by an élite.[4] Defined in this way, socialism was nevertheless opposed to individualism and the undue concentration of wealth.

Pearson was not alone among racial biologists in advocating this kind of socialism. In Germany, Ludwig Woltmann, who had been a Marxist, became an overt racist toward 1900 as a result of the influence of Darwinism. The class struggle was transformed into a war between races. Workers under this kind of socialism would receive equality of status, if not of function.[5] By contrast, the more usual attitude was to praise the capitalist system as beneficial for the process of natural selection. For example, the economic expert of the *Journal for Racial and Social Biology*, A. Nordenholz, saw capitalism as increasing productive capacity and the power of accumulation, and felt that it could be blamed only for not having done enough to spread the knowledge of racial eugenics.[6] Capitalists themselves responded favorably to Darwinism. For example, Alfred Krupp sponsored an essay contest in 1900 on the topic "What can we learn from the principles of Darwinism for application to domestic political development and the laws of the state?" Wilhelm Schallmayer, who won the first prize, was a constant collaborator on the *Journal for Racial and Social Biology*, while Alfred Ploetz, its editor, received recognition for his entry as well.

Schallmayer, a physician, rejected socialism because of its emphasis upon the environment. He advocated racial hygiene and, of course, was opposed to mixing between inferior races and the superior Aryan race. But for all that, he was a pacifist, believing that war was the enemy of the survival of the fittest, since the best would be killed and the slackers survive. Instead, the race must encourage the propagation of its fit, and childless couples should be required to remarry in order to bear children. It would be declared illegal to remain unmarried.[7] Schallmayer defended capitalism, but this was not his prime concern, for racial hygiene, however enforced, would set the nation upon its proper path.

These men, whether in England or Germany, were not concerned with stigmatizing an inferior race as the villain in the drama of survival. While the principal founder of racial biology in Germany, Alfred Ploetz, did emphasize the Germanic race as the chief culture-bearing race in the world, he did not do so in the simplistic manner with which we are familiar. He believed that all peoples were racial mixtures and that environment also influenced their evolution. Yet the Germanic race represented the best selection of the competent and able. The "blond and tall" people marched at the head of the racial procession, but Jews here were also considered a part of this superior race. For Ploetz the majority of Jews were Aryans, and had few ties to the ancient Jews of the Bible. Thus, Jews tended to have more Aryan than Semitic blood.[8]

Ploetz stood the Christian anti-Jewish argument on its head. Usually, the biblical Jews of the Old Testament were considered admirable and worth defending against anti-Semites, for they were also a part of the Christian drama of salvation; but modern Jews, standing stubbornly outside the last act of this drama, were to be condemned. Ploetz turned this argument around in favor of modern Jews. For the journal he edited, however, such Jews had something else in their favor—their blondness. The statistical discovery that a goodly percentage of Jews were blond and blue-eyed seemed to legitimize them as Aryans.[9] Often in the pages of this journal it was denied that Jews were a separate race; indeed, they were part and parcel of the Germanic Aryans.

At times Darwinism even led to the designation of Jews as a superior race. Arnold Dodel, a botanist at the University of Zürich, in his *Moses or Darwin?* (*Moses oder Darwin?*, 1892) claimed that the bloody persecution of the Jews had triggered a process of natural selection among them which made those who had survived superior to all other races. Dodel's assertion sparked a debate during which several "anti-Dodels" indignantly denied such Jewish superiority. Thus from Ploetz to Dodel the Jews at times were seen either as Aryans or as a superior race.[10] Not all social Darwinism was dedicated to their destruction. Indeed, this science of race in general tended to reject anti-Semitism. Fritz Lenz, a leading member of the German Society for Racial Hygiene founded by Ploetz in 1904, held that fanatical anti-Semitism and racial hygiene were not compatible. Consequently, there is no warrant for the claim to see in the German and English doctrine of "racial biology and hygiene" an immediate forerunner of the Nazi policy against the Jews.

Much of the contemporary writing in German lacked hostility not only toward the Jews but also toward the French, the "hereditary enemy" of the Germans. "There is no reason to talk about the degeneration of the French," said a physician in the German journal (1906), "for we must beware of falling into the same kind of chauvinism that the French ascribe to the Germans."[11] Mixing between French and Germans was heralded as useful for both parties. Alfred Ploetz called for an end to the tensions between German and English as well on behalf of a common solidarity against colored races (a belief Hitler was to share).[12] It is typical that racial mixing among whites was contrasted to that among "total strangers"—meaning Negroes. And indeed, however much the contributors to the journal proved friendly toward the French, English, and Jews, there was never any doubt about their hostility to the faraway blacks. In fact, the separation of the black and white races practiced in the United States was usually singled out for praise as an example of proper racial eugenics.

The demands for racial hygiene even went so far as to call for the sterilization of the unfit, but more normally appealed for voluntary abstinence from mating by those who had a history of congenital sickness. At times there was a call for registration of all citizens in order to keep track of their physical condition. The Society for Racial Hygiene founded by Ploetz did not even mention race in its statutes of 1904 or 1922. This Society thought itself the German equivalent to Galton's Eugenics Education Society.[13] Education and propaganda were the means by which national policy was to be changed. Such a program was not geared either to the elimination of inferior races or even to the necessity of race war. These ideas circulated instead among those who emphasized the "mystique of race"—men and women whose interest focused upon the so-called spiritual aspects of race rather than upon Darwinism and science.

The Nazis later brought the two strands of racial thought together again. Then Ploetz, Fischer, and other leaders of racial biology joined the Nazi Party and supported the law for the prevention of bearing hereditarily diseased offspring of June 28, 1933, which set up courts to judge hereditary health and in certain instances decreed sterilization. With some reason, Ploetz could applaud this measure, for it incorporated most of what he had desired for the protection of the fit. It was perhaps logical that such enthusiasm should lead him and Eugen Fischer to join the party and to sing the praises of National Socialism, the first European government to make racial hygiene a matter of public policy.[14]

For all the differences between racial biologists and the Nazi racists, both talked about "race and degeneration," and of the "fit" and "unfit." An élite was thought necessary for the governance of the nation, and it would be a product of natural selection helped along by the state. Moreover, the black was always seen as clearly inferior, and here the usual accusations of fecklessness and inherent lack of metaphysical thought were once more repeated. Only after 1935 were such signs of inferiority transferred to the Jews in the pages of the *Journal for Racial and Social Biology*.[15] Before this, even when a man like Fischer distinguished between German and Jew and showed some reservations about so-called Jewish characteristics, he was quick to add that racial hygiene benefitted all races.[16]

The fear which haunted racial thought after the mid-nineteenth century was that of degeneration. (For the use that the Nazis would make of this concept, see Plate 15.) Gobineau had already used this term to describe the fatal and inevitable consequence of miscegenation. But in the second half of the nineteenth century, the term gained a new force and respectability which made it a staple of all racial thought. Anthropologists had used it as one possible result of chance variation and biologists had seen in degeneration a return to primitivism. Benedict Augustin Morel in 1857 gave degeneration its classical definition: "Degenerations are departures from the normal human type, they are transmitted through inheritance and lead progressively to destruction."[17] While degeneration could come about through environmental factors (such as poisoning by disease or alcohol), the most dangerous infection, according to Morel, was caused by a combination of physical and moral factors. As this infection progressed, the first generation of a degenerate family would only be nervous, the second neurotic, the third psychotic, and the fourth as cretins would die out.[18] Physical changes accompanied changes in attitudes and feeling. Morel was a physician whose ideas influenced only a limited circle, but through Cesare Lombroso and Max Nordau "degeneration" became a powerful slogan.

Cesare Lombroso (1836–1909), himself no racist, was a liberal and sometime Socialist, a Jew who until the end of his life believed in complete assimilation.[19] But as the founder of the science of criminal law, and the advocate of psychology which made physical characteristics symbolic of the state of the mind, he had a major impact upon that racial thought which he himself condemned. Degeneration became a sign of inherent criminality, of a mind locked into perdition.

Lombroso defined degeneration in the manner of Morel, giving a detailed list of its outward signs: among others, a retreating forehead, low-lying eyes, an upturned nose, and obvious asymmetry of the face. Perhaps there is an influence of Lavater here; certainly, the ideal of harmony and moderation becomes crucial, for to Lombroso, exaggeration of feeling, inconstancy, lack of character, and egomania were the signs of degeneration which accompanied outward appearance.[20] Lombroso's theories praised the normal, the golden mean; all else was degenerate.

His *Genius and Madness* (*Genio e Follio*, 1863) popularized these ideas, arguing that even genius, for so many the height of human achievement, was dependent upon the pathological condition of the body. Elsewhere he wrote that hallucination, epilepsy, and lust were all characteristics of men like Molière and Beethoven whose outward appearance reflected both their genius and their degeneracy. The genius and the madman have no love for order and

no instinct for the requirements of practical life. They lack stead-
fastness of character and are dreamers—the very opposite of good
citizens and liberals.[21]

Lombroso was subject to Darwinist influence as well, which led
him to cruel and harsh attitudes toward habitual criminals. He
regarded such criminals as bearing outward signs of degeneracy
which pointed to atavism; they had reverted to a barbaric, primeval
race. Enormous jaws and high cheekbones characterized such men
and women, as well as, among other signs, handle-shaped ears,
"found in criminals, savages and apes."[22] Lombroso thought that
these were signs of habitual criminality, and he distinguished such
people from occasional criminals or those led on by momentary
passions. The latter two types could be reformed and must be
treated humanely; but a person doomed to a life of criminality
must be killed as this was the only way to protect society. Capital
punishment would therefore be part of a process of "deliberate
selection," which might serve to supplement and strengthen natural
selection.[23] Lombroso was more radical in his solution to racial
decline than the eugenics movement, but he shared its fundamental
presuppositions.

There is no question that the Nazis and the Fascists in general
rejected Freud and advocated Lombrosian psychology. Nazi euthanasia was based upon the proposition that degeneration as exemplified by habitual criminality or insanity was structural and final. But
since the Nazis also believed the Jews to be degenerate as well as
habitual criminals, Lombroso's definition of criminality became a
part of Hitler's final solution of the Jewish problem.[24]

Max Nordau (1849–1923) was the real popularizer of the concept of degeneration. He was a close friend and student of Lombroso, matching him in personal accomplishment: as a physician;
as the author of nine novels and volumes of short stories, seven
plays, fifteen essays; and finally as a journalist and ardent Zionist,
who wrote many articles as the Paris correspondent of Berlin and
Vienna newspapers, as well as giving Zionist speeches later in life.
Perhaps it is significant that both Lombroso and Nordau pitted degeneration against a so-called normal life of sweat and toil. They

certainly typified that bourgeois normality which Nordau repeatedly praised: those who rise early and are not weary before sunset, who have clear heads, solid stomachs, and hard muscles.[25] Such virtues were needed for their own multifarious accomplishments.

Nordau was more popular than Lombroso, for he was concerned with simple explanations of science and culture, not with clinical analysis or legal briefs. His *Degeneration* (1892–93), which was dedicated to Lombroso, swept Europe, finally establishing the concept in the vocabulary. Nordau was a liberal, not a racist, and until his conversion to Zionism, certainly a cosmopolitan Jew. Even his Zionism tended toward the necessity of charity for the persecuted rather than nationalism. The basis of his thought was formed by the "irresistible and unchangeable" physical laws, which applied as much to man as to nature. Man must discover these through clarity of thought and mind if he was to cope with the perils of natural selection. But Nordau held that men could achieve such clarity only through observation and knowledge based on mental discipline— "whoever preaches absence of discipline is an enemy of progress."[26] Scientific positivism stood opposed to degeneration. For Nordau, such positivism also involved proper working habits, appearance, and sexual morality.

"Degenerates" were all those who stood against this scientific method and middle-class morality: Tolstoy, for example, because he lacked clarity; the sculptor Auguste Rodin because he imagined muscles where none existed; and modern artists or writers who substituted imagination for self-discipline and accurate observation. These signs of degeneration were not merely confined to the artists' works, but were demonstrated through physical abnormalities as well. Thus, Nordau believed that the decay of the nervous system accounted for the Impressionist painters, while the exhaustion of old age explained the work of the naturalists. Obviously, for Nordau all modern artists and writers were incapable of "rational convictions arrived at by the sound labor of the intellect."[27] He supported the traditional artistic forms because they arose out of an orderly evolution (in analogy with Darwin's principles of natural selection). To be sure, Nordau also advocated a community of men based upon solidarity, but *Degeneration* praised the liberal middle-class virtues and stigmatized those who rejected them.

Degeneration was the enemy of that middle-class morality which was, implicitly or explicitly, always the ally of racial survival and dominance. From Camper's ideal-types to Nordau's "normal men," these were bourgeois ideal-types, the "clean-cut American" or "right-living Englishman" of our own day. As we have seen repeatedly, racism annexed the middle-class morality which came to dominate Europe during the nineteenth century, just as it annexed nationalism and indeed all ideas that seemed to have a future. That was its strength. Neither Morel, Lombroso, nor Nordau were racists. But their ideas became a staple of racist thought.

The racists believed that degeneration might be averted through eugenics, but such a prosaic solution to the maintenance of the race was not destined to last. Racism always felt the pull toward the irrational, the urge to become a secular religion. Racial biology attempted to prevent this flight into irrational heights, but it could not prevent a considerable area of eugenics from escaping into a mystique. This was especially true for the popularizers of racial Darwinism, who became infused with a religiosity which Lombroso and Nordau deplored. Yet racial biology, in spite of its pretension to remain in the realm of fact, had always been a myth and thus open to irrationalism of all kinds.

In particular, German Darwinists not closely associated with the *Journal for Racial and Social Biology* thought of evolution and science as partly in the domain of religion. Ernst Haeckel (1834–1919), the leading German advocate of evolution as a cosmic force manifesting the creative energy of nature, stood midway between science and metaphysics. He was an excellent zoologist but remained always a child of romanticism. For Haeckel, matter was a mystical force rather than something earthy and mechanical. Evolution, he asserted, saw man and society as a consistent whole, infused with a pantheistic spirit. He called this understanding of Darwinist theory "monism," and contrasted it to all other explanations of the world which lacked such material and spiritual unity.[28]

Evolution, then, was not a change from one species to the next.

Instead, it was a cosmic force, which worked through the instrumentality of diverse races according to a determinist scheme, where every effect had a natural cause. Thus, Darwinism made for that clarity which Nordau praised so much, and gave an appearance of science even while leaving room for idealistic and subjective content. Haeckel not only constructed a genealogy for the whole human race, but also combined a sharp distinction between races with a desire to eliminate the unfit. Unlike the racial biologists, whose respect for facts and observation, however tenuous, set limits to their racism (after all, they thought of themselves as enlightened men of science), Haeckel and his disciples lost their grounding in empiricism. Eventually, patriotism displaced "reliable facts," and for them, the Germans became the superior race. The Germans had deviated furthest from apelike man and had therefore outstripped all others in higher mental development and civilization. Jews and Negroes were placed at the bottom of the chain of being.

Eugenics must be practiced on behalf of the superior race, to keep it from degeneration, and that meant the elimination of the unfit. Racial biologists had sporadically criticized the medical profession for keeping the unfit alive; but Haeckel and his disciples were consistent in their opinion that individuals damaged by disease must not be permitted to survive, and like Lombroso they advocated the death penalty for habitual criminals. Haeckel even proposed a commission which would decide over life and death.[29] Clearly, the racial biologists were only indirectly forerunners of Nazi euthanasia, while Haeckel can be claimed as a direct ancestor.

Haeckel made one additional contribution to racial thought in his biological hypotheses, which he formulated into a "biogenetic law." This law stated that the biological history of an individual must in abbreviated form repeat the biological development of his ancestors. The ancestors were always present not just in the mind but in biological reality, thus assuring the continuity of the race.[30] Haeckel's *Riddles of the Universe* (*Die Welträtsel*, 1899) became a best seller, for it gave the reader a feeling of being in on science while at the same time gaining the comforts of a new pantheistic religion. Haeckel based his arguments on the higher biblical criticism, which analyzed the biblical story from a historical perspective to find that it lacked truth and conviction. He gratefully annexed the findings of David Friedrich Strauss and Ernest Renan for his own contention that Christ was human and not divine. At the same time he agreed with Houston Stewart Chamberlain, his contemporary, that Christ's religion of love could not have anything in common with the Jews and their typically oriental fantasies.[31] Haeckel regarded the Jews as an inferior race, who had falsified the teachings of Christ in their own interest. Christianity was a pantheistic religion of love, which infused matter and which must be freed from the encumbrance of both the Old and the New Testaments.

Haeckel founded the Monist League in 1906, but its members did not necessarily follow Haeckel's own Volkish and racist doctrine. Many members of the League, as well as those who were influenced by monism without belonging to the organization, believed that nature pointed in a humanitarian, liberal direction. The beneficent evolution of nature would create a new man who would exemplify love and rationality. The literate working classes in particular probably derived their belief in progress from such Darwinist monism as much as from Karl Marx.[32] The "temple of nature" was not necessarily built upon a narrow nationalist and Aryan foundation; but the fact that Haeckel and some contemporary monists believed this to be the case did give racism one more so-called scientific justification.

The attempt to make racism into a science, and the flight into a new Darwinian religion, did not exhaust racial thought at the *fin de siècle*. Anthropology also added its share, which was perhaps all the more important because of its consistent attempts at proof.

If eugenics was pioneered in England, and racial biology as well as monism in Germany, anthropology made its greatest strides in France. Paul Broca's (1824–1880) summary of the work done by the Paris Anthropological Society between 1859 and 1863 demonstrates an ambivalent attitude toward race. On the one hand, the distinction between races is admitted; on the other, they are said to form a harmonious group, and it is man as such who must be examined.[33] Working in Paris, men like Paul Broca and William Frederick Edwards (1777–1842) believed in the existence of race, but also in the beneficial effect of the mixture of races and in the importance of environmental factors. Ideas of superiority and inferiority were rejected; even beauty was not confined to one race or type. Yet for Edwards, beauty was not universal, each race having its own typical beauty.[34]

Broca criticized both Gobineau and Knox for being overly simplistic. In his view mixed races tend to dominate civilization, and the French were certainly such a mixture, varying according to geographical region. Everywhere there were tall men and short men, blond and brown, long heads and round heads.[35] French anthropology thus had a liberal tradition. Not even the Negro was excluded by this view. François Pruner, thought to be the leading authority on this subject, pictured him as prone to extreme attitudes, although he concluded by saying that this was not the rule. Instead, most blacks were seen as sober, industrious, and patient workers who guided their families with wisdom and dignity.[36] Certainly, this was a refreshing viewpoint but, fortunately, not an unusual one.

Of course at times different ideas were expressed in the Anthropological Society. For example, in 1865 J. A. H. Périer told his fellow scholars that pure races were noble, mixtures of blood inferior, and that Europeans were the noble races in contrast to blacks.[37] But Joseph Deniker was more typical of the most influential anthropologists. His book on *The Races of Europe* (*Les Races de l'Europe*, 1899), while based upon skull measurements as a test of race, denied that race and nationality coincided. France was made up of several races: Frenchmen were tall in the east and small in the southwest. Deniker did believe in racial heredity and denied environment as a factor. He posited a more or less pure Nordic race which, however, did not coincide with any nation. He falls somewhere in between Broca and Périer, but even so, refused to entertain ideas of racial superiority.[38] Indeed, he consciously attempted to avoid value judgments.

Armand de Quatrefages de Bréau (1810–1892) who, after Broca, was the leading member of the Anthropological Society, also affirmed that racial mixtures were fruitful. Moreover, even if the Negro skull was different from that of whites, this did not prove black inferiority. Indeed, Broca himself had made the same statement. Not only was Quatrefages opposed to Knox, who was generally attacked as guilty of faulty racial analysis; he even attacked Camper for deducing intellectual superiority from the facial angle. Once again these praiseworthy sentiments and scientific ideals were vitiated by ambivalence. The white race was regarded as having the highest intellectual development and thus able to raise others by mingling its blood with theirs. Such exhortation to intermarriage was, of course, anathema to most racists. The Jews, incidentally, were definitely seen as members of the superior white race, while those in most dire need of improvement were the yellow and black races.[39]

After the Franco-German War of 1870, Quatrefages lost his sense of proportion. The German bombardment of Paris had hit the famed anthropological museum in the Jardin des Plantes, destroying collections dear to him, and he believed that the Prussians had purposely sought to exterminate French anthropology. The war of 1870 had been transformed by the Prussians from a national war into a race war in which France must be destroyed; indeed, Quatrefages now held the Prussians to be a nation separate from the blond Germans. They were racially Finns, that is, a dark Mongoloid race. By destroying French anthropology, the Prussians would prevent the discovery of their inferiority.[40]

Rudolf Virchow (1821–1902) answered Quatrefages in the name of science and reason, reaffirming the absence of pure races in the tradition of French anthropology.[41] Virchow was one of the founders of German anthropology and certainly the most influential member of the German Anthropological Society (founded in 1870). He was one of the last universal scientists our civilization has produced, and he made major contributions in a wide variety of fields, from cellular pathology (which he discovered), to epidemiology, public health, archeology, anthropology, and politics (as a leading progressive member of the Prussian and German diets). His contributions to anthropology must concern us here not just because he was a superb organizer, but above all because of his famous racial survey of German schoolchildren, which was to be imitated in Austria, Holland, and Belgium.

In 1871, the newly founded German Anthropological Society resolved to accumulate statistics on all skull shapes in Germany, and a year later it added examination of hair and eye coloring. Virchow, who had been entrusted with executing this plan, suggested that the survey be made among schoolchildren. The Society decided to examine the differences between Jewish and Christian schoolchildren. The Federal German states agreed to help in this survey and the schools were told the purpose of such examinations—to see how much of the primeval race remained. This was said to be necessary in order to gauge the peculiarities of peoples and cultures. The teachers gave the examinations, first to Germans and then to the Jews separately, by filling in questionnaires prepared by Virchow. Only the city of Hamburg refused to cooperate, believing that the examination interfered with personal liberty; elsewhere there was little difficulty. Finally 6,760,000 children were surveyed as to color of eyes, hair, and skin, although skull measurements were not taken so seriously.[42]

The separateness of the Jewish schoolchildren, approved by Virchow, says something about the course of Jewish emancipation in Germany. However rationalized, the survey must have made Jewish children conscious of their minority status and their supposedly different origins. The effect on them must have been similar to the shock which German Jewish soldiers received during the First World War when they were singled out and counted in order to test the accusation that they shirked front-line service. The "Jew count" of 1916 drove some assimilated Jews into the arms of Zionism.[43] Admittedly nothing like this is reported about Virchow's survey, but then we have no details about the feelings of those involved. His examination, however, had positive results. Virchow was enabled to prove that there was no such thing as a pure German or a pure

Jewish race. His findings were intended to bury the myth of race once and for all.

The survey showed that nowhere were the Germans racially uniform and least of all predominantly blue-eyed and blond. In the entire German Empire, according to Virchow's statistics, the blonds constituted 31.8 percent of the population, the brunettes 14.05 percent, and the mixed types 54.15 percent.[44] Among the 75,377 Jewish schoolchildren examined, 11 percent were pure blonds, 42 percent black-haired, and 47 percent of mixed type.[45] It is interesting that by the outbreak of the First World War, the statistician Arthur Ruppin believed that the percentage of blond Jews in Germany had increased to between 20 and 25 percent.[46] Virchow was quite justified in denying the existence of pure races.

Yet the German *Anthropological Review* remained uneasy about racial mixtures which blurred the differences between Germans and Jews. When Virchow's survey was completed and the results published in 1886, the *Review* did its best to exaggerate the statistical differences. There were fewer blonds by percentage among the Jewish than among the German population, it asserted blandly. The Austrians, always more radical and interested in separating Jew from Gentile, concentrated their survey upon Galicia and Bukowina, where the Jewish race was said to have maintained its purity. They did find fewer Jewish blonds in that region.[47]

This survey should have ended controversies about the existence of pure Aryans and Jews. However, it seems to have had surprisingly small impact. The idea of race had been infused with myths, stereotypes, and subjectivities long ago, and a scientific survey could change little. The ideal of pure, superior races and the concept of a racial enemy solved too many pressing problems to be easily discarded. The survey itself was unintelligible to the uneducated part of the population. For them, Haeckel's *Riddles of the Universe* was a better answer to their problems.

There were protests against Virchow's findings, of course, by students and by those who claimed that the famous doctor of medicine was either a slave of the Jews and part of the Jewish world conspiracy, or indeed himself of Jewish blood.[48] Virchow, however, was not shaken in his conclusions that the Jews were a nation but not a race. He continued to believe in a Jewish separateness from Germans such as we have seen operating since the outset of his racial survey. Looking back at his survey, Virchow mused that if there was to be a "German type," then a great part of south and west Germany must be excluded from the Reich. For Virchow, "race" was nothing other than hereditary variations.[49]

Virchow's enemies disregarded his scientific spirit. Instead, people preferred to believe in the myth, symbol, and mystery of race, regardless of the largest racial survey ever made. In Germany this development added to ideas of racial warfare, and in France liberal anthropology was challenged by racial ideas relevant to the political turmoil of the Third Republic.

CHAPTER SEVEN

The Mystery of Race

SIDE BY SIDE with the development of racial biology, a strong
mystical impulse made itself felt in modern racism. The "mystery of race" emphasized the irrational nature of racism, the
supposed mythological roots of race, and the so-called spiritual
substance which was said to create and inspire it. Thus any connections with science, however tenuous, were rejected, and with them
such rational structures of thought and observation as the science of
race had sought to maintain. Those who believed in the mysterious
sources of race lacked the ambivalence toward racism as a doctrine
of superiority and aggression which the advocates of the science of
race demonstrated from time to time.

The mythological and spiritual roots of the race were equated
with the national origins: the past of a race and its history was
identical with the history of the nation. As we saw earlier, racism
from the very beginning had been linked to the rise of national consciousness. Particularly in central Europe, the language and history
of the people was used to explore its racial origins, and the virtues
of a race were ascribed to the qualities of its roots. The science of
race and the mystery of race had been related to one another, in that
all racism used anthropology and phrenology, as well as historical
myths and the classical aesthetic. But during the last three decades
of the nineteenth century, at the same time as the eugenics movements were founded, the idea of a "mystery" of race diverged from

race as science and instead propagated racism as part of a new national religion.

Two factors influenced this development. The first lay in the wave of spiritualism which descended on Europe from the United States; the second was a growing concern for national unity at a time of increasing class strife and competition for wealth and status. These two elements became integrated with one another, for national unity based upon religious and racial foundations would, so it was hoped, renew the national mystique, especially among the disunited nations of central and eastern Europe. The spiritualist influences and the quest for a new national faith were not mutually exclusive, for many who were attracted to spiritualism were also concerned with the people and the race. Nevertheless, they were distinct from one another, since the spiritualists sought to penetrate into the supersensible world of spiritual beings, while those who sought to transform nationalism into a religion attempted to annex for its use idealistic philosophy, especially that of Kant.

Spiritualism was nothing new in Europe. In the first half of the eighteenth century, the Swedish engineer Emanuel Swedenborg had "enjoyed the privilege of constant association with angels and spirits." [1] For him the spiritual and the corporeal world interacted, enabling some prophets to experience the universe filled with angels and spirits. Swedenborg founded his "new church" in 1767. Swedenborgianism would continue into the nineteenth century, but the major spiritualist impetus at this time came from the Theosophical Society, founded by Helen Petrovna Blavatsky and Colonel H. S. Olcott in New York in 1875. Active branches were soon established all over Europe and in England, starting with the British Theosophical Society in 1876. Madame Blavatsky in her chief work *Isis Unveiled* (1877) taught how the veil interposed between man and the astral bodies could be lifted. The adepts who could pierce the veil would be capable of knowing all that had been known or could ever be known. Every human being had an astral body besides his own physical body, and this enabled him, if he was adept, to make contact with the "life spirit of the universe." Such contact was estab-

lished through a "life force," an omnipresent "vital ether" that
drew man and universe into a single unity. In broad outline, these
were essential elements in the secret science of theosophy.

Madame Blavatsky's theories were based on Indian religions—
a tradition that, as we have seen, fascinated many Europeans. Indeed, the theosophic headquarters would eventually be established
outside Madras. Moreover, if the adept could grasp the unseen
universe through a secret science, then the concept of Karma, the
eternal cycle of birth and rebirth which she took from Buddhism,
robbed death of its sting. Such ideas were appealing to men and
women who sought to plumb the depth of the "race-soul," and who
were fascinated by secret conspiracies. Theosophy itself was not
racist (indeed, it was the first European movement to tell the Indians that their religions were superior to Christianity); but eventually racism allied itself with theosophy.[2] Theosophy could, in fact,
also support a new humanism. Rudolf Steiner's Anthroposophical
Society, founded in Berlin in 1913, linked spiritualism to freedom
and universalism. However, our concern is with racism, and here
Germany along with Austria was central to the fusion of theosophy
and race, for in German-speaking lands theosophy found a mystical
tradition ready made, and one that for a long time had been a part
of the rising national consciousness.

It was a sixteenth-century cobbler, Jacob Böhme, who became a
national symbol for a disunited nation. Böhme had exemplified
a Germanic religion which supposedly sprang from the people
themselves, and which was directed against priests and princes. He
held that the world was within man, and that man could consequently make contact with the cosmos through empathy with
nature. The God of the Bible was no longer imprisoned in legalistic
confessions of faith, but revealed himself in nature. Nature brought
harmony of spirit; through it, the individual soul could be united
with that of the universe. Böhme believed that all things were in
movement toward each other and thus toward a higher divine
unity.[3] His nature mysticism could be bent to mean that Germans
might overcome their anxieties if they were prepared to receive the
native landscape into their souls. Then, he believed, they would be

able to penetrate beyond material reality into God's universe. The German landscape thus became the means by which the German Volk was linked to the cosmos. The mystical tradition of Silesia which Böhme had founded remained alive among Germans well into the nineteenth century, expressed so well in the many famous cradle songs of the region.

Theosophy and this Silesian tradition in the late nineteenth century mingled with racism in the effort to counter the stark materialism of the age. Julius Langbehn's *Rembrandt als Erzieher* (*Rembrandt as Educator*, 1890) became the key work of this theosophist, racist, and mystical tradition. The book attained a vast popularity since it could be interpreted on several levels: culturally, it could be seen as a criticism directed against bourgeois opulence and complacency, and as an attack against realism and naturalism in the arts. But it could also be read as a racist work, which gave new depth to the concept of the German Volk. For Langbehn, mysticism transmuted science into art.[4] The German must be an artist (just as Rembrandt had been), a notion which was music to the ears of the younger generation. Their parents were entrepreneurs and businessmen, while the sons and daughters wanted to be "creative." That was, after all, the crux of the revolt of the young bourgeois generation of the *fin de siècle*.

Langbehn coupled creativity with racism in claiming that only the German race of artists could understand nature and God's universe. The Volk, based upon a common racial identity, was the mediator between man and the cosmos, infusing the individual with the life spirit, the vital cosmic ether about which Madame Blavatsky had written. The racial identity of the Volk was symbolized by the nature within which it lived. Thus, every race had its landscape: the Aryans were set in the German forest, and the Jews in the desert, which expressed their rootlessness and the barrenness of their souls. But Langbehn also believed in physical stereotypes, and he used physiognomy in order to prove the superiority of the Aryan. The Volk was exemplified through the landscape that surrounded it, as well as by the appearance of its members.

If the Volk transmitted the life force, Langbehn thought that the "life-fluid" which flowed from cosmos to Volk, and from Volk to its individual members, could be grasped not only through nature but also through extrasensory perception. Man's "racial soul," which constituted the essence of the Volk spirit, stood at the center of the process whereby the life-giving fluid flowed between God and the world, spiritualizing all outward and inner life and transforming all Germans into artists. Langbehn asserted that the Aryans had a monopoly on this life force and therefore upon artistic creativity; the Jews had long ago forfeited their souls, while the French had lost theirs through revolutionary conflict. Langbehn admired the Middle Ages because to him a society of medieval estates was the most desirable polity. Langbehn himself, after a life of poverty, was converted from Protestantism to Catholicism and joined a religious order. He liked to think of himself as a lonely prophet, but in fact, although his work did make an impact in Germany, other "cosmic philosophers" in Vienna were following the same line of thought, without referring directly to the Rembrandt German, as Langbehn was often called.

Thus, Guido von List, in his *German Mythological Landscape Pictures* (*Deutsch-Mythologische Landschaftsbilder*, 1891), stressed nature as the fount from which the life force flowed. Whatever was closest to nature would therefore be closest to the truth, and the Aryan past, being closest to nature, was farthest removed from modern materialism. List set himself the task of rediscovering that past. "We must read with our souls the landscape which archeology reconquers with the spade." Again, he advised: "If you want to lift the veil of mystery [of the past], you must fly into the loneliness of nature."[5] Later, he claimed to have found the language of the Aryan spirit in his *Secret of the Runes* (*Geheimnis der Runen*, 1908). List also shared with theosophy the belief in Karma, the cycle of birth and rebirth, and asserted that future Aryan leaders would be reborn from the ancient heroic dead.

List was never widely read. His importance lies in the adoption of his ideas by a group of intellectuals in Munich at the beginning of the twentieth century who called themselves the "cosmic philosophers." There another prophet, Alfred Schuler, carried on the belief in an ethereal life force and claimed that he could reconstruct the Aryan past by viewing it with his soul. As a young agitator, Adolf Hitler heard Schuler lecture much later, in 1922, at the house of his maternal friend Hélène Bechstein, in Berlin. Was he remembering that evening when he claimed that science must again become se- cret, or when during the war he talked about the occult forces of nature which penetrate our dreams?[6]

Jörg Lanz von Liebenfels was another Viennese prophet of Aryanism, a believer in life forces and sun worship. He had left the Catholic Church under the influence of the *Los von Rom* (inde- pendence from Rome) movement of the Austrian Pan-Germanist Georg Ritter von Schönerer. Lanz became a pagan, influenced by the talk about an Aryan religion among Schönerer's followers. Lanz wanted to breed a heroic Aryan race, blond supermen who were also adepts of the occult. Pagan sun worship through the goddess Ostara was combined with theosophical ideas in which fire was symbolic of the substance of the soul. Lanz called the enemies of the Aryans "ape-men," "dark people of inferior race," who must be regarded as animals, at best slaves, and whose physical extermina- tion he advocated. World peace could only be attained through the dominance of the blond Aryan race. Lanz's importance lies in the newspaper *Ostara, Journal for Blond People* that he founded in 1905, which until the outbreak of the First World War attained a respectable circulation among the many Viennese sectarian publica- tions. It is likely that the young Adolf Hitler read the paper.[7] It seems certain that he encountered these ideas in Vienna; the parallel between Lanz's Manichaean, spiritualistic world view and that of Hitler is striking. Undoubtedly, the artist in Hitler was attracted to this mysticism of race.

The equation of Aryan with the life force meant that those who opposed Aryanism were indeed people without a soul, cut off from nature and the universe. Hitler also believed that the Jews consti- tuted an evil "principle," opposed to life itself. The concept of the Volk as the mediating organ between the cosmic life force and man could not permit compromise with the forces of darkness. The bat- tle was joined between the people of life and those of darkness.

Guido von List had hoped for such a struggle, claiming that during the Ice Age the Aryans had built up their bodily and spiritual strength in the hard fight with nature. Their development was quite different from that of other races that had lived without struggle in a bountiful world. The myth of the Aryan migration, which we analyzed earlier, was once again refurbished. The element of struggle was always a part of this spiritualism, and great cosmic principles were locked in battle in which there could be only victory or destruction. Hitler's Manichaean world view must have emerged strengthened from this encounter and from his acceptance of the theosophic mystery of race.

The spiritualistic and theosophical ideas of race were always on the fringes of racial thought. Those who wanted to use the concept of race in order to create a national religion took advantage of idealistic philosophical traditions which were closer to the center of European thought. One man straddled these two approaches, just as he was ambivalent about racism itself: Paul Anton Bötticher, who called himself Paul Anton de Lagarde. His *German Writings* (*Deutsche Schriften*, 1878) early on pointed the way toward a new Germanic religion. Lagarde was concerned to preserve and vitalize the life force found in the genuine nation and Volk. Political leadership, economic growth, and national prosperity were merely superstructures, which bore no relationship to the inner, spiritual needs of the Volk. A new German faith was needed that would free the Volkish spirit from traditional Christianity. This Christianity had been perverted into a stifling legal system by the Jewish St. Paul. An inner religious dynamic must lead each Volk to realize its destiny, for through such a dynamic each man was linked directly to God.

The German Volk was endowed with a particularly vital spiritual revelation, a correspondence with the creative demi-urge more valid than that of other peoples. Vague and mystical, the spiritual dynamic was once again related to nature. Man, Lagarde wrote, should listen to the trees of the wood and the harvest in the fields. The Jews were the enemy, but Lagarde at times was willing to welcome into the Volk individual Jews who had rejected their religion. Elsewhere he castigated the "world Jewish conspiracy," and called for a mortal contest between Jews and Aryans.[8] Lagarde was a leading Orientalist. Nevertheless, only toward the end of his life did he become a professor at the University of Göttingen, and such academic frustration led to a bitterness in his search for the true Volk, lending a pedantic quality to his work which is missing from Langbehn's ecstatic writings.

Lagarde is a transitional figure, his Germanic religion vague and sometimes contradictory. Others who set out to revive the national mystique in a more thorough racist fashion overshadowed Lagarde's not inconsiderable influence from the 1880's onward. Richard Wagner, Houston Stewart Chamberlain, and Otto Weininger became names to contend with, racial prophets who oriented themselves to more respectable traditions than the spiritualism fashionable in their times. Yet Wagner stressed the Aryan blood strain; Chamberlain called for a race war; and Weininger annexed racism to his sexual fears. Blood, war, and sex form a triad which is constantly repeated in twentieth-century racism, though we have seen that each of these elements was allied with racism from the beginning.

The ideas of Richard Wagner are particularly important because of the influence exercised by Bayreuth not only during the composer's life but also long after his death. The Wagner circle, presided over first by his wife Cosima, and then by his daughter-in-law Winifred, came to symbolize culture for much of the German right. The operas performed annually ever since 1876 were "festivals" which rendered his abstract ideas concrete. They were supported by an unflagging barrage of propaganda from the *Bayreuther Blätter*, as well as from books and pamphlets. At the same time, Bayreuth as a cultural center became a center of racism, where neophytes could worship at the altar of Germanic blood and Teutonic myth (even though Cosima was half-French, and Winifred English by birth).

Richard Wagner had taken part in the revolution of 1848 as a young man, but in time had turned to racism as he became embittered toward a world that refused to bend to his wishes. Richard and Cosima Wagner exalted the quiet, rooted life against the big city, what they saw as the depth of Germanic feeling against the

menace of industrialism. The Jews represented all that was opposed
to the good and beautiful; in fact, Richard Wagner once dreamed
that he was murdered by a Berlin Jew.[9] At times Jesuits, Frenchmen,
and Socialists were added to those who exemplified a hostile race.
But Wagner's attitude toward Jews was far from consistent. Young
Jewish musicians like Anton Rubinstein or Karl Tausig were welcomed into the inner circle, while Hermann Levi was one of his
favorite conductors; patrons of Bayreuth such as the Jewish Alfred
Pringsheim were showered with praise. Wagner's attitude depended
upon the usefulness of individual Jews to his cause; even so, any
difference of opinion, any supposed slight by his favorites, was immediately connected to their racial disabilities: the Jewish restlessness, lack of reverence, or lack of soul.[10]

To be sure, such ambivalence was absent in Wagner's writings.
Thus *Jewry in Music* (*Judentum in der Musik*, 1850) transferred his
jealous hatred of Jacob Meyerbeer to all Jews—they were not able
to compose music because they lacked passion; they were devoted
to the lure of money and without any inner life of their own. Jewish
blood was inherently incapable of plumbing the depth of the Aryan
soul. Such stereotypes surface in Wagner's writings again when he
comes into musical contact with his other imagined rival, Felix
Mendelssohn. Meyerbeer and Mendelssohn provided the catalyst
for Richard Wagner's racism as an outlet for his bitterness toward
the world. Since Cosima was a mere shadow of her husband, and
Winifred imitated her mother-in-law, Bayreuth continued to propagate the Aryan myth until after the Second World War.

Yet Wagner's operas were not mired in a bitterness laced with
hatred for the Jewish race. Instead, they sought to put forward what
Wagner regarded as a positive Germanic world view. He wanted to
bring the so-called eternal German truths back to his people, who
seemed to be ignoring them and thus denying the heritage of their
blood. The Germans, he held, were characterized by an inner substance that had never changed; therefore, the ancient sagas were
also an expression of the present. From its conception in 1848, his
Ring of the Nibelungen stressed the freedom of the German Volk
against feudal oppression. Each individual soul must be freed so

that it could unite with the Volk and be truly creative. Wagner believed that the free moral conscience of man was directed by Germanic gods.[11] But this identification of conscience and pagan gods was not to last. Christian themes began to intrude, tied in turn to the Germanic past.

Wagner's drift to racism was accompanied by a certain Protestant fervor. Not only were Jesuits in particular regarded now and then as part of the conspiracy against Germany, but Protestantism enabled Wagner to detach Christ from his Jewish origins. As we shall see later, the so-called higher biblical criticism had prepared the way, and many Protestants in Germany would have agreed with Cosima Wagner's assertion that Christ was no relation to the Jewish God, but a personal messiah for those who knew and gave love—something the Jew could not do because he lacked the proper soul and blood.[12] Christianity seen without its historical Jewish roots but as an integral part of the Germanic mission informs several of the operas: sin, repentance, and salvation are the key to both *Lohengrin* (1850) and *Parsifal* (1882). *Lohengrin* is set in the Middle Ages, the "age of faith," and not, like the *Nibelungen*, among the ancient gods. *Parsifal* presents the Easter myth on stage. The unending dream of sacred Volkish revelation which Wagner wanted to present had tamed the ancient legends out of their pagan freedom into an acceptable Christian morality.

Lohengrin and *Parsifal* are both based upon the myth of the Holy Grail—the vessel that caught drops of Christ's blood as he died on the Cross. The "holy blood" of Christ, which constitutes a central element in the Easter myth, is in the custody of German knights. They guard it with their swords and through their moral purity. The blood myth was old, and, as we shall see, had been used against the Jews in accusations of ritual murder.[13] Here it was used positively to demonstrate that the Germans had inherited the mantle of Christ. The Saviour was indeed severed from his historical Jewish origins and entrusted to the custody of the superior race. The mythology of race had been fused with Christianity in order to define the eternal property of the German nation, its purity of blood. The salvation of the Germanic race will come, Wagner tells us, when it is worthy of this blood through repentance of its sins and through moral purity. Again, the penitence and death of *Tannhäuser*, first performed in 1845, were an atonement for his sensual pleasures in the Mountain of Venus; and his final salvation was due to the pious death of the chaste Elizabeth. Parsifal also resisted the temptations of the flesh as he guarded the Holy Grail. The heroic struggles of Siegfried and Brünhilde were paired with the sentimentalized Christianity of Lohengrin, Parsifal, and Tannhäuser. Middle-class morality enters once more to make the Germans fit custodians of the Holy Grail.

Purity of blood had become a symbol for the purity of the race and for its vigor. This symbolism was generally pervasive. For example, just a little later Martin Buber used the metaphor of blood to strengthen the national feeling of the Jews. Talking to a group of Zionist students in Prague in 1911, he gave an excellent definition of how the myth of the blood was supposed to function: "He (in this case the Jew) feels the shared community of blood through the immortality of previous generations; feels it as his previous life, as the everlasting nature of his personality within an infinite past. . . ." Blood is the root and the nourishment of each individual.[14] But for Buber these concepts were metaphors that defined nationality rather than race.

At much the same time that Buber gave his speeches in Prague, the poet Stefan George talked about the "lightening of the blood" (*Blutleuchte*), which was to demonstrate the existence of primeval, heathen residues within the soul.[15] But it was Wagner who blended the racial mystique and the concept of Christian salvation most effectively.

Wagner's racist ideal (which led him to befriend Gobineau)[16] is also expressed in his prose writings. But his operas were his "deeds" on behalf of Germany, as he called them. They were festivals, intended to introduce Germans to the Aryan dream. Then, once they had dreamed, they could transform the dream into reality.[17] This was a mysticism which respectable people could enjoy and be moved by. The festivals were supposedly for the many, not just the handful who read Wagner's prose. The operas were felt emotionally; Wagner communicated their theoretical foundations mainly through their texts.

The philosophical justification was to follow, and it was Houston Stewart Chamberlain who supplied it, even if there were others, less famous, who also lent a hand. Chamberlain admired Wagner although he never knew him in person. He was drawn into the Wagner circle at Bayreuth through Cosima Wagner after Richard's death. This was part of Cosima Wagner's continued effort to draw like-minded spirits to Bayreuth in order to strengthen her circle. Leopold Schröder, an expert on India, expressed well not only the ideal of the festivals but that of Bayreuth in general when he wrote: "for the first time since the scattering of the Aryan peoples they can, once again, gather at a predetermined locality [i.e., Bayreuth] . . . in order to witness their primeval mysteries." [18]

Chamberlain became such a witness (like Hitler much later), and eventually married one of Wagner's daughters. His famed *Foundations of the Nineteenth Century* (*Die Grundlagen des XIX Jahrhunderts*, 1899) were seen as expressing the official philosophy of Bayreuth. Indeed, nothing like the Wagner circle existed in other nations, and its role in rooting the mystery of race in Germany cannot be underestimated. For many Germans the Bayreuth festivals, the personality of Cosima Wagner, and the two volumes by Chamberlain represented German culture *tout court*.

For Chamberlain the Germans were held together by their shared blood, but he also believed in a Germanic Christianity quite similar to that of Wagner. To begin with, Chamberlain founded his theory on Kant, who, according to his interpretation, postulated an essence of things beyond reason and pragmatism. This essence was the "German religion," which bestowed infinite vistas upon the soul and served to keep science within narrowly defined bounds. And for Chamberlain, this religion was a monopoly of the Aryan "race-soul." Such a soul made Germans honest, loyal, and industrious; thus middle-class morality became once more a quality of the German race. Moreover, Chamberlain believed in the Aryan stereotype, and here he accepted anthropological and cranial measurements. But as not all Germans possessed the outward appearance proper to Aryans, it seemed best to retreat to the race-soul which they did share.

In the light of the Aryan ideal-type and its racial soul, Chamberlain transformed Christ into an Aryan prophet. Christ's disposition revealed an Aryan soul, for he exemplified love, compassion, and honor, and his soul was devoid of all materialism. A supposedly factual argument was also adduced, namely, that the Jews had never settled in Galilee and that actually an Aryan people lived in the place where Christ was born. This was however of secondary importance compared with Christ's "Aryan race-soul."

According to Chamberlain, the Germanic race entered history as the saviours of mankind and as the heirs of the Greeks and Romans. German Aryans had to wage a bitter struggle against their enemies in order to fulfill their civilizing mission; for Chamberlain, Catholic Christianity was one such enemy, which sought to enslave the race-soul under foreign laws first invented by St. Paul, the Jew. The Protestant Reformation put an end to that and liberated the racial soul. German racism was always to think of Luther as the great liberator from foreign oppression.[19] The real enemy of the Aryan, however, was the Jew. Chamberlain saw in the Jews an Asian people who had entered European history at the same time as the Germans, and like the Germans had managed to preserve their racial purity. He held that the Jewish soul was materialistic, legalistic, and devoid of tolerance and morality, drawing upon the Old Testament for his proof.

In Chamberlain's view, the Jews were the devil and the Germans the chosen people; between them existed a chaotic mixture of peoples—passive spectators at the crucial battle of history. The outcome of the battle between Aryans and Jews would decide whether the base Jewish spirit would triumph over the Aryan soul and drag the world down with it. Chamberlain wrote that the Germans had never strayed far from their original stock, while the Jews, though they had kept themselves apart from Gentiles for centuries originally, were a mixture of the most diverse peoples imaginable (Syrians, Amorites, Hittites) and therefore a bastard people.

The Aryans must struggle against this bastard race, which was the
very epitome of all evil.

The defeat of the Jews would lead not to social or economic
change, but to a spiritual revolution, as a result of which the Aryan
race-soul would dominate the world. A new culture would be born,
which would end the present degeneration. The German spirit
would revive the great tradition of art and letters which Chamberlain traced through past centuries, and the example of men like
Shakespeare, Michelangelo, and Beethoven would determine the future of the race. For Chamberlain, the triumph of the race-soul led
to a vision of salvation through culture.

Chamberlain mentioned the state, but again rather in terms of its
racial disposition than the details of its government. The true state
was based upon Germanic freedoms. The fount of these freedoms
was the *Magna Carta*, instead of the Comitatus (whose role was
analyzed earlier), but the basic idea was the same—Germans must
live a creative life, not stifled by foreign ideas and laws. Economic
problems get short shrift in the *Foundations* except for a vague
suggestion favoring a corporate state. The section dealing with such
realities is slim when compared with the discussion of religion and
art. The mystery of race is clearly more important in Chamberlain's
mind.

Racial mysticism culminated in an extended criticism of the culture, in contrast to the racial biologists, who put forward practical
schemes of eugenics and race improvement. Where the racial scientists had merely concentrated upon sterilization as a part of eugenics, here the struggle between Aryans and Jews was seen as a fight
to the death between creative and uncreative races. Art and religion
were pitted against the perversion of myth into matter. Racial mysticism posited a race war—a fight to the finish between two principles of life. It was a religion that allowed no compromise, for
the racial mystics believed that the faith that would lead to salvation must burn bright and pure.

While Chamberlain's influence radiated throughout the German
right, Hitler himself was not greatly influenced by his thought.

Indeed, he criticized Chamberlain for believing that Christianity could have any spiritual reality, even as an Aryan religion. But when Chamberlain met Hitler in Bayreuth in 1923, he was greatly impressed; here, Chamberlain wrote, was a man who showed a courage reminiscent of Martin Luther. The aged writer died in 1927 secure in the knowledge that he had discovered the prophet who would lead the Aryans to victory (see Plate 6).[20]

Wagner's and Chamberlain's Christianity had been puritanical; sex was to be resisted, in tune with middle-class morality. Three years after the *Foundations*, the Austrian Otto Weininger published his *Sex and Character* (*Geschlecht und Charakter*, 1903), a book which linked race and sex and which was to become almost as famous as Chamberlain's work.

By 1919, *Sex and Character* had gone through eighteen editions. In England it was published by the respectable publishing house of Heinemann, and from Scandinavia to Italy it found an eager and receptive audience.[21] In part, its popularity may have been due to the sexual analysis, and in part because this anti-Jewish book was written by a young Jew who committed suicide immediately after its publication. Above all, Weininger constructed an Aryan ideal-type on the basis of sex and race.

Weininger claimed that the Aryan male emphasized clarity of thought, showed decisiveness in attitudes, and rose to metaphysical heights of belief. On the other hand, women of every race were incapable of thinking in concepts, being indeed devoid of any clarity whatsoever, for they were great compromisers, for whom everything was a "formless wobble." "Clarity" here connoted a clear distinction between enemy and friend. As in all racial mysticism, no middle ground was to be allowed. For Weininger, the polarization was symbolized by the sexual differences between men and women: the male stood for heroism, battle, and "clarity," while the woman represented indecisiveness. When Weininger wrote that a woman was incapable of being radically evil or radically good, he voiced a longing for simplification which would become ever more pronounced with the growing onslaught upon liberal values. Weininger believed that Friedrich Nietzsche had blazed the trail by his opposition against compromise and his challenging call to accept the dangers life holds. But Nietzsche had put this into a framework of individualism, and his "Know thyself" knew no nationality or race. Yet Weininger could claim that Nietzsche shared his view of women to whom, after all, Zarathustra took the whip.

Weininger's Aryan male was exemplified by classical models, not only as part of the Aryan ideal-type but also as an unambivalent reference point in a confused and complex world. The woman represented the liberal democratic principle, based on compromise, opposed to all strictness of artistic form. These qualities are abstract principles in *Sex and Character*, for Weininger saw that in reality the woman may have something of the male and the male something of the female attitudes. But the Aryan woman still has a redeeming quality. Although she is incapable of true spirituality, she is capable of belief in the man or in her child. As Weininger put it, in the last resort to believe in something at all is what matters in life.

By contrast, according to Weininger, the Jew lacked any belief. He had no soul, no concepts of a higher order, and therefore, no idea of the state. In short, the Jew was at once a materialist and an anarchist who denied the polity. But for Weininger the Jew was also a Communist, for "communism" meant the absence of spirituality. Race and nationality were taken as identical, and those who were outside the tribe could possess neither spirituality nor creativity. Weininger went even further to assert that Jews and women, because they lacked national feeling, could not acquire any personality whatsoever. As dehumanized stereotypes, the Jews were non-people to Weininger.

Weininger was not unique in his comparisons of sex and race. F. Gellion-Danglar in France had made the same argument in 1882: the Semitic race had the weakness of women, who were emotional, superstitious, rapacious, catlike, to give only a few of his characterizations.[22] The depersonalized nature of this stereotype was noted by Émile Zola, who in his *J'Accuse* (1898) wrote that Dreyfus was to his enemies not a man but an abstraction.[23] Maurice Barrès proved him right when shortly afterwards he asserted that no proof was needed that Dreyfus had betrayed France—"that he is capable of treason I believe by knowing his race."[24] For all these men—Weininger, Gellion-Danglar, Barrès, and Chamberlain—the Jewish stereotype took on metaphysical dimensions that had no connection with reality. The battle against the Jews was therefore once more seen as a struggle of light against darkness, in which there could be only victory or death.

Nationality and race focused on the male ideal-type. In the words of a Nazi journal, where Aryan man is the sun, all others are moon-people.[25] Weininger represented a heightened irrationality, since he rejected all science as materialistic and all environmental theories as absurd. For him, the ideal Germanic man was the artist—the representative of all higher aspirations. Moreover, in common with Houston Stewart Chamberlain, Weininger held to the emphasis on Kant as the pacemaker for Aryan clarity of thought and spirituality. Weininger, however, also attacked Chamberlain in a most revealing passage asserting that Christ was indeed a Jew. For Weininger himself quite logically believed that only a Jew could truly know the evil of his race and thus try to transcend it.[26] This attempt to transcend Jewishness was in conflict with the book's racism, but not with Weininger's own desires. Poor Weininger; he must have seen himself as attempting such a feat, and failing, decided to end it all. It was to be expected that the author of *Sex and Character* would take his own strange theories seriously. The fact that many others did so as well is proof of the extent to which racial mysticism had penetrated the national consciousness.

Weininger's *Sex and Character* constituted a critique of modern culture. He wrote that in his own times anarchy reigned; his was a world without state or law, originality or ethics. This "degenerate age," as he called it, was symbolized by the *demimonde* which had replaced the virgin, and where sexual intercourse had become a duty. In order to remedy this state of affairs, a new religion must be founded, one that would distinguish clearly between Judaism and Christianity, business and culture, man and wife, species and personality.

Adolf Hitler knew Weininger's book and used it to bolster his own hatred of the Jews.[27] There is a definite resemblance between

Weininger's theories and Hitler's account in *Mein Kampf* of how he
perceived the east European Jews in Vienna, who were so different,
he tells us, from the assimilated Jews of Linz. For Hitler the dirty
and unheroic Jew with sidelocks and caftan was immediately linked
to sex. We hear about Jews in charge of white slavery and prostitution, but also get a description of Jewish boys lurking at street corners ready to attack Aryan virgins at any moment.[28] Weininger was
not needed to make these connections, for just as the Negro had
aroused the sexual fantasies of Europeans, so the Jew was feared as
the sexual rival. (For the consequences of this belief, see Plate 7.)
But this image owed something to the supposed perversion of sex
into lust by the inferior race, which was a part of the absence of the
higher faculties as far as Weininger was concerned.

Sexual fantasies were also stimulated by the greater sensitivity to
smells among Europeans from the mid-nineteenth century onwards.
There was more emphasis on bodily cleanliness, and sanitary ar-
rangements were improving, so that "bad smells" were no longer so
easily tolerated in the house, especially as by this time the supposedly curative power of the "clean air" of the countryside had
been discovered. Eventually, too, Darwin's *The Descent of Man*
(1871) stirred interest in the role of smell in sexual life.[29] Smell and
race had always been associated, and Jews as well as blacks were
endowed with peculiar odors, even during the Middle Ages. In the
nineteenth century, the overcrowded conditions in east European
ghettos and in the Jewish quarters of west and central European
cities bred foul odors. All too many people connected these not to
the endemic poverty in which Jews lived, but to the inherent "dirtiness" of their race.

The link between race and smell was actually elevated into some-
thing of a world view toward the end of the nineteenth century.
For example, the German biologist Gustav Jäger, founder of the
Viennese Zoo, in 1881 tied the "origin of the soul" to odors pro-
duced by chemical processes which determine all life and thought.
Different races have different and unique smells. As he also be-
lieved that "Disease is stink," Jäger advocated woolen underwear
("Jäger's underwear") in order to keep the skin warm and to lock in

body odors.[30] Iwan Bloch in 1900 called the Negro problem an "olfactory question" and cited as witness the famed anthropologist Quatrefages mentioned earlier.[31] Gustav Jäger himself thought that the "Jewish smell" was particularly unpleasant and that every Jew could be recognized by his odor. Thus, he repeated some seventy years later the opinion of a headmaster who had asserted in 1809 that some Jewish toddlers because of their "foul vapors" could never share a bench with Christians.[32]

Racism, which allied itself with all movements, also attempted to embrace sex and smell, thereby completing the stereotype that had already received wide currency. Cleanliness and lack of smell were thought to be middle-class virtues that must be added to the others we have mentioned so often. Inferior races were inherently dirty and smelly.

The Aryan race-soul made a higher spirituality possible; the outward expression of this inner spirit was emphasis upon middle-class morality and confrontation with the Jewish enemy. Whether the Aryan substance was a life force similar to Madame Blavatsky's ether, a "lightening of the blood," or certain male characteristics, it could only break through to reality by fighting a war to the finish against the Jews. This call to war climaxed the development of racism which we have traced from the eighteenth century into the beginnings of the twentieth. So far we have largely focused on the Aryan. Now we must turn to the Jew.

CHAPTER EIGHT

The Jews: Myth and Counter-Myth

THE MYSTERY of race transformed the Jew into an evil principle. This was nothing new for the Jew; after all, anti-Christ had been a familiar figure during the Middle Ages. But in the last decades of the nineteenth century and the first half of the twentieth, the traditional legends which had swirled about the Jews in the past were revived as foils for racial mysticism and as instruments of political mobilization. Accusations of ritual murder, the curse of Ahasverus the wandering Jew, and fantasies about the universal Jewish world conspiracy had never vanished from the European consciousness even during the Enlightenment. Now they were to be revitalized and given renewed force.

The accusation of ritual murder—the so-called blood libel—had medieval roots in the legend that Jews murdered Christian children and drank their blood during the feast of Passover. As part of their religious ceremonial, the Jews allegedly performed a "ritual murder," typical of the perverse nature of their religion and the evil it represented. Moreover, this Jewish use of blood blasphemed the sacrifice of Christ on the Cross, for Easter and Passover coincided. The blood libel provided the basis for an accusation of atavism, because in contrast to civilized people, Jews supposedly practiced human sacrifice. The so-called Jewish conspiracy against the Gentile world was also built into this myth from the beginning, for no Jew, so it was thought, would inform on any other Jew, while talkative Gentiles were bribed with gold to remain silent about this ritual of human sacrifice.

The myth of the use and misuse of the sacred substance of blood served to separate out the Jews from the Christians. Blood libel had always surfaced in periods of stress. At the end of the nineteenth century, the times seemed out of joint and ritual murder accusations once more swept through eastern Europe. Between 1890 and 1914, there were no less than twelve trials of Jews for ritual murder; the last murder charge was leveled as late as 1930, in the Rutho-Carpathian Mountains by the prosecutor of the Czechoslovak government.[1]

The blood libel remained alive chiefly in the underdeveloped countries of eastern Europe and the Russian Empire. Within the Russian Empire the government shrewdly exploited the belief in order to provoke pogroms, and every lost Christian child was a menace to the local Jewish community, one of whose members might be accused of murder. Western and central Europe had also made use of this legend, but in these regions the accusations receded in time, especially among urban segments of the population where secularism had made large inroads. In rural regions the myth continued, encouraged in particular by the Catholic Church, which had trouble ending its long association with the accusation of ritual murder. Local priests still proclaimed its truth at times during the nineteenth and even into the twentieth century, and medieval saints like Simon of Trent, who were worshiped into our own day, kept the legend of martyred children supposedly brutally murdered by the Jews before the eyes of the pious.[2] (For the Nazi use of the legend, see Plate 8.)

If the blood libel encouraged Christians to look upon the Jew as harbinger of evil, the legend of the wandering Jew exemplified the curse laid upon that race by Christ himself. The figure of Ahasverus appears in legend as a Jew who sped Christ along to his crucifixion and refused him comfort or shelter. As a result, Ahasverus is doomed to a life of wandering, without a home, despised as rootless and disinherited. The wandering Jew, who can neither live nor die, also heralds terror and desolation.[3] This medieval tale of the "wicked Jew" (as Ahasverus was often called) did not fade in the nineteenth century but instead became symbolic of the cursed fate of the Jewish people (see Plate 9). The restless age and the restless Jew both became symbols of a desolate modernity.

Ahasverus in legend is also associated with conspiracies against the righteous. In France, he symbolized the conspiracy of Jews and Masons against the nation. However, at times the wandering Jew could become a hero and the conspiracy be laid on other shoulders. Eugène Sue's *The Wandering Jew* (*Le Juif Errant*, 1844–45), the most famous Ahasverus story of the century, turns him into a hero who foils a Jesuit conspiracy. Then again, during the First World War the English satirized Emperor William II as Ahasverus who had driven Christ from his door and was now wandering through Europe in the vain search of peace.[4] Nevertheless, for the most part the ancient legend retained its original form, and remained symbolic of the curse which the Jewish people brought upon themselves and all they touched. These legends, whether the blood libel or that of the wandering Jew, offered explanation and coherence in a world of industrialization, instability, and bewildering social change, just as they had earlier been used as explanation for famines, sickness, and all manner of natural catastrophes.

The legend of the wandering Jew reenforced the view of the Jew as the eternal foreigner, who would never learn to speak the national language properly or strike roots in the soil. This myth, in turn, was linked to the supposed oriental origin of the Jew as described in the Bible. The Jew was assumed to be fixed for all time as a desert nomad wandering through the Sinai. The Viennese Orientalist Adolf Wahrmund popularized this image in his *Law of the Nomads and Contemporary Jewish Domination* (*Das Gesetz des Nomadenthums und die heutige Judenherrschaft*, 1887). The Jews had been nomads in the past, and were still nomads today, claimed Wahrmund. This explained their shiftlessness in commerce, and their rootless, cosmopolitan way of thought, as opposed to the rooted Aryan peasantry. Wahrmund carried on the tradition of proving Aryan peasant origins through linguistics. Both as nomads and Asians, the Jews were indeed Ahasverus, not because of the curse of Christ, but because they were still a desert people.[5] Thus, an anti-Jewish image rooted in religion was secularized and given new credence by means of a pseudo-scientific environmentalism.

Such legends catered to the love of the romantic and the unusual. The nineteenth century, which popularized Frankenstein and human vampires, was fascinated by horror stories that had a real people as their foil. The novel *Biarritz*, written in 1868 by Hermann Goedsche (under the pen name Sir John Redcliffe), was not only typical of this love of the unusual, but also significant as one of the chief sources of the notorious forged *Protocols of the Elders of Zion*.

The setting of *Biarritz* is the Jewish cemetery of Prague. Significantly, other more famous writers, such as Wilhelm Raabe, used the identical setting to tell stories of Jewish mysteries and secret deeds. The Jewish cemetery in Prague was a romantic site; moreover, it was accessible, for Prague, although part of the Austrian Empire, was considered a German city. It was easy to travel there and to see for oneself the sights of the ghetto, while the other ghettos of eastern Europe were in regions with "obscure" languages and difficult to reach. The tourist from Germany or Austria, for example, would feel at home staying in the large German section of Prague and visiting the picturesque sights. The clash of different cultures, which was exemplified by the ghettos still existing in eastern Europe, could be symbolized through the Jewish cemetery in Prague with its mysterious graves and caftaned figures—at least as seen by the tourist from the West. Goedsche summed up this symbolism when he wrote that Prague was the only German city where Jews still lived in isolation.[6]

In this way, Goedsche set the scene for a meeting of the thirteen Jewish elders in the cemetery. He named them the "cabalistic Sanhedrin," referring to the many legends associated with the Jewish Cabalah and thus giving a wider historical dimension to the assembly at the cemetery. For Goedsche, the mystery of the Cabalah consisted in "the power of gold."[7] Thus through the Cabalah he cemented the traditional association of the Jews with base materialism. One of the elders is Ahasverus, the wandering Jew; his presence among the thirteen clearly shows how Goedsche exploited old anti-Semitic traditions.[8]

The elders meet as the representatives of the chosen people, who show "the tenacity of a snake, the cunning of a fox, the look of a falcon, the memory of a dog, the diligence of an ant, and the sociability of a beaver."[9] The association of Jews with animal imagery should not surprise us; it was noted earlier when discussing the rise of the stereotype in the eighteenth century.[10] The blacks suffered an identical fate when they were constantly compared to monkeys. Likening the so-called inferior races to animals put them low on the chain of being and, by analogy, robbed them of their humanity.

In the eerie setting of the cemetery, the elders conspire to take over the world. They plot to concentrate all capital into their hands; to secure possession of all land, railroads, mines, houses; to occupy government posts; to seize the press and direct all public opinion. This bizarre plan was later to be borrowed from *Biarritz* and, as a "Rabbi's speech," circulated all over the Russian and Austrian Empires.

The myth of the sinister Jewish conspiracy was not confined to eastern Europe. Only a year after *Biarritz* appeared, Gougenot de Mousseaux in a polemic against the Jews of France depicted them as devotees of a secret mystery-religion presided over by the devil himself.[11] Thus, the rapidly growing belief in occult forces during the last decades of the nineteenth century intersected with a revitalized medieval demonology. Indeed, Mousseaux declared that the devil was the King of the Jews, and his version of the Jewish plot would become part of the more famous *Protocols*, just as *Biarritz* also fed into this forgery.

The Protocols of the Elders of Zion became both the climax and the synthesis of these conspiracy theories (see Plate 10). They were forged in France in the midst of the Dreyfus Affair, with the assistance of the Russian secret police, probably between 1894 and 1899. The French right wanted a document in order to link Dreyfus to the supposed conspiracy of his race, and the Russian secret police needed it to justify czarist anti-Jewish policy. This time the "learned elders of Zion," again meeting in the Jewish cemetery of Prague, reflected every aspect of the modern world which the reactionaries in France and Russia, but also in the rest of Europe, feared so much.

The weapons that the elders were to use to achieve world domination ranged from the use of the French Revolution's slogan, "Liberty, Equality, Fraternity," to the spreading of liberalism and socialism. The people of the world would be deprived of all faith in God and their strength undermined by encouraging public criticism of authority. At the same time, a financial crisis would be provoked and gold in the hands of the Jews would be manipulated in order to drive up prices. Eventually, "there should be in all states in the world, besides ourselves, only the masses of the proletariat, a few millionaires devoted to our interests and our own police and soldiers." [12] Blind obedience would then be demanded to the King of Jews, the ruler of the universe. In short, the conspiracy myth fed into the uncertainties and fears of the nineteenth century, bridging the gap between ancient anti-Semitic legend and the modern Jews in a world of dramatic change.

What if the Gentiles discovered this plot and began to attack the Jews? In this case the elders would use a truly horrible weapon, for soon all the national capitals of the world would be undermined by a network of underground railways. If there should be danger to the Jews, these tunnels would be used to blow up the cities and kill their inhabitants. Such a nightmare bears traces of the fear of a new technology, but also of the stories of horror and fantasy so popular at the time. Furthermore, the elders would destroy the Gentiles by inoculating them with diseases.

Opposition to inoculation was to become a part of racist thought. In 1935 the *Weltkampf*, a Nazi anti-Jewish journal, stated that inoculation had been invented by the Jews in order to subvert the Aryan blood, citing the *Protocols* as its evidence. [13] Racism is basic to the nightmare of the *Protocols*, for the Jews were considered an evil race, coherent and well organized. The mystery of race had found one of its most popular supposed proofs in the conspiracy of the elders of Zion.

Conspiracy theories might have been less popular and effective had it not been for certain past and present Jewish organizations which to some Gentiles seemed to serve a sinister purpose. In Russia it was charged that the Jewish communal organizations, which had been dissolved by Czar Nicholas I in 1844, were still alive and active as a secret Jewish government linked to foreign interests.[14] An element of spurious reality was lent to these conspiracy charges with the founding of the "Alliance Israélite Universelle" in 1860 by French Jews. The Alliance was intended to aid Jews in nations where they were deprived of civic rights, and to support schools for North African Jews. These worthy purposes were, of course, ignored and the Alliance seen as the exposed tip of an iceberg of conspiracy.

Aside from the reality of the Alliance, anti-Semites and racists pointed to the Masons as another existing secret conspiracy directed by Jews—the *Protocols* had linked Jewish and Masonic conspiracies. The fight against Masons in turn called the Catholic Church into action. The Anti-Masonic World Congress of 1897 was supported by Pope Leo XIII, and was placed under the protection of the Virgin Mary. During the Congress, the Jews were specifically linked to the anti-Catholic Masonic conspiracy, and the Union Antimaçonnique which was founded at that time received support from Drumont and other French racists.[15] An anti-Masonic movement also existed in Germany, and eventually, under the Nazis, an anti-Masonic museum was established, but this particular myth was strongest in Catholic France.

Powerful though the groups might have been that at times supported such theories and pointed to the Alliance or Masons as proof, they were still a minority (except, perhaps, among the Catholic clergy). Such myths and legends about the Jews were used in order to mobilize those who wanted to protect both traditional Christianity and traditional society. But much of the future importance of these anti-Jewish myths consisted in their association with a secular nationalism which lacked the traditional Christian inhibitions against embracing racism. Certainly, as we shall see, the line between Christian anti-Semitism and racism was thin; but the national mystique could without question accept these myths as inherent in the Jewish race. There was no need for secular nationalism to confront the problem of how Jews could be changed into Christians through baptism if their race was inherently evil, nor was it necessary as a part of the drama of Christian salvation to disentangle the Jews of the Old Testament from their inferior racial status. All racists did better to ignore Christianity whenever possible.

In this regard, a journalist like Wilhelm Marr in Germany was typical. His *Jewry's Victory over Teutonism* (*Der Sieg des Judentums über das Germanentum*, 1879) rejected the Christian accusations against the Jews as unworthy of the enlightened, but then repeated all the myths about rootless and conspiratorial Jews. For Marr the Jews were stronger than the Germans, for they were winning the racial battle for survival. He suggested a counteroffensive, spearheaded by anti-Semitic Russia.

The one-time member of the German diet, Hermann Ahlwardt, became more famous than Marr with the publication of his *The Desperate Struggle Between Aryan and Jew* (*Der Verzweiflungskampf der arischen Völker mit dem Judentum*, 1890). Two years later, this primary school principal wrote a book in a similar vein entitled *New Revelations: Jewish Rifles* (*Neue Enthüllungen Judenflinten*, 1892), in which he once more sounded the alarm against the Jewish threat. Here, he contended that the Jewish armament firm of Löwe was selling defective rifles to the German army as part of a universal world Jewish conspiracy to destroy the Reich. And for all the absurdity of the allegation, the government initiated an inquiry into the charges.[16]

As yet, the attempts to act as if the Jewish conspiracy were true remained on the fringes of European thought and, apart from Russia, unsuccessful in immediate terms. They were forerunners of the concerted war against the Jews which began only after the trauma of the First World War, in 1918, and of men like Hitler who not only believed in the *Protocols* but eventually had the means to act as if they were true. The anti-Masonic and anti-Jewish lodge founded by Jules Guérin in Paris during the 1890's was seen as ludicrous.[17] And the first international congress of the tiny rival anti-Semitic groups (mainly from Germany, Austria, and Hungary) meeting in Dresden in 1882 seemed scarcely more important, though it conceived itself as a rallying point against the Jewish world conspiracy. Its purpose was to consolidate the anti-Jewish struggle, but the congress could not overcome tensions between Christian anti-Semites like Adolf Stoecker and the racists, who were prone to violence and who denied that a baptized Jew differed from the rest of his race. The second meeting of this congress in 1883 bore the title "Alliance Antijuive Universelle" and clearly pointed to the Alliance Israélite as symbolic of the enemy.[18]

The legends about the Jews, as part of racial mysticism, penetrated beyond the relatively small groups who were obsessed with the Jewish conspiracy and had little time for other concerns. More important, however, such legends became a mechanism through which rightist movements sought to change society. The imaginary threat posed by the Jews could be used to rally people behind such interest groups as agricultural unions and conservative parties in their battle with liberals and Socialists. But Catholic and Protestant movements could also appeal to traditional legends about the Jews in order to fight atheism more effectively. Above all, those who wanted to reinvigorate the national mystique by emphasizing equality among the people used the Jews as a foil. Here, typically enough, an agitator like Wilhelm Marr, who was a democrat believing in universal suffrage and freedom of thought, accused the Jews of being liberals—a people without roots, who sought to substitute the slavery of finance capital for that of oppression by kings.[19] Such National Socialists, as they were called long before Adolf Hitler usurped the term, will occupy us later. Moreover, racism was firmly allied to nationalism through the mystery of race and even to science through Darwinism. Within these frameworks, the legends about the Jews which we have mentioned were kept alive, now as part of the race war that seemed imminent.

Even "The Universal Races Congress" of 1911, held in London and intended to reflect humanistic and Christian values, assumed that "pure" races could be said to exist, though such opponents of racism as John Dewey, Annie Besant, and the American black leader W. E. B. DuBois attended.[20] This Congress was one more sign of the abiding and deep interest in race.

Were the Jews themselves exempt from the influence of racial thought which seemed so widely spread throughout European society? Did the Jews themselves counter the myth of the Jew as an evil principle with a myth of the Jew as a pure and noble race? Many, indeed most Jews who were highly assimilated in central or western Europe regarded themselves as full members of the nations in which they lived—not as a separate people but rather as one of the tribes, like the Saxons, Bavarians, or Alsatians, which made up the larger nation. The First World War enhanced such tendencies, and after 1918 Jewish veterans associations in many European nations provided the principal support for such attempted national integration. However, those Jews who regarded themselves as a separate people must be our special concern. Did Jewish nationalism follow European nationalism in making an alliance with racism?

The racial ideas of Gobineau had been introduced to the readers of the Zionist *Die Welt* in 1902, not merely to sing the praises of racial purity, but mainly to counter the accusation that Jews were a degenerate people. Gobineau had admired the Jews precisely because they had not given in to modern degeneracy, and now his theories could be used to best advantage in order to prove that "Jewry has maintained its . . . toughness, thanks to the purity of its blood." Miscegenation must be avoided at all costs. The Jewish and Aryan races could not interpenetrate, they could only live side by side in mutual understanding.[21] The influences of racism were clearly accepted here, even if the concept of the blood was not defined in terms of "blood and soil," but rather as the vehicle of the drives and peculiarities of the soul. Yet, this annexation of Gobineau (and of Houston Stewart Chamberlain, as we shall see later) proved the exception rather than the rule among Jews. If some Jews were attracted to racism, it was the science of race which seemed to have more appeal to them.

Jews, for example, contributed to the German *Journal for Racial and Social Biology*. But like most of the contributors to that journal, a belief in the reality of race did not mean that any one race was necessarily superior to another. For example, Elias Auerbach, one of the pioneers of Zionist settlement in Palestine, wrote in 1907 that while the Jewish race had been a mixture in the dim past, it was now pure because it had kept itself separate through centuries. He concluded his article with a quote from Gobineau to the effect that a Volk will never die while it can maintain its purity and uniqueness of composition.[22] Yet Auerbach advocated a binational Jewish-Arab Palestine, and opposed any domination of one people by another. It was possible to believe in pure races and still not be a racist; indeed, this was a trait shared by most Jews who believed in a Jewish race, and by many Gentiles as well.

Auerbach did not stand alone in his belief in race. The German writer J. M. Judt in *Jews as Race* (*Die Juden als Rasse*, 1903) was more specific, for he wrote that, as a race, Jews share common physical and physiognomic traits.[23] Even earlier, in 1881, Richard Andree, a German who was not a Jew but the founder of the discipline of ethnography and demography as applied to the Jews, had asserted that they represented a definite racial type kept intact through thousands of years. But for Andree, Jews and Aryans had a common root: both were Caucasians. Both were also the bearers of modern culture, in contrast to blacks who had remained in their primitive state.[24] Andree, like Judt, attempted to base his arguments on anthropology as well as physiognomy.

But it was the Austrian physician, anthropologist, and Zionist Ignaz Zollschan (1877–1948) who became the most famous theoretician of the Jews as a race. His major work, *The Racial Problem with Special Attention to the Theoretical Foundation of the Jewish Race* (*Das Rassenproblem unter Besonderer Berücksichtigung der Theoretischen Grundlagen der Jüdischen Rassenfrage*, 1910), held that race is transmitted by the human cell and thus not subject to outside influence. In this large work Zollschan praised Houston Stewart Chamberlain's racial ideals, such as the nobility that racial purity confers on a group and the necessity of developing the race to ever greater heights of heroism. Zollschan thought that Chamberlain was right about race, but wrong about the Jews. He felt that the evolution of culture could not be due to one race alone (such as the Aryans), but must be created by a series of pure races, including the Jews. The undesirable, materialistic aspect of the contemporary Jewish race would vanish when it found nationhood and escaped the ghetto.[25] Zollschan's ideal, as he restated it in 1914, was for a nation of pure blood, untainted by diseases of excess or immorality, with a highly developed sense of family, and deep-rooted, virtuous habits.[26] The linkage of racial mysticism and middle-class morality could hardly be demonstrated with greater clarity.

Zollschan broke with Zionism after the First World War, believing quite erroneously that the postwar world would see the decline of anti-Semitism and the end of ideas of national sovereignty.[27] At the same time, he also began to reject his earlier belief in races—a process which culminated in his *Racism Against Civilization* (published in London in 1942). By this time, the lengthening shadow of the Nazis in Europe made it difficult for any Jew to uphold ideas of race, even if he had done so earlier.

However, before the Nazis, and especially before the First World War, the debate among Jews as to whether or not Jews were a race had been a lively one, especially in the German *Journal of Jewish Demography and Statistics*. The guiding spirit behind this journal was the social Darwinist Arthur Ruppin. Ruppin was in charge of Jewish settlement in Palestine from 1908 until his death in 1942. Like Auerbach he believed, however ambivalently, in the existence of races. Yet during his many decades in Palestine he was a committed binationalist. At first Ruppin thought race to be an instinct which could not be changed, though typically enough his *Darwinism and Social Science* (*Darwinismus und Sozialwissenschaft*, 1903) advocated eugenics, and not a doctrine of racial superiority. Beauty and strength depended on factors of inheritance, not on environment, and in this connection Ruppin did talk about racial types. When he contemplated *The Jewish Fate and Future* (*Jüdisches Schicksal und die Zukunft*) in 1940, however, he condemned the confusion of "people" with "race," and referred to Virchow's findings among the German schoolchildren which denied the existence of pure races.

Jewish acceptance of the notion of race was ambivalent at best; being the foil of racism did not necessarily mean imitating the enemy. What about those orthodox religious Jews who believed in the reality of the concept of the chosen people? For the majority of such Jews, chosenness meant giving a living example of how life should be lived, and did not entail any claims to domination. Moreover, all peoples could be considered righteous, even Gentiles, provided they observed the seven Noahic laws instead of the 613 commandments binding on pious Jews. Thus belief in monotheism, and obedience to commandments against stealing, murder, false judgment, and adultery, as well as abstinence from eating live limbs of animals, would qualify anyone as chosen. No racism was inherent in this orthodoxy.

To be sure, the Hasidic rabbinical dynasties believed that qualities of leadership were at times transmitted by the blood; but this was not held to consistently, and in any case was no more racist than traditional notions of royal descent. But for all the denial of racism in theory, the borderline to racism was at times as furtively crossed by such orthodox Jews as by believing Christians, who were also supposed to reject it. The true believer in the nineteenth and twentieth centuries always retained some secular elements of superiority and domination within his belief.[28]

Again, Zionism was not in fact racist in its orientation, in spite of the occasional ideas of Zollschan or even Auerbach, both of whom were not really important in the movement. Yet, Theodor Herzl himself once wrote that whether Jews remained in their host nations or emigrated, the race must first be improved wherever it was found. It was necessary to make it work-loving, warrior-like, and virtuous.[29] Herzl often reflected his Viennese environment, whether in his vague and general use of the word "race" or in his condemnation of "kikes" who refused to follow his lead. Nevertheless, he stated that "No nation has uniformity of race."[30]

Much more typical were those influential young Zionists who at the beginning of this century believed in a national mystique without at the same time believing in race. Whenever the Zionist movement attempted to be scientific, they proclaimed in 1913, it got mired in skull measurement and all sorts of "racial nonsense."[31] Judaism, instead, was an inner cultural unity, the revelation of belief in the substance of Jewish nationality. World history, as the young Zionist Robert Weltsch put it in 1913, is not made by zoologists but by ideas. He compared Jewish nationality to Bergson's *élan vital*. The mystery of the Volk was accepted, but the racism which was often part of these mysteries in Gentile society was rejected.[32]

Even during the 1930's, when Max Brod asserted that race was basic to Jewish separateness, he meant this as an exhortation to eugenics; but for Brod, as for Martin Buber, the Jewish Volk became only a stepping stone to human unity and equality reflecting the oneness of God. Jewish nationalism did not embrace racism at a time when other nationalisms in Europe were becoming ever more racist themselves.

Those who did not believe in the existence of any Jewish race—and they were the overwhelming majority among the Jews—referred to the Jewish physician Maurice Fishberg's influential *Racial Characteristics of Jews* (*Die Rassenmerkmale der Juden*, 1913). Fishberg, a famed doctor and anthropologist living in New York, held that Jews have no such characteristics, and attacked Elias Auerbach for believing in a Jewish race. As proof for his contention, Fishberg cited the existence of those blond Jews who could be found all over Europe, tall Jews with long heads, Greek noses, and blue eyes. This "Aryan type among Jews," as he called it, must be the result of miscegenation with the Nordic and the Slavic races.[33] But another, even more influential and non-Jewish voice was raised to contend that Jews were no race or even a separate people. Felix von Luschan, an Austrian professor at the University of Berlin, had already replied to Auerbach that there was no Jewish race, but only a Jewish religious community, and that Zionism seemed opposed to all culture by forcing Jews back into the Orient where barbarism ruled. This highly respected Gentile anthropologist asserted that Jews, like everyone else, were a racial mixture. Indeed, for von Luschan there was only one race, *Homo sapiens*. No inferior races existed, only people with different cultures from our own; and the characteristics which divided men had their origin in climatic, social, and other environmental factors. Men like Chamberlain, he wrote, were not scientists but poets.[34]

Many Zionists who used words like "blood" or "race" actually agreed with von Luschan. Despite the scientific predilections of the nineteenth century, the use of terms like "blood," "race," "people," and "nation" was often imprecise and interchangeable. Blood and race were sometimes shorthand for the transmission of spiritual factors and had nothing to do with appearance or racial purity. The "new man" of whom both racists and Zionists dreamed was opposed to rationalism, but for the Zionists he represented a "humanitarian nationalism" that was both voluntaristic and pluralistic.[35]

Ideas about the mystery of race remained strongest in central Europe, though the legends about Jews found a home in France as well as in the more primitive Balkan regions. Rootless and conspiratorial, the Jew became a myth. As revealed by Ahasverus or by the *Protocols of the Elders of Zion*, he was the adversary, all the more effective in that medieval myths were applied to modern times. The fears and superstitions of a bygone age had sunk deeply into the European consciousness, and could be used to mobilize people against the frustrations of the present. Still, European civilization was, after all, a Christian civilization, in spite of the increasing inroads of secularism. If racism had presented itself as a science and as a national belief, what was to be the attitude of the Christian churches toward race?

CHAPTER NINE

Infected Christianity

RACISM HAD sought an alliance with the main trends of the century: nationalism, spiritualism, bourgeois morality, and the belief in science. But it also reached out to Christianity, in spite of its own claim to a monopoly over salvation. Christianity, in turn, was handicapped in embracing racism, for this would imperil the sacrament of baptism, which was supposed to convert men into Christians regardless of origin or race. There were many pious Christians and good churchmen who consistently rejected racism, and others, such as the Quakers, who equally consistently helped the oppressed. But the record of most Protestant churches and of the Catholic Church was not one clearly opposed to the idea of racism.

In order to understand the interrelationship between Christianity and race, we must retrace our steps. The permanence of the Jewish and black stereotypes had been accepted by many Christians and their churches, even if in theory baptism should have washed them away. Moreover, as long as European civilization was still thought to be a Christian civilization and the state a Christian state, Jews who kept their faith would always be in danger of appearing as foreigners. In England at the turn of the eighteenth and nineteenth centuries, for example, enemies and even friends of Jewish emancipation had sought at times to safeguard the Christian nature of their state and society by making a sharp distinction between the "God of Moses" and the "God of Christians."[1] In Germany at the same time the young Johann Gottlieb Fichte deplored Old Testament religion as being built upon nationalism and hate, and foreign to ideals of freedom and equality. Indeed, hand in hand with Jewish emancipation at the beginning of the nineteenth century went a dislike of the Old Testament, which was seen as either belonging solely to the Jews and of no interest to Christians, or as subordinate to the Christian drama of salvation.[2] The Jewish stereotype was imbedded in the Christian way of looking at the world; and it is striking how many men of tolerance and goodwill thought of Jews as foreigners, devoid of the proper civilized behavior.

The various attempts to cut Christianity's Jewish roots made it all the easier for racism to sweep aside the Old Testament as a barrier protecting the Jews as indispensable actors in the drama of salvation. The old covenant always threatened the new, and some Christian theologians thought that the time had come to cut, once and for all, the bond between parent and child. Not only was Judaism regarded as a fossil by those who, with Hegel, believed in the inevitable progress of man's self-consciousness through history; but nationalists attempted to connect Christianity to their own tribal rather than to an Israelite past.

Hegel's attitude led his disciples to attack traditional Christianity in order to discover the true world-historical spirit. These "young Hegelians" determined the course of the new biblical criticism. David Friedrich Strauss in his *Life of Jesus* (*Das Leben Jesu*, 1835) applied what he called the strictest historical method to the biblical story. But at the same time he attempted to leave untouched the "inner core" of Christian belief. Strauss called Christ's birth, the miracles he wrought, and the resurrection, eternal truths whose existence was independent of historical facts. The life of Christ himself could never be written as history, for it symbolized the unending struggle for spiritual perfection. The Bible stories were to be treated either as simple history or as myth. In either case, Jews and Judaism were irrelevant to the message of Christ. Such was the gist of the higher biblical criticism and of the popular nineteenth-century attempts to come to grips with Christ's life.

Ernest Renan in his influential *Life of Christ* (*La Vie de Jésus*,

1863) had written that Christ did not renew the ancient religion (Judaism), but proclaimed instead an "eternal religion of humanity" opposed to Old Testament dogmatism and intolerance. Jesus was free from the provincialism of his Jewish race. Moreover, for Renan, intolerance was a Jewish and not a Christian characteristic. It sprang from the rigorous application of the law in biblical Judaism which, he felt, stifled the power of love. These accusations were not unique; indeed, they recur frequently throughout nineteenth-century biblical criticism. But for Renan, at least, biblical Judaism lost its relevance even for the Jews themselves as civilization advanced. Thus, modern Jews were no longer handicapped by their past and were able to make important contributions to modern progress.[3]

Much earlier in Germany, Karl August von Hase, a Lutheran theologian and professor in Jena, had made the same points as Renan. His popular *Life of Jesus* (*Das Leben Jesu*, 1829) was intended as a textbook for schools.[4] There he contrasted Christianity, a religion for all mankind, with the narrow particularism of the Jews. Judaism was imprisoned within the laws and the faith of a single Volk. The Jews were a product of historical evolution, and while the life of Christ on earth took place in a historical context, the Saviour himself stood outside history. He symbolized the spark of the divine in every man. Thus Christianity was a faith valid for all seasons, while the Jews and their religion existed only within one historical period of time. Neither Strauss, Renan, nor Hase advocated the persecution of modern Jews, nor were they racists, but their views of Jesus and the Old Testament prepared the way for the Germanic Christ of Houston Stewart Chamberlain.[5]

Bruno Bauer, a leader of the young Hegelians, had in the mid-nineteenth century attacked Christianity as alienating man from the state which alone should be his integrative force. But German nationalism had as a matter of fact already sought to annex Christianity by cutting away its Jewish foundations and substituting the ancient tribal past. Protestants from the early nineteenth century onward desired "a new union, new and better principles for the inward worship of God, without Mosaic law, which belongs to

Jews only."[6] This opposition to the Old Testament persisted throughout the rest of the century. It was deepened by analogies of national to Christian salvation, especially popular in Germany ever since the wars of liberation against Napoleon. The annual meetings of the German Protestant Church (*Kirchentage*) after 1848, for example, were filled with sermons that equated Christianity with the Volk; the lives of nations were singled out by providence in order to create a truly chosen people. Christian revelation must therefore have grown out of the history of the nation and not from some foreign, Semitic root.[7] The "Protestant Association" founded in 1863 attempted to further such a national Christian Church.

Militant German Protestantism also supported a foreign policy hostile to both France and England. It held that "Papists" (equated with the French) enslaved man, and protested toward the end of the nineteenth century that the "external Protestantism of England does not attract the German people, for it is hypocritical in its pretended humanitarianism which in reality seeks to conquer gold and empires."[8] French nationalists, in turn, lumped Protestants and Jews together as materialist and aggressive. These national enmities rarely became racist however, and between Germany and England, for example, the door was always left open, depending on whether one nation supported the ambitions of the other.[9] The Jew, on the other hand, stood outside this give-and-take among the nations of Europe.

Anti-Semitism was built into such Christian thought. At the end of the nineteenth century, it was bound to lead to the nationalist religion of Paul de Lagarde or Julius Langbehn, which made the Volk the vessel of God, the true revelation of the divine spirit. The religious dynamic exemplified by Christ, who had revealed himself to the Volk, must be cleansed of the law which the Jews had fastened upon Christianity.[10] St. Paul was accused of loyalty to the Jewish traditions from which he sprang, and of attempting to imprison Christianity within the Mosaic law.[11] The narrowness, provincialism, and legalism which many Protestant theologians discovered in the Old Testament were projected upon St. Paul, who became a kind of fifth column within Christianity. In this way the break between the old and the new covenant could be made complete and Christianity freed of its traditional base.

German Protestantism fought rationalism and rationalistic religion and tried to restore the mysteries of Christianity. In reality, like the new biblical criticism, it secularized religion. Christian incarnation now took place within the Volk. The result was that mere conversion of the Jews was no longer good enough. They must not only be dipped into holy water but also into the Volk itself. Yet how was that possible for those who had not been part of the Volk since time immemorial? Obviously, the question arose whether Jews could ever become Christians, and while the answer was shirked in large measure, it was clear that Jews who remained Jews could have no place in national life. Though Catholics found it difficult to follow here, many came to share similar views.

Protestantism, especially in Germany, found it easier to become part of the national mystique because Martin Luther had been regarded as a great patriot in contrast to ultramontane Catholicism. Throughout the nineteenth and into the twentieth century, Luther was praised as the great liberator of the German spirit from Catholic and Roman bondage.[12] A self-conscious German Protestantism fought against Catholic France, and later Bismarck's *Kulturkampf*, which was meant to cut the foreign ties of German Catholicism, encouraged the quarrel. But a part of German Catholicism also sought to prove its patriotism by excluding the Jews from the "Christian nation."

The barriers against Jewish assimilation had not always been raised so high, and Volkish Christianity, whether Catholic or Protestant, must not be read backward into the early nineteenth century. For example, as we have seen, in some German villages and towns Jews, Catholics, and Protestants worshipped together in the same church in order to celebrate the victory over the French at the Battle of Leipzig (1815).[13] At that time Jews did not have to deny their Judaism in order to become full members of the Volk, any more than did Protestants or Catholics. But by mid-century, with the attacks on the Jewish foundations of Christianity and stress upon a Christian state, being a Jew meant being a foreigner. Those who, while assimilating the individual Jew, wanted to do away with Jews as a group because they were non-Christian, projected their own intolerance upon the Jewish stereotype. Those who raved about freedom and equality thought that in order to possess these ideals the Jew had to be stripped of his religion. Racism could easily make use of this contraction of values.

Such men repeated the Enlightenment ideal: to the individual every right was due; but to the Jew as member of the archaic religion, none. This was one way to solve the clash between Jewish and Christian cultures in Europe. At first the Jewish stereotype had tended to exist side by side with advocacy of emancipation. Thus the letter written by the principal of a school to the city council of the small German town of Bruchsal in 1809 advocated educating Jewish and German children together in primary school, in spite of the difficulties to be overcome. These difficulties included not only the ingrained hatred by Christians of Jews, but also the Jewish lack of cleanliness and their foul odor. Some Jewish children would never overcome these handicaps, the letter added, and must always be seated separately from Christian toddlers.[14]

The continued existence of ghettos made the differences between Christian and Jew starkly manifest. The clash between these different cultures in Europe was difficult to overcome. In Rome the ghetto existed until 1863, and in Bohemia and Moravia until 1848; and since 1814, the pale of Jewish settlement had been newly constituted in Russia and Poland. Yet we must distinguish between Christian and racial persecution. Anti-Jewish riots in Europe remained largely traditional up to 1918, whether in Russia or in the West. Their slogans were culled from the past, concentrating on Jews as Christ-killers, usurers, and practitioners of ritual murder.

The principal anti-Jewish riots in Germany (1819, 1830, 1844, and 1848) were partly due to economic causes such as famine and the decline of handicrafts. Here the lower classes—men, women, and children—as the victims of society, rioted against the Jews. Yet the symbols they carried spoke of ancient tradition: a white flag with a blood-red cross or a doll representing the hanged Judas. Accusations of ritual murder preached from the pulpits in churches encouraged such riots.[15]

In France the accusation of ritual murder was also kept alive in rural regions, furthered by the Catholic Church.[16] For the Russian Empire, of course, such accusations sometimes leading to pogroms were government policy, a situation not duplicated anywhere else in Europe. These riots and pogroms would not result in the extermination of Jews, but rather either in their forced conversion (as in Russia) or in their emigration. Racism was eventually to mean extermination, but this needed a more sophisticated bureaucracy, and indeed all the trappings of the advanced modern state, rather than random killings, brutal though they were.

Christian theology never advocated extermination of the Jews in the first place, but rather their exclusion from society as living witnesses to deicide. The pogroms were secondary to isolating Jews in ghettos. As the Catholic bishop Alois Hudal wrote in 1937, trying to curry favor with the Nazis, it was not the Church but the state that abolished the ghetto.[17] Christianity attempted to transform Jews into stereotypes of guilt, objectified through ugliness, dirt, and lack of spirituality. The crowded ghetto where the Jews retained their peculiar dress and religious laws did indeed transmit such a picture of Jews to an outside world easily frightened by the unusual and the different. Forcing Jews to live in ghettos thus gave a semblance of truth to the myths about the Jews in the eyes of the Gentile world.

The transformation of the stereotype into reality was a constant endeavor; thus the accusations leveled against Jews were made into self-fulfilling prophecies, a theme to which we will constantly return. Here once more, racism was helped along even while being overtly denied. As we have seen earlier, the stereotype was based on the kind of classical beauty which symbolized a superior race. Christianity accepted this stereotyping into ugly and beautiful. Indeed, the Christian art of the nineteenth century is full of it. Christ on the Cross is often portrayed as blond, tall, and lithe.

All these developments took time. It was not until after mid-nineteenth century that the Jews rather than the blacks became the foil of racism, and that Christian churches became increasingly hostile to Jews as the symbols of a threatening atheism and rootlessness. This was especially true for Catholicism, which saw itself besieged by the new liberal and scientific trends of the age. Typically enough, when anti-Semitism awakened in Poland toward 1880, it was largely due to a Catholic reaction against scientific positivism, as well as to a more general fear of capitalist development among the population. At that time Jan Jelenski, who had previously been an advocate of Jewish assimilation, took the helm of the long-lasting Catholic anti-Semitic movement.[18]

In Germany the Catholic Church, in addition to fighting modernity, had to prove its national loyalty; it advocated a return to the pre Reformation tradition of union of Church and state. The Jew became symbolic of all that had gone wrong with history since this golden age, and Jews took the place of the demons of old who had played various tricks on pious Christians.[19] To be sure, Catholic doctrine was for the most part hostile to a racism which seemed to attack the Bible, and which asserted that the sacrament of baptism was useless for Jews. Yet in reality, Catholicism as it evolved during the nineteenth century, like its Protestant counterpart, was separated from racism by a very thin line which could be easily crossed.

Baptism could not be denied, but the ancient hope of conversion was in the last decades of the nineteenth century overshadowed by hatred of Jews. Whether in Germany, Austria, or France, and whether he appeared in the disguise of atheist, liberal, or Freemason, the Jew symbolized the enemy of a besieged Catholicism. In France, many local Catholic weeklies showed respect for Édouard Drumont, the most celebrated anti-Semite of his time, despite his racism and his condemnation of the weak-kneed clergy.[20] German Catholics condemned individual Jewish emancipation because it was based upon the philosophy of rationalism and the Enlightenment; but they also saw the Jew lurking behind Bismarck's fight against the Church.[21] At times Catholics in French- and German-speaking lands liked to make a distinction between the individual Jew and Judaism; the one was redeemable, the other was not.[22] But

no matter what the attitude toward the individual Jew, the stereotype was always present. "What is a Jew?" asked the Catholic
weekly in Nantes in 1892, answering, "A Jew is a crook, a thief
and all the rest." [23]

These trends in Catholicism were duplicated in Protestantism,
though the latter was less paranoid, since it had no allegiance outside the national boundaries and was controlled by the state. Nevertheless, both feared a rising tide of atheism, liberalism, and science,
and both attempted to recapture lost territory by emphasizing their
nationalism and their social concerns. Catholicism and Protestantism drew sustenance for their anti-Semitism from their rural
roots, from the "unchanging countryside"—which in reality was
changing only too fast. Agricultural interests were bound to provide
powerful support for and direction to churches that were losing
their appeal in urban areas. The German Agricultural League
(founded in 1893), for example, fervently believed in a Christian
and Protestant state. And the big German landowners who dominated the League considered both racism and Protestantism an integral part of their effort at agricultural protectionism. [24]

The Catholic and conservative agricultural unions in France were
not racist but preserved the traditional Catholic anti-Semitism.
Founded in 1886 by H. de Gailhard-Bancel, these unions based
upon local autonomy were organizations of farm workers and
peasants led by landowners. They were strongly religious in character; indeed, Catholic rites and the union festivities were identical.
The keystone of union politics was opposition to government centralization. The provinces were exalted as the true France (in the
tradition of Gobineau). Jews and capitalism were equated, and both
were seen and feared as instruments of destruction descending upon
the countryside from Paris. [25]

All over Europe, the agricultural crisis of the *fin de siècle* used the
Jew as symbol for the hated city, for uprootedness, and for modernity. In many rural regions, the Jews as cattle dealers were also the
bankers and thus stood for mortgages and expropriation. It was no
coincidence that Xavier Vallat, one of Gailhard-Bancel's young
friends and admirers, would become Commissioner for the Jewish

Question in Vichy France. Vallat, an important leader of the French Veterans Association and of a national Catholic federation, typically wanted to isolate Jews from French life, but refused to collaborate with the Nazis in the deportation of French Jews.[26] Face to face with the Nazis, he represented a traditional anti-Semitism as against their racism, which knew no inhibitions. Gailhard's own son became a Nazi collaborator.

The agricultural unions and the Catholic countryside shared the anti-Semitism that was common to all underdeveloped regions of Europe. The Jew was anti-Christ and a usurer. Perhaps a tract on ritual murder which originated in Bayonne in 1889 can illustrate this feeling. It asserted that Jews were merchants and bankers who bled the nation, and through ritual murder literally became "eaters of Christian blood."[27] This undercurrent of medievalism persisted also in many other European rural regions. At the border of Serbia and Austria, it was estimated that some 10,000 cigarette papers were sold which contained pictures of the murder of a Christian child by Jews.[28] Modern habits and ancient superstitions may have blended similarly elsewhere as well.

The largely inchoate feelings of the countryside were articulated by those Catholics who were fighting secularism and liberalism. As far back as the revolution of 1848 in Vienna, where Jews had taken a conspicuous part, many a priest accused them of wanting to take over Austria by means of their liberal politics and capitalist exploitation. Friedrich Heer, the modern historian, is correct when he describes the atmosphere among some Catholic Viennese circles as providing the background for the young Hitler's anti-Jewish thought. Pope Pius IX himself had set the example for such hostility toward the Jews in accusing them of fomenting anarchism, Freemasonry, and general hostility to the Church. And after 1870, when the Church was seemingly hard-pressed by its enemies, Pope Pius gave free rein to anti-Jewish polemics in Vatican publications.[29]

Yet such Catholic anti-Semitism was not really violent, for it believed fervently in law and order. Thus the founder of social Catholicism, the Austrian Karl von Vogelsang (1818–1890), was typical when he fought against overt racism and condemned the Pan-German anti-Semites who had used as one of their symbols a Jew hanging from the gallows.[30]

For Vogelsang, the Jews were a foreign people, liberals and individualists who were opposed to justice and community. But he refused to attack the Jewish religion itself, even while calling for the conversion of Jews and Protestants to the true Catholic Church. That, he wrote, "is Catholic anti-Semitism."[31] Vogelsang's French friends, Alfred du Mun and La Tour du Pin, shared his admiration for the Middle Ages and also viewed Jews as the heralds of a modern world that was anti-Catholic because it had destroyed a moral society based upon medieval estates and the "just price." The emphasis was always on a shared Christianity, and not on a shared race. Much later Vogelsang's pupil Ignaz Seipel, a priest and a future Austrian chancellor, wrote that it was a mistake to put the idea of race above the idea of nation, since the latter unites within it both state and Church.[32]

The depth of the anti-Jewish strain in Catholic thought was excmplified in the accusations against the Talmud leveled by August Rohling, canon, professor of Catholic theology, and subsequently professor of Semitic languages at the German University of Prague. His *Talmud Jew* (*Talmud-Jude*, 1871) was a rehash of Eisenmenger's earlier *Judaism Discovered* (*Entdecktes Judentum*, 1700), which had sought to prove the immorality of Jews through excerpts from the *Talmud*. The attacks on traditional religion during the eighteenth century had deepened such accusations against a people apparently hopelessly under the spell of superstition. Christians joined this chorus against Jews. For example, Magnus Schleyer, a Benedictine, wrote in 1723 that the *Talmud* exemplified the stiff-neckedness for which the Jews are condemned in the Bible. The *Talmud* was said to be full of exhortations to cheating, lustfulness, usury, and hatred of Christians.[33] (This opinion was shared alike by the secularists and the Catholics, who otherwise fought each other.)

The *Talmud* had come to symbolize the secret and "perverted" religion of the Jews, largely because it was not part of Christian theology like the Old Testament. To attack the Old Testament,

however much it was a part of the function of higher biblical criticism, was to risk condemnation as going contrary to Christianity.
But the *Talmud* stood outside the drama of Christian salvation.
This fact was officially acknowledged in Germany when the Jewish community of Berlin attempted to counter the attacks against
the *Talmud* in 1881. The Jewish community cited the German law
which forbade slander of all religious communities. The state prosecutor, however, refused to indict the newspaper that had attacked
the *Talmud*. First, the *Talmud* was not a religious code of law, he
wrote, but merely of historical interest. Second, and still more
ominously, this royal official held that in attacking the *Talmud* the
paper had not attacked the Jews as a religious community (which
would give them a basis for legal protection), but only as a race and
a Volk.[34] Thus the *Talmud* was viewed as a Jewish racial tract,
unrelated to religion.

August Rohling himself treated the *Talmud* as an anti-Christian
breviary. He claimed that it regarded Christians as the servants of
Baal and that it permitted Jews to take any amount of interest from
Christians, to practice sodomy with them, and violate their women.
Indeed, it was charged that in this "Jewish gospel" Christians were
called swine, dogs, and donkeys. The animal imagery often used
against inferior races was supposedly turned against Christians.
The *Talmud*, he concluded, was a program for the domination of
the world by the chosen people.

Rohling's *Talmud Jew* was taken up not only by Austrian and
German Catholics but also by a part of the Catholic press in France.
There, under Rohling's influence, the *Talmud* was now no longer
considered a mere book of magic but instead said to advocate "fla-
grant immorality."[35] Édouard Drumont wrote a preface to the
French edition of Rohling's work, in which he suggested that the
Talmud was Jewry's revenge against the New Testament. This preface was translated back into German, so that *Talmud Jew* could
now be read in the context of the struggle against Jewish domination in both France and Germany. Moreover, the book included
passages about ritual murder which asserted that whoever spills the
blood of a Christian offers a sacrifice to God. Rohling also volun-

teered his testimony to the prosecutor in the Hungarian ritual murder trial at Tisza-Eszlar in 1883 that Jews were commanded to per-
form such practices.[36]

Rohling's own solution to the Jewish question was self-contra-
dictory. Jews should not be deprived of human rights but rather
stripped of their rights as citizens. They should be expelled from
host countries as "pirates against humanity."[37] In the last resort,
Rohling perceived in the Jews not a religious community but a
nation that had committed deicide. He saw the Jews from a conventional Christian viewpoint as living witnesses of their own guilt,
and hoped for their conversion.

The Jewish community was almost paralyzed with fear before
Rohling's onslaught, as it was to be once more in the 1890's during the Dreyfus Affair. It seemed inconceivable to the prosperous
and settled Jewish bourgeoisie of central and western Europe that
such an accusation could be leveled against them by a supposedly
responsible canon and professor. For such Jews this passed all understanding, happening, as it did, in the midst of an age they considered liberal and enlightened. However, once they became conscious of the enormity of the accusation, discretion seemed a logical
consequence of the politics of assimilation. It was possible to ignore
this slight, as it was possible to ignore the Dreyfus Affair, and to
carry on as if nothing had happened.[38] Sadly enough, the Jewish
bourgeoisie was to try the same tactics against the Third Reich,
where it would no longer work; but at the end of the nineteenth
century, it must have been successful for a great many Jews. Rabbi
Joseph Bloch of Vienna, an eccentric outsider, took Rohling to
court and obtained a judgment (1885) that "not a single text exists
in the whole of the *Talmud* in which Christians or pagans or
idolators are given the name of an animal." But this made no more
difference to the myth than the final exposure in a Swiss court in
1934 that the *Protocols of the Elders of Zion* were a forgery.

Rohling's *Talmud Jew* updated the myth of the Jew as anti-
Christ, and racists like Drumont in France took it up everywhere.
Houston Stewart Chamberlain considered the *Talmud* a typical
example of Jewish lack of spirituality; Alfred Rosenberg saw in it

the roots of both Bolshevism and capitalism—in his view the two instruments of Jewish domination. Ultimately, the *Talmud* as a code of laws which revealed the evils the Jews supposedly practiced upon non-Jews would figure prominently in Nazi anti-Jewish exhibitions, such as that held in Paris in 1941.[39] The inferior race now possessed its breviary of immorality.

If apart from Rohling's work there was little borrowing from German to French anti-Semitism,[40] then the parallelism is all the more instructive. Conspiracy theories flourished in France as well as Germany, but in France they were more widespread because of the financial scandals of the *fin de siècle* in which Jews were involved, and also because of the Catholic hate of "Jewish" Freemasonry—a conspiracy which was said to rule the Third Republic. In Germany such ideas became important only after 1918. Initially Gobineau had been rejected in France, although as we have seen, the metahistory and racism for which he stood reached France as it did all of Europe by the 1880's. Catholicism, then, left a crack in the door, even while accepting the Jewish stereotype and all that went with it.

Catholic attitudes toward Jews did not remain confined to sermons or polemics, but were carried to the masses of the population through political movements in Austria and France. Karl Lueger, as lord mayor of Vienna between 1897 and 1910, instituted the first régime on the continent based on an anti-Semitism anchored in militant Catholic faith. Lueger was a disciple of Vogelsang, and his anti-Semitism and Catholicism were combined with promises of social reform. He called his movement the Christian Social Party. Lueger's promises were eagerly accepted in a city long mismanaged by liberals, whose problems were compounded by startling growth. Moreover, the large Jewish immigration into Vienna, from Galicia and the Russian Empire, lent a spurious reality to Lueger's designation of the Jew as the powerful enemy of a righteous Christian society. Indeed, the lord mayor was elected by huge majorities, much against the will of the emperor Franz Joseph II, who disliked both Lueger's anti-Semitism and his demagogic leadership of the masses.

Lueger equated Jews with atheism, liberalism, finance capitalism, and social democracy—the evils which social Catholics had always denounced.[41] He pursued a policy which sought to counter these so-called Jewish instruments of power, and he succeeded in freeing Viennese municipal transportation and utilities from the stranglehold of foreign (largely British) capitalist control. As a result, he gave Vienna a good streetcar system, as well as better electric and gas services, both now owned by the municipality. Lueger also reformed public welfare, creating such institutions as hostels for the poor, municipal orphanages, and a municipal employment office. The liberal idea of self-help was discarded, and health services as well as schools were opened to the poorer elements of the population. Finally, Lueger created a green belt around the city. The Social Democratic city administration after the First World War merely took over where Lueger had left off.[42]

In this manner "honest labor," meaning independence of finance capitalism, was to triumph and Christian private property to be safeguarded. Lueger was a popular mayor, and his successful administration based upon a profession of anti-Semitism frightened many Jews in Vienna. In reality, Lueger did not persecute Jews; some of them remained his close friends. He once quipped, "I decide who is a Jew," thus coining that famous phrase.[43] Anti-Jewish rhetoric took the place of the exclusion of Jews from Viennese life which the Christian Social Party's platform had promised. Lueger was careful to show himself as a practicing Catholic, a faithful son of the Church as well as of the Habsburg Empire.

In spite of his indecisive Jewish policy, Lueger did not lack admirers among racists. Thus Édouard Drumont praised Lueger as having demonstrated that anti-Semitism was no mere rhetoric but also led to practical reforms. Hitler, who in his youth witnessed the mass funeral of Lueger, admired him as a great mayor, and though more insightful than Drumont, criticized him for not being a true racist and thus never executing a consistent anti-Jewish policy.[44]

In France, too, the most important right-wing political movement proved to be both militantly Catholic and anti-Semitic, though it never attained power on any level of government. The Action Française was born during the Dreyfus Affair (1899) in order to take advantage of anti-republican feeling and to proclaim a return to the

France of the Ancien Régime. The restoration of the monarchy stood in the forefront; once this had taken place and the Jews were regulated again as they had been during the Ancien Régime, the Jewish problem would no longer exist.[45] Yet attitudes toward race were not so simple in an organization born during the Dreyfus Affair, and directed against the atheistic republic of Jews and Freemasons. Charles Maurras, the leader of the Action Française, contended that race as a physical fact did not exist while in the same breath positing a Gallo-Latin French race.[46]

Not only did many anti-Semites flock to the banner of the Action Française, which was supported by a large section of the Catholic hierarchy, but Maurras was at times allied with Drumont's overtly racist enterprises. Moreover, the "Camelots du Roi," the youth movement of the Action Française, was vastly more radical than its leaders. The Camelots held street demonstrations and did not shy from violence. The climax of their activism came in 1908, when they occupied the Sorbonne in protest against a Professor Thalmas who had supposedly slandered Joan of Arc. This Catholic and royalist youth group even reached out to anarchists, who in turn were attracted by its violence.[47]

But the alliance they sought of royalists and workers never came about, for their membership comprised predominantly students, commercial employees, or apprentices. Youth from an identical background had allied with Adolf Stoecker's anti-Semitic and Protestant Christian social movement in Germany, which we shall discuss presently. The Association of German Students (founded by Stoecker in 1881) and the Union of Commercial Employees (1895) shared the Camelots' opposition to finance capitalism and to socialism also symbolized by the Jews. Moreover, the German students, like those in the Camelots, were less interested in their Church than in a national mystique. But both radicalisms were spawned by Christian movements.

There was much posturing among these organizations; for instance, the blood-stained handkerchief of the first Camelot wounded in the riots of 1908 was kept as a substitute flag of martyrs.[48] The French students of the Camelots du Roi were full of esprit, while the German Student Association was less activist and instead debated and polemicized. Moreover, while French youth proclaimed a "holy war" against Jews, Masons, and republicans, their German comrades had no republic to fight and were loyal subjects of the crown. Therefore, they concentrated upon the Jews and became overtly racist, while the Camelots themselves proved ambivalent on this issue. Nevertheless, these students and commercial employees foreshadowed the radicalization of bourgeois youth toward the right in the first half of the twentieth century. Then movements like Italian fascism and National Socialism in Germany were widely supported by such youth in search of activism, enthusiasm, and camaraderie. In Rumania, the edition of the *Protocols of the Elders of Zion* translated by future Iron Guard leaders (1922–23) was dedicated to the "Rumanian students," the future shock troops of that movement.[49] But though support of the radical right by students and other largely middle-class youth increased after the First World War, it already existed in the last decades of the nineteenth century.

Some intellectuals belonging to the Action Française formed the "Cercle Proudhon" in 1911, which was inspired by Georges Sorel and presided over by Charles Maurras. The Cercle contained nationalists and syndicalists, both united in their opposition to parliamentary democracy and capitalism. The invocation of the name of Proudhon symbolized the will to destroy these instruments of bourgeois power. But did Proudhon's hatred of the Jews also enter the Cercle for good measure?

The Cercle Proudhon proclaimed that the Action Française wanted to take political power away from "Jewish gold," and give it to "French blood." They tried to support associations of small producers as being especially suited to fight both the middle classes and parliamentary democracy. The bourgeois had become "Judaized"; the republic was a creation of Jews and Masons; and to this list of the enemies of Catholic and royalist France were added Protestants and Germans as well.[50]

Members of the Cercle shared with Charles Maurras a love for the symmetry and order of the Ancien Régime, which they equated with reason, even while seeing in the use of violence a catharsis for their own frustrations. It was typical that the Cercle praised the "beauty of violence in the service of reason," though no more than Charles Maurras did they practice what they preached. Yet some members of the Cercle did forge a more militant association. Georges Valois, the founder of the short-lived French Fascist movement "Faisceau" (1925–27), was one of the guiding spirits of the Cercle; and Édouard Berthe, another important Cercle member, became a Communist in 1920.[51] Their urge to activism found scope between the world wars, when it became a more general phenomenon, not confined to France. What had been talk and debate before the war seemed within grasp during the chaos of the postwar years.

The transition to activism and a more militant racism was made by groups which sprang from the Action Française rather than by the parent organization itself, which never adjusted to the new *élan* of the postwar world. The Action Française produced men more radical than Maurras wished, who on leaving the movement became the Fascists of the 1920's and 1930's in France. This illustrates an important distinction: the more reactionary and traditional the right, the less overtly racist; the greater the desire for social reform and popular support, the greater also the pull toward racism as a weapon against finance capitalism and liberalism. As the nineteenth century closed, the overwhelming problems of capitalist concentration, the rationalization of all aspects of life, and the consequent depersonalization brought to the fore a radical right which sought a remedy in social action and in racism. Catholic movements followed a similar course, but with their usual ambivalence stopped short of a racism that denied Christian regeneration.

The Catholic standpoint on Jews and race was well summed up by Bishop Alois Hudal, who headed the German Catholic community in Rome in the 1930's and 1940's. His *Foundations of National Socialism* (*Grundlagen des Nationalsozialismus*, 1937) pleaded for an alliance between Catholicism and the newly awakened "Germanic man."[52] National Socialism should reject neo-paganism, and become a purely social and political movement without claims to a new, potentially anti-Christian world view. The bishop rejected racism and condemned Gobineau, Chamberlain, and Alfred Rosenberg. Christianity could not approve of a membership limited to Aryans, nor could it countenance attacks upon the Old Testament, he wrote. These ideas made the Nazis ban the bishop's book. Yet, in the same tract, the Jews themselves were accused of racism in their claim to a pretended superiority, being said to menace Germany's culture and her economy.[53]

For Bishop Hudal, the Jews symbolized liberalism and hostility to the Church. He looked back nostalgically to the time when Jews were excluded from Christian life and lived in ghettos. Indeed, Bishop Hudal justified the Nazis' Nuremberg Laws, which sought to exclude the Jews from German life as an act of German self-defense. It was not merely fear of modernity that motivated the bishop's pen, but also the need for allies against Bolshevism.[54] The Church was driven into the arms of the right in the fight against the left, as well as against liberalism and republicanism. As the Church became the prisoner of the right, it was also pushed ever closer to racism, a constant temptation. The fact that the pope entrusted Bishop Hudal with the rescue of the Jews of Rome in 1942 is not without irony,[55] but it also demonstrates the result of an infected Christianity. Needless to say, the bishop's polite and hesitant request that Germans stop arresting Jews was met with contempt.[56]

Protestantism was similarly infected with anti-Semitism and racism, especially where it was in the majority. Adolf Stoecker's political action was part of his missionary zeal. The court preacher to William II first confronted the condition of the Berlin working classes when he attempted to win them over to active Church membership. He founded his Christian Social Party in 1878, partly in order to improve the worker's standard of living, but also in order to better integrate him into the newly united German state. Stoecker's social program was conservative compared to that of Lueger. It advocated a tax on the stock exchange and laws against usury, and like the social Catholic movement, encouraged trade unionism as a welcome revival of the medieval guilds. Finally, Stoecker called upon the state to protect native labor against foreign competition. The Christian Social Party opposed liberalism, social democracy, and finance capitalism. The enemies were the same as those of the Catholic social movement.

Stoecker changed his tactics after a dismal showing at the polls in 1878 of less than 1,500 votes.[57] Now he focused upon the Jew as the obstacle to social justice. Once again, anti-Semitism proved effective politics. We know that whenever Stoecker preached in 1880 and 1881 on the Bible, only a few hundred attended church; but when he lashed out against the Jews, he had an audience of several thousands.[58] Stoecker did not exhort his audiences to violence; indeed, he adopted a moderate tone in distinguishing between good Jews who earned their bread through their own labor and those who controlled the stock exchange. Moreover, he believed that baptism could wash all Jews clean. Stoecker's success shows the depth of a Christian anti-Semitic tradition which could easily be brought to the surface, not only in Germany but in every corner of Europe.

Not surprisingly, Stoecker himself moved ever closer to the German Conservative Party. This was founded on so-called Christian principles (even if by Julius Stahl, a converted Jew), and toward the end of the century increasingly allied with anti-Semitic movements. At a meeting in the Tivoli Hall in Berlin in 1892, the conservatives adopted a platform which followed Stoecker's ideas: Christianity, monarchy, and fatherland were praised, finance capitalism was condemned, and the call went out to roll back undue Jewish influence in Germany. The opinion in the hall against the Jews was more radical than the "Tivoli program" actually adopted, and in the provinces the conservatives sometimes collaborated with racist groups.[59] As Stoecker's star waned, the conservatives were pushed ever closer to outright racism through alliance with the Agricultural League.

The conservative right in Germany, as in France and Austria, was restrained from outright racism by Christian ideals and by allegiance to law and order. Charles Maurras in France and the conservatives in Germany believed that an overt substitution of racism for Christianity would destroy traditional order and authority and run the risk of uncontrolled violence. Such attitudes were reflected in the Action Française's opposition to fascism, as well as in the Prussian conservatives' hostility to National Socialism.

This very attitude made the Catholic or Protestant anti-Semitism we have discussed respectable as one way to bolster up the old order. But the anti-Jewish cause could also gain respectability through an association with academic prestige, especially in Germany, where the professor ranked high in the social scale. This explains the effectiveness of the famous article on the Jewish question by Heinrich von Treitschke (1879), professor of history at the University of Berlin. Treitschke attacked the east European Jewish immigration into Germany as the shock troops of a foreign invasion destined to dominate the stock exchange and newspapers. These "trouser-selling youths" were hostile to a Germany in which Christianity and nationality were identical. The famous professor was no racist. He advocated the complete assimilation of settled German Jews into the Christian nation, but excluding the ghetto Jews from the east. The latter exemplified a "Semitic being," and were denigrated as "German-speaking orientals." As such they were opposed to Germanic and Christian ideals of social justice, lacking reverence for both monarchy and fatherland.[60]

Treitschke's attempted objectivity, like Christianity, allowed for the complete assimilation of individual Jews. Such a viewpoint simply continued the conditions of assimilation laid down by the Enlightenment, but adding Christian baptism to the prerequisites of honest work and good citizenship as further obstacles to membership in the "elect." As in the Enlightenment, the stereotype of the Jew was still kept intact, and the individual Jew was supposed to run fast in order to escape from its shadow.

Nominally, it was true, he could still escape; but racism and Christian anti-Semitism shared all other prejudices against the Jew. The traditional medieval and Christian accusations against the Jews were not dropped. Instead, they became intertwined with the fear of finance capitalism and the deprivations of modern society. The First World War turned Christianity in an ever more patriotic direction as ministers and priests blessed their respective sides in the conflict. Moreover, for the various nationalities in the Austrian and Russian

Empires, their Church had become the symbol of the fight for national liberation. However understandable this linkage between the churches and the national ambitions of their congregations, it did work to undermine further a universalism and tolerance that most Christian Churches had all but given up long ago. The Christian Churches did not prove an effective barrier to the implementation of racial policies, even though some courageous individual churchmen were to oppose the Nazi policy of Jewish extermination.

The Jews were made to seem the obstacle to a return to a just, Christian, and hierarchical society. Cutting the ties with the old covenant had left the Jews unprotected before Christianity. Now they were seen not merely as the traditional villains in the drama of salvation, but as the driving force behind the atheism and materialism of the age. The social concerns of a modern Christianity had found their foil in the Jews as well, however moderate the anti-Semitism of a Vogelsang, a Lueger, or a Stoecker may seem when contrasted with pogroms and calls for extermination. The line between such apparent respectability and a dynamic racism was easily crossed, especially as side by side with this infected Christianity there arose a National Socialism which was to prove as seductive as it was without compromise. Most pious Christians stood apart from this National Socialism at first, although eventually it would inflame a cross section of the population, including several Churches, with its enthusiasm.

CHAPTER TEN

The Rise of National Socialism

C ENTRAL EUROPE seems to have loomed large in the development of racism during the nineteenth century. The elements of racial mysticism seemed, above all, to fulfill the longing for a true national community and an organic approach to life and politics. The building blocks of racism took in all of Europe, however, and were not confined solely to Germany or Austria. Indeed, during the last decades of the nineteenth century, when racism forged ahead everywhere, it was France that seemed destined to be the country within which racism might determine national politics.

Contemporaries thought that racism had penetrated France suddenly and rapidly from the 1880's on, unleashed by financial scandals, the corruption of the Third Republic, the loss of Alsace-Lorraine to Germany, and last but not least, the Dreyfus Affair. In reality, however, Catholic anti-Semitism had always existed in France and had prepared the ground for racism. It was particularly strong in the countryside, where, as we have seen, Catholic priests and laymen often denounced Jews, Freemasons, and republicans. The failure in 1882 of the Union Générale, a Catholic and royalist bank—the first of the great financial scandals that were to rock France—was blamed by the clergy on all forces hostile to the Church, but particularly upon the Jews.[1] Yet racism itself was not necessarily involved in this thunder from the right, even if at times there was ambivalence on this issue.

The mainstream of French anti-Semitism attempted to link nationalism to social and political reform. The anti-Semites were interested above all in national unity; they rejected class war in favor of class integration, without, however, approving of the existing capitalist and bourgeois order. They desired a more equal distribution of wealth, and demanded that all classes of the population participate in the political process. It is necessary to explain the social and political attitudes of this anti-Semitism somewhat more fully because it gave racial thought in France its dynamic. Ever since mid-century the men and women who held such views had been known as National Socialists, a name Adolf Hitler adopted for his political party long after it had become common currency for a political theory which desired a government both social and national.

National Socialism did not accept the existing capitalist order, nor did it condemn all private property. On the contrary, social hierarchy was to be maintained, even while the right to work must be guaranteed and insurance schemes for the working classes initiated. The enmity of National Socialism was directed toward finance capitalism only: the banks and the stock exchange. The abolition of the "slavery of interest charges" would produce both social justice and national unity. Édouard Drumont described shortly after 1870 the fears which haunted the National Socialists: "The expropriation of society through finance capital takes place with a regularity which resembles the laws of nature. If nothing is done to arrest this process within the next fifty to a hundred years, all European society will be delivered tied hand and foot into the hands of a few hundred bankers."[2]

Arresting this development meant eliminating the Jews from national life, for they had become the symbol for the dominance of finance capitalism. We have seen earlier the role which the House of Rothschild and even the legend of the wandering Jew played in the growth of this myth, while the Jew as usurer presented a traditional image reaching far back into antiquity. Now within the economic crises of the last decades of the nineteenth century in which Jews were prominently involved, the Jew as finance capitalist stood re-

vealed, symbolic of the power of unproductive wealth confronting
the producers who unjustly lived in misery and want. The emphasis
upon production is important here; for although the Jew as usurer
had always presented an image opposed to "honest work," this image, especially in the second half of the nineteenth century, was now
projected upon the strains and stresses of a developing capitalism.[3]
Critics of finance capitalism turned to the past, when productivity
had been defined as money earned through the sweat of one's brow,
while making money multiply without individual labor was traditionally branded as unproductive. The association of Jews with
finance capitalism was Europe-wide, as indeed were the banking
interests of the Rothschild family; but in France this myth dominated all others and from time to time received considerable working-class support.

Alphonse de Toussenel (1803–1885), a onetime disciple of the
utopian Socialist Charles Fourier, was influential in popularizing
National Socialism. He was to write one of the most important
attacks upon the inborn and irremediable faults of the Jewish rule.
The Jews, Kings of the Age (Les Juifs, Rois de l'Époque, 1845),
subtitled *History of the Feudal Aristocracy of Financiers*, linked the
medieval image of the Jew as usurer to the populism of a society
suddenly plunged into the maelstrom of early capitalism.[4]

The Jews, according to Toussenel, dominated the world through
their control of finance capital. Toussenel supported his contention
by attacks on the House of Rothschild, and indeed just after his
book was published, a flood of pamphlets was unleashed against
this symbol of capitalist and Jewish conspiracy (see Plate 11). Toussenel came from a rural background, and for him the Jews were also
the despoilers of the countryside—a view shared by many German
writers for whom the Jew was the enemy of the peasant. Other anti-
Semitic Socialists, like Fourier and Pierre Joseph Proudhon, also
came from a rural background; however, Toussenel's rural orientation, unlike Proudhon's, did not entail opposition to centralization.
Indeed, he praised the centralizing efforts of the Ancien Régime and
castigated the decline of authority which, to him, meant the aban-
donment of weak and defenseless workers.

Patriotism made Toussenel long for the kings of old, whom he conceived not as despots but as the voice of their people. He expressed his hatred for the English and Dutch as well as Jews, for these Protestants had sought to reduce the power of France. Toussenel's ideas at mid-century were not markedly different from the National Socialism of men like Édouard Drumont at the end of the nineteenth century. Toussenel's "socialism" consisted in his preoccupation with the right to work, his opposition to finance capitalism, and his demand for equality among all the French. He believed such equality had existed in the Middle Ages, when Frenchmen had formed a true community.

Pierre Joseph Proudhon (1809–1865) differed from Toussenel, above all in his belief that free association should be the basis of government and that individual moral reform would make any use of force among men unnecessary. But such optimism about man's potentialities was, once more, combined with a rather primitive cast of mind, which saw in Jews and finance capitalism the implacable, hated enemy. The social concerns of men like Toussenel and Proudhon were based upon a rejection of modernity, a hostility to civilization as an urban accomplishment. Here they agreed with Richard Wagner, their younger German contemporary, that equality among people and a nation committed to social justice meant the destruction of the "power of gold." Jews symbolized this power, hence the exploitation of the people among whom they lived.

The Jew who used gold as a weapon was thought incapable of honest labor; therefore, Proudhon could write that the Jew "is by temperament an anti-producer, neither a farmer, nor even a true merchant"; in short, he had solely negative characteristics.[5] Proudhon was circumspect in public. But in private, he called the Jews the enemy of the human race, who should be excluded from all employment and expelled from France, and whose synagogues should be closed. Like Toussenel, Proudhon was driven by his anti-finance capitalism to a racist stance. "One must send this race back to Asia or exterminate it," he declared.[6] Proudhon wanted to establish communities based upon the individual consent of all members; indeed, voluntary agreements made between all of those who entered such a community would render it truly reciprocal without the use of force or authority. That the call to exclude the Jewish race came from a man committed to communitarianism is of more than passing significance.

Through such men and their successors, racism became a part of the communitarian experience for which so many longed toward the end of the nineteenth century. Racism attempted to provide the cement for a human community linked by affinity, not created by social compulsion. Both the nationalists and some Socialists advocated such a community. For Fourier, Toussenel, and Proudhon, this meant a communitarian socialism which had nothing in common with Marxism. Moreover, they agreed with those nationalists who defined community through shared history, the native soil, and a vague inner necessity. The communitarian ideal of Toussenel and Proudhon centered upon the nation. Universalism had no part in their theories, for they were primarily concerned with the fate of France.

The Jewish race, as they put it, was predatory, competitive, and without morality, and was therefore to be excluded from participation in a genuinely national and socialist community. The First World War encouraged an emphasis upon cameraderie, which in turn deepened the longing for such a community. Fascism would subsequently take up this heritage, but starting from the thought of these early French National Socialists, racism had already allied itself with this ideal.

While Toussenel and Proudhon did not hold any socialist ideas in common with Karl Marx, they did share with him a similar approach toward the Jews. In his articles on the Jewish question (1844), Marx argued that the Jew symbolized not only finance capitalism, but all types of capitalism. Yet Toussenel would have endorsed Marx's exclamation that "Money is the zealous God of Israel."[7] The bill of exchange, said Marx, was the Jewish God, while Jewish law caricatured morality. Small wonder that Marx's tract was reprinted by anti-Semitic Socialists from time to time, for it had the additional merit of the kind of Jewish self-confession which all racists took as proof of the truth. Marx had ended his tract with the sentence, "The social emancipation of Jewry is the emancipation of society from Jewry," arguing that the abolition of "usury and its preconditions" (i.e., capitalism) would abolish the Jew because his convictions would no longer have any object and he would therefore become humanized.[8] This argument was opposed to all racism, for it advocated complete assimilation, and the abolition of conflict between men. In the end, Marx differed drastically in his conclusions from those French Socialists who wanted to expel or to destroy the Jews.[9]

But it was Édouard Drumont (1844–1917) who became the controversial and celebrated National Socialist of *fin de siècle* France. His *La France Juive* (1886), which sold over a million copies, spread the message that the mercantile, covetous, scheming, and cunning Semites were responsible for the existing state of national and social degeneration. Drumont's newspaper, the *Libre Parole,* and his remaining fourteen books were also widely read. Moreover, Drumont was indefatigable in founding leagues and making alliances with the like-minded. Throughout all of this activity, he looked to the lower classes and workers for success in his venture of instituting a national and social state by getting rid of the Jews.

Drumont believed that the Jewish question was the key to French history. He called for a revolt of the oppressed masses against the Jew as oppressor, and the *Libre Parole* was fond of featuring sentimental descriptions of the misery of the lower classes (see Plate 13).[10] The expulsion of the Jews from France would lead to social justice; in the process their property would be confiscated and redistributed among all those who had shared in the struggle. Since he believed that this property was immense, dominating all economic life, the redistribution would entail considerable economic change.

Typically enough, Drumont associated Jews with Freemasons and Protestants—all of whom would have to vanish from the French scene. Although he respected Catholicism as necessary for social cohesion, he was not himself a devout believer, and he despised the French Catholic clergy as weak, and bought by Jewish capital.[11] Thus his Catholicism did not stand in the way of considering the Jews as a race.

Drumont continued the struggle started by Toussenel, whose anti-Semitism he adopted, and his analysis of France as decadent was bolstered by references to Jean-Baptiste Morel and Cesare Lombroso. The evil Jew could be recognized by his physical decadence: the hooked nose, shifty eyes, protruding ears, elongated body, flat feet, and moist hands.[12] The image of the rootless Jew was present in Drumont, linked, in this case, to the Jews' supposed origins as a desert and nomadic people. Drumont asserted that the Jew had the "soul of a Bedouin who will burn down a town in order to boil his egg."[13] He considered Russia the only nation which had been spared decadence as a result of its anti-Jewish policies.

Drumont repeatedly disclaimed any intention of proclaiming a holy war or of attacking the Jewish faith. "I have never insulted a Rabbi," he wrote.[14] Thus he deftly avoided religious issues, and his war against the Jews became a racial one. Drumont's preface to Rohling's *Talmud Jew* made this book exemplary for a description of the Jews' lust for power and absence of morality. Here was a source that had no relevance for Christianity and was thus a more welcome proof of Jewish evil than passages culled from the Old Testament. Finally, Drumont also propagated the blood libel against the Jews.[15]

Drumont was above all a publicist; but unlike Gobineau or Chamberlain, he attempted to found political and social movements that would advance his cause. The "Ligue Anti-Sémite," for example, founded in 1890, proclaimed the need for new trade unions which would expropriate financial monopolies and advocated the granting of credit without interest charges. But this and several other leagues which Drumont called to life were tiny and without significance. It was only through indirect control that he finally managed to become associated with a larger movement.

The trade union called "Les Jaunes" (The Yellows), which was founded in 1900, had over 100,000 members between 1903, when it came under Drumont's shadow, and 1908, when it collapsed.

Pierre Biétry, its leader, adopted Drumont's anti-Semitic anti-capitalism. The union, which received its name when workers who refused to join a strike used yellow paper to stop up the smashed windows of their meeting place, was no mere company union at the time. Les Jaunes sponsored strikes, if only after a waiting period, and supported cooperative workers' factories. But their vision of the future was centered upon workers rising to the rank of proprietors; patriotic workers who fought Jews, reds, and Freemasons alike.[16]

The union advocated job security, insurance schemes, and the trappings of that National Socialism we have discussed. Membership was diverse, embracing butchers in Paris, textile workers in Lille, and weavers in Albi, and a considerable number of industrial workers. Other members of the French right besides Drumont joined with the Yellows, rejoicing in a new type of union which was patriotic, seeing the workers not as proletarian but as future proprietors and yet taking some industrial action against the capitalist enemy.

This enthusiasm was well warranted. Nowhere else before the First World War in central and western Europe had the right penetrated so far down into the population through a mass organization, except in the case of Karl Lueger's election as lord mayor in Vienna in 1897. The brief success of Les Jaunes was due to the workers' bitter disillusionment with a wave of unsuccessful strikes that had preceded its founding. But once the radical unions were no longer bent on a policy of confrontation with their employers, the workers drifted back to the older unions. Even the agitators Drumont furnished could not prevent the Yellows' demise; but then by 1908, Drumont himself had become a lonely figure.

Yet as late as 1931 Georges Bernanos resurrected him as a model for French youth. The praise of Drumont in Bernanos's *La Grande Peur des Bien-Pensants* (*The Great Fear of Prudent Men*, 1931) is based on an appeal no different really from that he exercised at the height of his influence: the stubborn radical who refused to compromise with conservatives, liberals, or Socialists who, in his eyes, had betrayed their aim of the liberation of man. They had made

their peace with the soulless and avaricious bourgeoisie. In Bernanos's hands, Drumont became an example to the younger generation of the good fight against a society which was without a God,
and therefore without meaning. Drumont exemplified the heroic
fight for a life with meaning, dedicated to individual fulfillment
against the bourgeois enemy—symbolized by the soulless Jew.[17]

For Bernanos in 1931, the Jew himself was probably less important than the general tenor of Drumont's ideas; but the symbol of
the Jew could not readily be disentangled from the fight which
Drumont had waged against the supposed degeneracy of his time.
In *La Grande Peur des Bien-Pensants*, no such attempt was made.
However much Bernanos repudiated these views a few years later, it
was Drumont, and not any of the other possible heroes of the right
or left, who exemplified a relevant opposition to the weakness of
the modern world, showing both heroism and courage in exposing
the universal Jewish world conspiracy. Drumont the racist was held
up before French youth in 1931 as an example of a heroic man of
uncompromising independence who dared tell unpalatable truths to
his countrymen. This was a powerful image for a racist in an age
that sorely lacked heroes.

The young rightists who were attracted to racism in the 1930's
also rediscovered Drumont; men close at the time to the Action
Française and the newspaper *Je Suis Partout*.[18] Louis-Ferdinand
Céline in *Bagatelles pour un Massacre* (*Trifles for a Massacre*,
1937) continued the attack against Jews in the tradition of Drumont, if possible even more violently and indiscriminately.

Indeed, there was something hysterical and violent about all
French anti-Semitic racism as it evolved from the end of the
nineteenth century into the twentieth. Jules Guérin actually believed
that Masonic lodges were a cover for Jewish conspiracies. To beat
the Jews and Masons at their own game, he founded the anti-Jewish
and anti-republican "Grand Orient." There in the rue de Chabrol,
he collected arms for a *coup d'état*, and in 1899 resisted a siege by
the police for several days. The episode of the "fort Chabrol" in the
middle of the city was the sensation of Paris for weeks.

The marquis de Morès, wealthy and eccentric, financed a coach-men's and foodhandlers' strike in Paris in 1892, and founded bistros in working-class quarters where, in return for free beer, customers had to listen to Morès's workers' credit scheme and denunciations of the Jewish race. Guérin and Morès, both at one time close to Drumont, organized gangs whose nucleus was the butchers of the La Valette district of Paris, who demonstrated and caused distur-bances on the streets. Royalists, Bonapartists, and some industrial-ists contributed to their cause, enabling them to pay the butchers for demonstrating according to a fixed table of fees.[19]

To some young men, Guérin and Morès symbolized an "epic life," "happy and committed."[20] This was not unlike Bernanos's praise for Drumont. The meetings of these groups and the many leagues dedicated to the protection of the fatherland and the spread of anti-Semitism were filled with songs ("chansons anti-juive"), shouts of indignation, and polemical speeches. These were enjoyable catharses in a world of apathy. The demands were nearly always the same: expel the Jews from France, confiscate their property, and so bring about a more just economic distribution of goods. But in-sofar as audience reaction was recorded, this was often more vio-lent. "Death to Jews," and "String them up," were usual shouts.[21] Violence on the streets found its outlet in marches and demonstra-tions which entailed clashes with the police; but calls for physical violence against the hated race were largely confined to rhetoric at meetings.

These were National Socialist movements. Their adherents often wanted some kind of popular democracy with strong leadership and frequently called for rule by plebiscites. The political as well as the economic and social programs of the National Socialists at-tracted men and women who stood in the Jacobin tradition: anti-establishment, but fervent patriots, calling for an authoritarian form of government based on popular support, proclaiming the ideal of justice and equality. The Paris Commune of 1870 had, in the minds of some participants, exemplified this program. Above all, a majority of the followers of the eternal putschist, Auguste

Blanqui, passed from involvement in the Paris Commune to National Socialism under the guidance of Ernest Granger, one of Blanqui's closest friends.[22]

These Blanquists moved closer to Drumont and the anti-Semitic leagues without shedding their Jacobinism. Ernest Roche, their leader at the close of the century, embraced Drumont's ideals while proclaiming workers' solidarity.[23] Such men and women included Henri Rochefort, the editor of *Intransigeant*, as well as the celebrated anarchist Louise Michel. All of them had suffered punishment or even temporary exile for their part in the Paris Commune. Now the nationalism which was involved in this uprising came to the fore, combined with a goodly dose of anti-Semitism or even racism, plus an incurable penchant for violence.

French National Socialism was reenforced from Algeria. Algeria was not properly speaking a colony, but a department of France herself. The tension between the mixed population of French, Jews, and Moslems there was a daily fact of life. The Jews were highly visible as merchants, bankers, and professionals, forming a native middle class which was the envy of both the impoverished Moslems and the struggling French *colons*. Against the will and over the protests of Moslems and *colons*, Algerian Jews had been naturalized *en bloc* by the Crémieux Decree in 1870. Ever since that time, Algeria had provided fertile territory not merely for anti-Semitic but for overtly racist agitation.[24] The great success which an Algerian National Socialist and racist movement achieved at the polls in the 1890's seems to foreshadow the future more clearly than almost any single contemporary racist movement in Europe itself.

The racist movement in Algeria first elected the mayors of Oran and Constantine in 1896, and then captured the city government of Algiers in 1897. Max Régis, who headed the movement, dynamic and unrestrained in his racism, was only twenty-five years old at the time of his election as mayor of the city of Algiers. He called upon Algerians "to water the tree of liberty with Jewish blood,"[25] and together with a city council dominated by his supporters, he attempted to drive the Jews out of the city. Régis instigated a week of pogroms which left several Jews dead, a hundred wounded, and a multitude of Jewish shops plundered and destroyed.[26] At that point the French governor-general intervened and dismissed Régis after only one month in office.

Drumont, elected as deputy from Algeria to the French Chamber of Deputies with Régis's help, truly represented the violent racist spirit of many of his constituents. Contemporaries compared Régis to Robespierre, and his disciple, the mayor of Constantine, to St. Just.[27] Indeed, after his fall, Régis in exile in Paris frequently shared the platform not only with Drumont but also with those former communards whose Jacobinism was mentioned earlier; and he continued to call for that war of the races which he had not been allowed to wage in Algiers.[28]

For the first time, a violent and consistently racial policy had been implemented against Jews who were caught in a vice between French *colons* and Algerian Moslems and exposed to popular hostility as middlemen and shopkeepers. It is significant that racial policy first succeeded on the local level, for here the people could directly express preferences and frustrations which were not diluted by national concerns or policies. To be sure, the national government had pursued a racist policy against blacks in the French Empire for a long time past, but in Algeria the anti-Jewish policy was opposed by the national government and consequently dependent upon grass roots support. Racism was linked to democracy, and it was this connection that would largely determine the future of racism in Europe.

National Socialism was not merely confined to France, though it first struck its deepest roots in that nation. Central Europe also saw the rise of several movements and theorists who advocated the national and social state in a similar way.[29] Yet the specific conditions under which such social and national concerns were proclaimed mattered, not so much for the ever present hatred of Jews and the concern for the workers, but how these were related to other enemies not existing in France. Thus Georg von Schönerer and his Pan-German movement in Austria over the period 1881 to 1907 shared the national and social concerns of Drumont, but in the struggle against the Slavs other targets had to be taken into consideration as well. The Catholic Church had to be destroyed as one of the chief supporters of the Habsburg's multi-national Empire and therefore as an enemy of the supposed desire of German Austrians to join their brothers within the Reich. Schönerer's slogan, "Independence from Rome," reflected the struggle of German Austria against the other nationalities of the Empire. He wanted to annex Austria to Germany, and as a Pan-German he condemned alien peoples as well as Habsburg rule. Yet the Jews became his obsession, symbolizing all his enemies. At the same time, Schönerer combined racial abuse and the demand for Aryanization with the defense of the civil liberty of the workers, demands for advances in political and economic democracy, and a denunciation of police censorship. Schönerer put forward a typical National Socialist program. His approach was similar to that of Drumont in tying all social and political questions to a central theme—"the Jews versus the people." [30]

Schönerer had a certain success among the Viennese students, similar to Stoecker's success with German students at roughly the same time. Austrian fraternities began to exclude Jews and to adopt an Aryan clause for their membership, something the German fraternities as yet refused to do, though Jews were also being blackballed among many of them. But Schönerer was much more radical than Stoecker, who as a devout Protestant had not been a racist. From the very beginning of his political career, Schönerer wanted to fight the Jews "an eye for an eye and a tooth for a tooth." Baptism made no difference, for "the filthiness lies in the race" (*in der Rasse liegt die Schweinerei*).

Schönerer called for manhood suffrage as a democratic weapon against Habsburg rule. This suffrage would be restricted to the German population, who would use it to rejoin the German Reich.[31] Schönerer's slogans threatened death indiscriminately to Jews, Habsburgs, and the pope. While the first demand might have attracted support, the other two prevented this Pan-German movement from penetrating the Catholic masses.

At one point Schönerer made contact with skilled and industrial workers in Bohemia, hard-pressed by a Czech immigration which threatened their livelihood. Indeed, friction between Germans and Czechs in this region led to a pervasive and lasting racism. The Czechs were regarded by German Bohemians as vermin, biologically inferior but menacing the superior race through their toughness and population growth. This *Furor Teutonicus*, stoked by Schönerer, was originally sparked by the Badeni Decree of April 26, 1897, which placed the Czech language on an equal footing with German in Bohemia. Once more language was thought to be the core of nationality, and all elements of the German population joined in defense of their former monopoly with the students, who, as always, took the lead. But the workers joined in this opposition as well. Though the German workers were nationalist because of Czech pressure, they were also militant trade unionists. Perhaps earlier in his career, Schönerer could have become the Führer of Ostmark (as this part of the Austrian Empire was called by Pan-Germans), but by 1904 he had become more concerned with the welfare of students and shopkeepers than that of labor.[32]

That same year the German Workers Party (*Deutsche Arbeiter Partei*) was founded in Bohemia; and in 1918, shortly before the party's collapse, it changed its name to the German National Socialist Workers Party. The later title was a more accurate description of the goals pursued by the Bohemian workers.[33] The German Workers Party called for their liberation within the framework of the German Volk. This meant a strong trade union organization, freedom of the press and assembly, as well as the transformation of Imperial Austria into a Volkish democratic German state. The idea of such a state was really little more than a vague slogan directed against liberalism, meaning at most the advocacy of a popular consensus behind an aggressive national policy. Under the aegis of a young leadership, and supported by youth organizations, the party's struggle was directed simultaneously against Czechs, "Jewish" social democracy, and "Jewish" capital.[34] Within the Volk itself there was to be no class struggle, but violence against Czechs and Jews was permitted. Clearly, this was an extension of the National Socialism which also informed workers' movements like Les Jaunes in France.

These diverse National Socialist movements were not aware of each other's existence. Each was a response to a particular situation. The fact that these responses had so much in common is important as part of that general search for a more equalitarian community within the national mystique which took place throughout Europe. The Bohemian workers discussed ideas that Hitler's National Socialism would take up later, but there is no evidence that Hitler knew of these forerunners. Moreover, when the German Workers Party changed its name, the Hitler Party had not yet been born. Yet by 1923, most of the leaders of the older National Socialism had joined the new, which was making inroads in Bohemia and Moravia. Meanwhile in Germany herself, this National Socialism had some scattered success before the First World War both in theory and in practice. The theory elaborated by Eugen Dühring in Berlin provided some inspiration for the Austrian movement across the border as well.[35]

Karl Eugen Dühring (1833–1921) might justly be called the Drumont of Germany. Indeed, he and Drumont were aware of each other, but Dühring was more serious about his economic and social views.[36] He never acquired the organized following which Drumont managed to arouse, though at one point Friedrich Engels saw him as a threat to socialism and wrote his *Anti-Dühring* (1876), which long outlived in fame the subject of its attack. Yet Dühring was no negligible figure, and his appeal was in one way close to that of Drumont. He was a man who despised compromise, who upheld his independence and supposed integrity in an age of compromise and corruption. Many Germans saw Dühring in such a light, although he was not an easy man to admire. After the turn of the century, blind and fired from his teaching position at the University of Berlin, he became a paranoiac close to insanity, believing that everyone had stolen his ideas and plagiarized his works.[37]

But the young Dühring, whom the socialist leader August Bebel praised in 1874 and who impressed Eduard Bernstein, was a promising radical who surprisingly had entered the anti-socialist faculty of the University of Berlin, and who in his lectures championed the workers' right of association and their right to strike. However, contrary to Marx, Dühring gave the state a role as mediator between workers and employers, while at the same time denying that economics were regulated by immutable laws. Friedrich Engels sounded the alarm against Dühring's deviations from Marxist orthodoxy. Indeed, his danger to socialism seemed proven when Karl Liebknecht publicized letters from workers supporting Dühring's theories rather than Marx's.[38] But Engels need not have worried, for Dühring's career was about to change abruptly with his expulsion from the Berlin faculty in 1877 for having slandered his colleagues. Dühring now struck out on all sides, against the Social Democrats who had supported him, as well as against Richard Wagner who had tried to befriend him.

Dühring's racism came to the fore, while his economics changed as well. He began to reject the state (which as the employer of the university faculty had rejected him), and advocated self-help within independent communities. By 1900 he was writing about the superman who was needed to put things right. At the same time he condemned strikes and unions; the worker must be propelled into the middle classes.[39] This drastic revision of his views went hand in hand with stress upon the spirit of the Volk as the prerequisite for a sound society and economics.

In 1880, Dühring published his *The Jewish Question as a Problem of Racial Character and Its Damage to the Existence of Peoples, Morals and Culture* (*Die Judenfrage als Frage des Racencharakters und seiner Schädlichkeiten für Völkerexistenz, Sitte und Cultur*), and by 1901 the book had gone through five editions. The title adequately describes the contents; there is no sin, no failing for which the Jewish race is not held responsible. Unlike Drumont, Dühring also condemned Christianity as an invention thought up by the Jews in order to enslave the world. The wide, if spurious, learning of Dühring was impressive, and so was his reputation as a champion of the workingman, his concern for all peoples, not just for Germans. For though he singled out the German virtues of loyalty, trust, and work, by and large he saw the Jewish race as fatal to all mankind.

Race war was a living reality for Dühring, as it had been for

Wilhelm Marr in his *Victory of Jewry over Teutonism* (*Der Sieg des Judentums über das Germanentum*, 1867) and later for Houston Stewart Chamberlain in his famous *Foundations of the Nineteenth Century*. Dühring's confused National Socialism, however, made him influential in certain left-wing circles long after he himself had passed from the scene.

Neither Dühring nor other anti-Semitic agitators in Berlin could break out of their political isolation. Whereas in France some workers became involved in anti-Semitic and racist movements based in Paris, in Germany the countryside provided the setting for the one successful breakthrough of National Socialist racism during the nineteenth century. The Peasant League of Hessia (1885–94) under the leadership of Otto Böckel had no equivalent further west where, for example, the French agricultural unions remained under Catholic and conservative leadership. Indeed, the conservatives in Germany proved to be Böckel's worst enemies, for he seemed to endanger their alliance with agricultural groups. Otto Böckel was an academic type, who had dabbled in folk poetry and was trained as a librarian, but unlike Dühring he had a flair for organization and propaganda.

Böckel was a National Socialist whose anti-Jewish program was combined with social reforms and popular education.[40] He held that the Jews were a race of parasites and exploiters—a view that had great appeal in Hessia, where small-town Jewish settlement was dense, and where Jews were the cattle dealers and bankers as well. Böckel plagiarized Toussenel when he entitled his own book *The Jews, Kings of the Epoch* (*Die Juden-Könige Unserer Zeit*, 1886), and his Peasant League began its career by sending greetings to Eugen Dühring.[41] The book followed these models, Toussenel and Dühring, by asserting that the Jewish question was a matter of race and not of religion. If Böckel lacked originality of thought, he at least succeeded in putting his beliefs into practice.

Böckel and his Hessian Peasant League wanted to end all abuse of capital, but without abolishing private property. Böckel emphasized self-help through cooperatives run by the peasants, which bought and sold not only agricultural goods but eventually most of the other necessities of life as well. Factories were taken under contract producing cheap goods for the cooperatives of the Peasant League as the middleman was abolished. Equally important was the founding of banks which lent money without interest charges. Nor was Böckel afraid to call for the nationalization of essential raw materials like coal.[42]

Racism was embedded in this cooperative movement: the League attempted to run "Jew-free" cattle markets and to eliminate Jews as moneylenders. It unfolded an active propaganda campaign by means of newspapers, but also through some twenty speakers who went from village to village and town to town, exhorting, explaining, and condemning Jews and capital. Böckel liked to compare his Peasant League to the Social Democratic Party, yet radicalism in practice was tempered in theory. He called for loyalty to Church and monarchy against all attempts at revolution, and designated his League a party of law and order.[43] Thus he annexed to his National Socialism some of the conservative program congenial to rural regions. At the height of his power in 1893, Böckel controlled eleven deputies to the Reichstag.[44] The figure indicates his considerable support in Hessia; indeed, for a few years, the Böckel movement dominated the politics of that state. It was, without doubt, the most important early National Socialist breakthrough in central Europe, even though it contained some conservative features in Böckel's Protestantism and monarchical loyalties. Some Nazis later realized what they owed Böckel and built a museum to his memory in Marburg—an electoral district he had managed to hold even after his fall from leadership.

Böckel resigned from his League in 1894 when it became obvious that the cooperatives were facing financial collapse. He had never been able to achieve a proper financial base for his widespread cooperatives, nor had he managed to unite the various credit and loan institutions. Böckel was not interested in questions of administration, and this proved fatal in organizations so closely linked to his person and his leadership.[45] Though he remained a member of the German diet until 1903, Böckel rapidly passed into obscurity, the common fate of all these pioneers of National Socialism. Dru-

mont and Schönerer also left the scene within the first decade of
the twentieth century. The movements they had led had been too
closely tied to their abrasive and inflexible personalities, and their
misjudgments of the political and economic situation. In the first
fifteen years of the twentieth century, they were crushed between
conservative, liberal, and socialist forces. The economic crises of the
late nineteenth century seemed to have run their course by 1900,
giving way to what has been called the Indian Summer of the
bourgeois world. For the final National Socialist breakthrough, a
catastrophe of the dimensions of the First World War was needed.
Böckel's League speedily became an agricultural pressure group
without any National Socialist pretensions, though the anti-Semitism was preserved and eventually the surviving leaders joined the
postwar Nazi Party. Yet Hessia did not become National Socialist
in the 1920's any earlier or to any greater degree than other regions
with a similar social and economic structure.[46]

Ironically, before the First World War, it was France rather than
Germany or Austria that seemed likely to become the home of a
successful racist and National Socialist movement. Germany had no
Dreyfus Affair or Panama scandal and no Third Republic. Anti-
Semitism without racism was common enough, but racism itself
still seemed to find its home mainly in academic discussions, cultural coteries (like the Wagner circle), eugenics movements, or in
some popularizations of Darwinism.

The First World War and its aftermath revitalized racism in all its
forms, whether National Socialist, conservative, or merely nationalist, whether as the science or the mystery of race. This could not
have been foreseen in 1914, when relative security and well-being
characterized the middle classes, and when the differences which
had rent apart nations like France seemed to have ended in compromise. By 1914 racism seemed to be largely confined to the European
colonies, and in Europe itself it looked as if it had run its stormy
course. Yet it was in Europe that a few decades later racism would
be put into practice on an unprecedented scale. War and revolutions propelled racism into a more durable and awesome practice.

PART III

The Execution

CHAPTER ELEVEN

War and Revolution

THE FIRST WORLD WAR, whose outbreak was greeted with the same patriotic enthusiasm by European Jews as by Gentiles, was to be the prelude to the gruesome implementation of racist policy in Europe. The theory of racism had already penetrated important groups and made its impact upon the popular consciousness. But it was the war and its aftermath that would transform the theory into practice. As the principal minority in Europe, the Jews had already become the foil of racist thought; now, because of the war and the revolutions which followed, their visibility was accentuated and they became isolated and easily victimized. Indeed, the very violence which continued from the war into the postwar world provided another prerequisite for the triumph of racism. The history that we have unfolded so far now approaches its climax.

The attitudes springing from the war itself, and from the postwar chaos, as well as from the revolutions of 1918–20, all set the stage for the future. In general, the war encouraged longings for cameraderie, activism, and heroism within the nationalistic mystique. Nationalism was strengthened whatever its traditions or aims, whether to win victory against the enemy or to achieve national liberation. The national unity proclaimed in all nations at the outbreak of war, however, was often dissolved even while the war itself was in progress—through accusations of cowardice against Jews, or by tensions between competing groups fighting for national lib-

eration in eastern Europe. Finally, the fact of mass death added to
the consequences of the war a certain brutalization of the European
conscience, which also pointed to the future. None of these results
of the war were necessarily racist; but all of them would be subject
to racist penetration once the time was ripe.

The internal unity which had been evoked at the outbreak of the
First World War was broken most ominously in Germany. The
statistics about Jewish participation in the armed forces that the
high command collected on October 11, 1916, came as a deep
shock to German Jewry, which had regarded the war as completing
their process of assimilation. The army asserted that it had received
complaints that Jews were either being freed from armed service or
were evading it in order to find safe positions behind the front.[1]
Perhaps this collection of statistics was a part of General Erich
Ludendorff's proposal for a more general mobilization; but there
were also anti-liberal and anti-Semitic forces at work in the high
command who, like Ludendorff's closest adviser, Max Bauer, believed in secret international conspiracies.[2] While the army refused
to let known anti-Semites see the statistics, Jewish organizations
themselves welcomed this head count, which would disprove un-
founded accusations against their members. The Jews were made
highly visible in the midst of the war, singled out from the rest of
the population. Their patriotism alone was questioned and, whatever the motive, this fitted in nicely with the prevailing stereotype.
Nothing like the "Jew-count" occurred in other warring nations.
Already Germany was moving to the fore in questioning Jewish
emancipation and assimilation.

More important in the long run were those basic ideals of activism, heroism, and cameraderie that were so strengthened by the
war. Harmless though these might have been alone, in the context
of the war and the postwar world they were easily annexed by racism. Trench warfare gave a new impetus to such attitudes, in a
way of fighting that had no precedent. For those in the front lines
the war was a total experience: always facing the enemy and under
constant fire.

Such warfare emphasized the sense of cameraderie of those who spent days and nights together in the damp trenches; it also glorified that élite of soldiers who led the onslaught upon the enemy, for such storm troopers (as they were called) jumped over the tops of their trenches right into the murderous fire of the enemy. The call for cameraderie—that "overcoming of self," as the future leader of the French veterans, François de La Rocque, put it—was to echo long after the war was over, and everywhere it spelled opposition to liberal democracy as complacent and uninspiring. Hand in hand with this call went a glorification of the "*élan*" of the battlefield. In Italy, too, Gabriele d'Annunzio exalted the symbol of the "black flame" as the emblem of the Italian storm troopers.[3] This flame symbolized personal and national regeneration, and heroic passion exemplified by the storm troopers as opposed to modern degeneracy.

The warriors who symbolized cameraderie and the heroic reflected these virtues in their outward appearance as well. The First World War strengthened the stereotype whose growth we have analyzed ever since the eighteenth century and whose inner worth was expressed through its appearance. Otto Braun, killed during the war, whose letters from the German front, *From the Legacy of a Prodigy (Aus Nachgelassenen Schriften Eines Frühvollendeten,* 1921), went through many editions, praised the "manly beauty" which this "age of steel" had produced. By manly beauty he meant a strictly classical form. And such ideas were not confined to Germany. In England, much of the war literature paired the manly beauty of soldiers with blondness and classical form, as in the popular legend that enshrined the poet Rupert Brooke (also killed early in the war) as "A young Apollo, golden-haired"—to quote a part of Frances Cornford's epigram. The "general sunniness" of the stereotype was emphasized during the war by writers most of whom were not racists but who sought in the male society of the trenches living symbols of a genuine community, of human beauty and of sacrifice.[4] All over Europe the need to cope with the war experience tended to emphasize this stereotype, even if in France the blondness was absent, or in Italy the stress was on the spirit of the war rather than the appearance of the heroes. Postwar racism surely benefitted from the reemphasis upon this human ideal-type, especially in nations where many still saw themselves at war in their fight for social change and their struggle against national humiliation.

Germany was therefore not the only country where the war deepened these myths and propelled them into the postwar world to the confusion of liberals and parliamentarians. But it was Ernst Jünger in Germany who became their most celebrated theoretician, elevating battle to man's innermost experience, capable of producing a new race of heroes. "This was a totally new race, energy itself and filled with *élan*. Supple, thin and muscular bodies, distinguished faces with eyes which have seen thousands of horrors. These were men who overcame, men of steel. . . ."[5] Here the term "race" was used as a literary flourish; still, such a new "race"—whether in Germany, France, England or elsewhere—was thought to be the finest expression of the national will. The putative enemies of these nations were a lower species: revolutionaries, Freemasons, and, as often as not, Jews.

The exaltation of cameraderie, heroism, and a new race of men was surrounded by mass death on a scale never witnessed before, and this fact had to be confronted. The result was a certain brutalization of conscience, which derived not only from the acceptance of the inevitable but also from attempts to come to terms with such carnage by glorifying it. Death in war was said to give new meaning to life—to cement further the bonds of comradeship between those who had rejected the trivialities of daily existence in order to experience the ultimate sacrifice. The passion of Christ himself was invoked to describe death in war as an *imitatio Christi*—the end of life on the battlefield would be followed by resurrection.

Germany, which faced defeat, emphasized in a special way that soldiers never die but, resurrected, continue to fight not only in Valhalla but in every patriot's heart. The patriots were exhorted not to give in to defeat, but to fight on until the nation itself had been resurrected. This argument is best summed up in the introduction to a book which described the 700 shrines of honor to the war dead built during the German republic. The book asserted that the dead of the war were not really dead at all, but returned in dreams in order to witness a German miracle. That miracle was the belief that Germany had not been defeated, and that the time had come to rebuild the Reich and to defend its honor.[6] In this new martyrology, death and life were one and the same, and they constituted a miracle which the Hitler Youth years later summed up in a spoken chorus on Heroes' Memorial Day: "The best of our people did not die in order that the living might perish, but in order that the dead may come alive."[7] In Italy, too, d'Annunzio proclaimed that death was not only abolished but buried beneath the continuity of generations, in which the youth automatically took the place of their elders, and the flag was passed from one to another, each with sword in hand.[8]

Such ideas of death entailed a constant rebirth within the national mystique for those who had done their duty, and in this light death became less frightening. However, the enemy was excluded from such comfort; he had to be killed and would never return. There was one kind of death reserved for the man who fought for the nation, and another for the enemy. Later we shall see the relevance of such ideas of death for the process of Jewish extermination.

To many, the mutilated bodies and grimaced faces of the battlefields came alive through the picture books then in vogue, and, far from causing revulsion, filled many a youth born too late to fight with regret at having missed this challenge to his manliness. Such young men would have agreed with that German clergyman who declared during the war that God blesses every individual who kills an enemy.[9]

These attitudes were aggravated by the effects of foreign occupation on Germany during the period of 1919–1920. France used Moroccan and Senegalese troops in its Army of the Rhine, and when black troops occupied the city of Frankfurt-am-Main in 1920, a coordinated and massive German response was inevitable. For the first time, Germans were confronted with a large number of blacks—and in the role of occupiers. Racial fears, never far beneath the surface, were activated and indeed encouraged by the infant government of the new republic. The "black rape of Germany" might bring the defeated nation badly needed sympathy abroad. Even the basically decent Social Democratic leader Hermann Müller exclaimed with indignation that "Senegalese Negroes" were profaning the University of Frankfurt and the Goethe House.[10] It was against blacks, not Jews, that the ominous accusation of "Kulturschande" (rape of culture) was first raised after the war.

Racial fears were immediately linked to sexual anxieties, a common enough combination, but now increasingly emphasized because blacks were traditionally thought to be more potent than whites. The journalist Alfred Brie wrote in 1921 with much embroidery about raped German women, describing how the colored French went on the rampage in occupied territory. Novels appeared on the same theme, among them *The Black Insult, a Novel of Ravished Germany* (*Die Schwarze Schmach, der Roman des Geschändeten Deutschland*), published in 1922 with a preface by Count Ernst von Reventlow, one of the earliest Nazi supporters. The memory of this occupation would persist, for in 1940 a Nazi tract looked back when it opposed the entry of blacks into European culture. The Jews were not forgotten; they were accused, together with the French, of being responsible for the occupation and for waging a "Negro-Jewish war" upon the Germans.[11] Black troops never reappeared in Germany, for in the Ruhr occupation of 1923 to 1924 the French were careful not to use them; the fuss had been too great and too effective in winning sympathy for Germany in countries like the United States.

Nevertheless, racism was in reality directed more against the Jews than the black soldiers. The French and Belgian occupation stoked the fires, but the heat was easily transferred from such troops to the traditional foils of European racism. If blacks ravished German women in pamphlets and novels during the occupation, Arthur Dinter's *Die Sünde wider das Blut* (*The Sin Against the Blood*, 1918) had transmitted a more typical message, and it sold in the hundred thousands. The novel told of the violation of a German woman's racial purity by a rich Jew (cf. Plate 7), and even though she left him to marry an Aryan, her offspring continued to resemble the Jewish stereotype. More ominously, in 1919 the Jewish community in Hamburg had to protest police posters which defined a criminal as a "fat Jew" with a "Jewish nose." [12] In that same year the police of northern Bavaria, while deploring the increase of anti-Semitism, wrote that no remedy existed, since it "has its roots in the differences of race which divide the Israelite tribe from our Volk." [13] The police expressed its opinions under the stress of defeat and revolution. They reflected a racism which attempted to provide an explanation for the brutality of the war and the internal disorder that ensued—the Jew was to blame.

The revolutions which followed after the war gave the Jews a greater visibility than they had before, and it is not surprising that the years 1918 to 1920 saw an upsurge of racism wherever revolution took place or threatened. Moreover, to many middle-class Europeans, the revolution at home was a part of the newly successful Bolshevik revolution in which, once again, Jews seemed to predominate among the leaders. People were apt to confuse brutal Communist leaders like Belá Kûn in Hungary (see Plate 12) with men like Kurt Eisner in Bavaria, though the latter abhorred violence. It was also true that 1918 was the first year Jews did enter continental European governments in any number, and that these were left-wing governments, the products of revolution in central and eastern Europe.

Jews played such important roles in these revolutions because for the first time in central and eastern Europe, as well as Russia, they promised true equality to Jews, and an end to discrimination. Some, like Belá Kûn in Hungary, had joined underground Communist parties long before the war, and found themselves in the lead when the old order collapsed. While Jewish participation in these revolutions was understandable and, in any case, took in only a tiny fraction of Jews within their respective nations, the old stereotype found new encouragement. Every myth must have a semblance of truth if it is to be effective; here Jews who were helping to overthrow the old order were associated with the Bolshevik revolution, so proving, some thought, that as a group they were "anti-national." The topics of conversation between the young Heinrich Himmler and his father in a Munich beerhall in 1922 were typical of the times: "the past, the war, revolution, the Jews, harassment of officers, the reds, liberation."[14] Heinrich Himmler's diary records an association of ideas which served a newly invigorated right. Men like the young Himmler joined militant groups which fought for liberation as they understood it—against reds and Jews, for the fatherland.

A radicalized right was born in the wake of the war and revolution. Central and eastern Europe were its home, for western Europe had not experienced the same cycle of defeat and upheaval. Only now did this region of Europe become more receptive to racism than the West. Earlier, from the standpoint of 1914 (as we saw), it might well have been France that would transform racist theory into practice. After 1918 it was Germany which proved most receptive to racism, while Austria and eastern Europe were involved as well. The Jews had become visible here as they were not in France or England during the early postwar years.

The Jews were not merely accused of being revolutionaries, for their old image as capitalist exploiters was still alive as well. These Jews were seen simultaneously as revolutionaries and as exploiters —a myth which had haunted them since their emancipation, and which after the war became transformed into the Jewish-capitalist-Bolshevik conspiracy, uniting all those forces that seemed to prevent national liberation. It was at this point that the conspiracy was integrated with the *Protocols of the Elders of Zion*, which the reactionary Black Hundreds carried with them in their flight from Russia.[15] The London *Times*'s correspondent in Moscow had no doubt that the horrors of the Bolshevik revolution were an act of Jewish vengeance.[16]

The belief in a Jewish-Bolshevik conspiracy ruling over Russia and already prepared to take over the rest of Europe cropped up in every nation. In England, writers like G. K. Chesterton and John Buchan were fascinated by such conspiracies.[17] Even the young Winston Churchill talked about the "dark power of Moscow," where cosmopolitan conspirators from the underworld of the great cities had gathered (though later he was one of the first Western statesmen to realize that the German question could not be divorced from the Jewish question, because Hitler's loathsome racism was built into the Nazi régime).[18] Nevertheless, the impact of such fantasies was negligible on a nation that had won the war and had not lost its balance. A French rightist paper in 1920 reviewed the *Protocols* under the simple but telling heading: "The Origins of Bolshevism."[19] In France such ideas did not lead to the activation of racism either, for here too there had been no national defeat and no revolution. But in Germany it was a more serious portent of the times when in 1921 Fritz Halbach published *Comrade Levi* (*Kamerad Levi*), in which a young Communist agitator was pictured as on the best of terms with his rich banker father. Each wanted world power, and they collaborated in order to obtain it, working both sides of the street. The idea of a Jewish-Bolshevik conspiracy haunted the imagination of many others besides Adolf Hitler, but his belief in the *Protocols* was to be fatal. During the Russian campaign in the Second World War, for example, he ordered the immediate execution of every captured Bolshevik political commissar, considering them the spearhead of the Jewish-Bolshevik conspiracy.[20]

The result of this newly gained Jewish visibility was immediate. Central Europe saw no pogroms, but instead a wave of anti-Jewish measures, not by governments but by important social and cultural organizations. German student fraternities now introduced Aryan qualifications for membership, and national student organizations throughout eastern Europe campaigned for a Jewish *numerus clausus*.[21] Conservative parties tended to adopt anti-Semitism as useful in electoral politics, while Jews were excluded from war veterans' associations. As yet, there was little overt violence against the Jews in countries like Germany or Austria. But apart from sporadic outbreaks (mostly at universities), hatred and fear was building up to be released after 1933. Every new anti-Jewish law proclaimed by the Nazis was preceded by popular outbursts that were directed, though not necessarily created, by the régime.[22]

In eastern Europe, by contrast, violence remained common after the First World War. Several factors accounted for this volatility on the Jewish question. The Jews were *the* middle class in these nations and thus an easy target. Here Jews had also been prominent revolutionaries; moreover, the close geographical proximity of the Soviet Union stirred up additional fears of revolution. The tinder lay ready to be ignited, for the Austrian and Russian Empires left in their wake a problem of rural overpopulation and not enough industrial development to absorb it. Some thought that social conditions and the Soviet influence would mean a revolution led by Jews, while others saw the Jews as perpetuating poverty and unemployment in their own interests. The image of the Jew as revolutionary-cum-capitalist exploiter existed in eastern just as it did in central Europe.

At the same time, Jews in eastern Europe were losing any power they might have possessed.[23] Here the Jew had once fulfilled an economic function which made him indispensable, but this was no longer so after the war. The Jews, as the middle class, were often allied to the big landowners who held the political power and still needed their economic services.[24] But the war created native middle classes in much of eastern Europe. Now Jews could become unfettered objects of hate as revolutionaries, capitalist oppressors, and middle-class rivals. In central and western Europe, the Jews had never been so indispensable; instead, they were surrounded by a middle class at first liberal and devoted to pluralism. Even when this vanished, moderation, law, and order forbade pogroms, though after the war these barriers against violent persecution were wearing thin.

In eastern Europe, no such barriers existed and popular fury struck out against the highly visible and dispensable Jews. The pogroms of 1918 were some of the most brutal on record. Especially in Poland, with its 3 million Jews, the idea of the Jewish-Bolshevik conspiracy came alive with the war against the Soviet Union of 1920. During the attempted advance of Polish armies into Russia, Jewish soldiers and officers of the Polish army were not allowed to fight and were even put into detention camps. The army and the Church openly professed an anti-Semitism which flared up during this conflict. The refounded state was Polish and Catholic, despite all the minorities contained within its borders. Throughout the entire interwar period, popular violence against the Jews flared up, although the dictatorship of Marshall Josef Pilsudski, set up in 1926, proved benevolent and even friendly. But after Pilsudski's death in 1935, conditions worsened as the Conservative Party and the rightist National Democrats allied themselves to the military who held the real power. The anti-Jewish measures now introduced varied from ghetto-benches and a *numerus clausus* in universities, to an economic boycott supported by Church and state.[25] Finally, in 1938, when the Nazis expelled some 15,000 Polish Jews from the Reich, Poland refused to receive her actual citizens.[26] Their life and death in the no-man's-land at the German-Polish border signalized a bleak future for the mass of Polish Jewry.

The Polish government after Pilsudski opposed Jewish assimilation and held that the Jews were a distinct nationality. The régime of the colonels asserted that it rejected all racism, yet forced the emigration of Jews from Poland. The Jewish stereotype was spread in spite of all denials of racism, and Jews were pictured by the state and by the Catholic Church as dirty and slovenly, as usurers and even white slavers. The government's policy was always ambivalent: it urged restraint upon the anti-Semites to its right, while at the same time itself using anti-Semitism in order to cement national unity.[27] Violence in postwar Poland was sporadic, and racism as yet ambivalent, being interlaced with the traditional Catholic anti-Semitism.

All over Europe radical rightist parties sprang up in the wake of revolution and counter-revolution, as white terror took the place of red terror. Yet régimes came to power which were reactionary rather than of the radical right; but even here anti-Semitism sometimes became a part of government policy. The accession of Nicolas Horthy in Hungary and the military dictatorship in Poland after 1935 provide examples of this development. But even further south, in Rumania, the Jewish problem remained alive. Yet it was not until the 1930's that such nations, governed by reactionaries, were influenced by radical rightist parties who desired a final solution of the Jewish question. Polish, Hungarian, or Austrian reactionaries in power, fearful of any unrest, in fact more effectively prevented anti-

Semitic violence by a radical right than the weaker parliamentary
democracies. They feared that radical anti-Semitism might lead to
the breakdown of law and order. Eventually, after the Nazi seizure
of power, the head of the representative assembly of German Jewry,
Leo Baeck, would dream of a military dictatorship in Germany as
the last hope for the Jews.[28] Neither Horthy in Hungary, the king
in Rumania, Ignaz Seipel in Austria, nor Pilsudski in Poland were
racists. Their anti-Semitism remained Christian and traditional;
Jews must be kept out of government and held at arm's length,
but left alone.

Eventually this attitude was challenged by the Iron Cross in Hungary, the Iron Guard in Rumania, the Nazis in Austria, and other
such movements. In western Europe, too, traditional conservative
nationalism was at first more important than the radical right.
France had her Action Française, but also a number of Fascist and
racist groups, although until the 1930's these remained small and
impotent. England was without any important radical right until
Sir Oswald Mosley founded his British Union of Fascists in 1932.
Initially, these groups were small, but then neither England nor
France had lived under the shadow of revolution or suffered from a
serious conflict of nationalities, and both had been victorious in the
war. But even in Germany the radical right was a minority during
the 1920's when compared with the conservative political party, or
other groupings of the center and left. That radical right, whether
the Volkish Defense and Offensive League (*Deutschvölkische
Schutz- und Trutz-Bund*) or the insignificant German Workers
Party, was founded as a direct reaction to the revolution. The small
German Workers Party—soon to be called the National Socialist
Workers Party—arose out of a rightist society (the Thule Bund)
which had organized itself during the Bavarian revolution of 1918.

The Volkish Defensive and Offensive League, founded by rightist
splinter groups in 1919, was the most important of such organizations in the early days of the Weimar Republic. At its height, in
1922, the organization claimed 200,000 members, and that may
have been an underestimation.[29] It revived ritual murder accusations, as well as reprinting Rohling's *Talmud Jew*. The *Protocols*

were distributed by the League, although they had been translated into German by the short-lived "Society Against Jewish Arrogance."[30] This Volkish Bund took the short step from theory to practice, encouraged by the revolutionary situation. It joined with other rightist groups in spreading violence. Such groups were often led by the so-called Free Corps of soldiers and their officers who had refused to demobilize. They took the law into their own hands and a wave of assassinations rocked the country, perpetrated by "foot soldiers without a nation," as one of them put it.[31] It has been estimated that between 1919 and 1922, some 376 political murders took place in the German Reich. Rightists committed 354 such murders, and the left 22. But despite such lopsidedness, the prison sentences meted out to the right totaled 90 years and 2 months, while those given to leftists amount to 248 years and 9 months, and 10 executions. Clearly the judges of the new republic favored the right, another portent of things to come. But it must be added that by and large the Weimer law courts did shelter the Jews from their detractors. The so-called Fehme murders (ordered by secret self-appointed courts) were usually committed by rightist high-school students, of whom many were hardly over seventeen years of age.[32] Those who followed the Volkish movements were from the beginning young and committed, in contrast to the much higher age structure of the other parties—once more a portent for the future.

The Volkish Defensive and Offensive League had a hand in such lynch justice, for instance in the attempted assassinations of Philip Scheidemann, the Social Democrat who had signed the Treaty of Versailles, and of Maximilian Harden, the Jewish publicist, and in the successful assassination (among many others) of the Center Party leader Matthias Erzberger, whom they blamed for Germany's surrender. The campaign against the Jewish foreign minister Walter Rathenau in particular was filled with incitements to murder,[33] and his assassination in 1922 finally led the republic to ban the League. At that point the National Socialist Workers Party in Munich became its principal legatee and successor.

The postwar violence of rightist groups proved to be a school for murder for many of those later involved in exterminating the Jews.

Martin Bormann, the dreaded head of Hitler's chancery during the war, and Rudolf Höss, the commandant of the Auschwitz death camp, were both Fehme murderers. In 1923 they executed a youth who was suspected of betraying the hiding place of illegal arms to the police.[34]

Following the war, violence persisted in much of central and eastern Europe. But it was in a defeated and disorganized Germany that the radical right found its most powerful allies from the very beginning. The agricultural union (*Bund der Landwirte*) and the trade union of commercial employees put themselves at the disposal of the Volkish Defensive and Offensive League.[35] The Kapp Putsch of March 1920, in which right-wing elements attempted to overthrow the republic, was important in demonstrating the relationship of the conservatives and the Free Corps to Volkish racism. Wolfgang Kapp was a Pan-German member of the Prussian aristocracy. His personal connections reached down to the playwright and journalist Dietrich Eckart, who as Hitler's political mentor was a member of the newly founded German Workers Party. Members of the Ehrhardt Free Corps who gave military support to Kapp's venture wanted to start a pogrom against the Jews, but Kapp restrained them, in spite of his own anti-Semitism.[36] The traditional conservatism, which valued law and order, won out. The Kapp Putsch was over in five days, for this time the army remained loyal to the new republic.

In spite of its temporary loyalty, the army itself was infected with anti-Semitism. For example, in 1920 a memorandum by a regiment directed to the Bavarian minister-president called for a massacre of the Jews if the allies blockaded Germany again.[37] The army's disenchantment with the republic eventually made it vulnerable to the ideas of the Volkish Defensive and Offensive League, whose literature was publicly distributed by one general in 1920. The army's view was summarized in 1924 by a lieutenant writing at a point when the early crises of the republic seemed to have been overcome: "Ebert [president of the republic], pacifists, Jews, democrats, black, red, and gold [the new flag] and the French are all forces which want to destroy Germany."[38] To be sure, the higher officers did attempt to differentiate between Jews in general and those who had distinguished themselves in the war and should be treated as if they were good Germans. Still, most of the army (as well as the even more radical navy) must be added to the large landowners and the conservatives as being infected with racism.

After 1918, nationalism was everywhere on the increase, for the war had not brought about the end of the nation-state but its apotheosis. Even the left showed a nationalist and patriotic spirit.[39] The Jews, more visible and isolated than ever before, were regarded as a foreign people if not yet as a foreign nation. They were thus in danger of being doubly abandoned—as a people without a nation, and as a separate group in the nation without a power base. Racism seemed to have an easy prey.

Yet such a view of the Jewish question would have seemed absurd to most European Jews until well into the Nazi era. For the moment there were allies: governments in western and central Europe who were committed to tolerance and hostile to discrimination, as well as political parties of the left and center who believed in furthering the process of Jewish assimilation. Center parties were strong in England and France, by whatever name they called themselves, for both Tory and Labor in Britain, for example, were committed to a pluralist society at home based on moderation and tolerance. This was also true of the center parties and of the Social Democrats in Germany, who in fact became allies of the Jews in their fight against anti-Semitism.[40] Basically, the liberal tradition still held, even though liberal parties were in decline. The liberal heritage was taken over in England by all major parties, in France by Socialists and Radical Socialists, in Germany by the Social Democrats. Even in eastern Europe where there were functioning liberal parties, as in Rumania, they proved to be friendly toward the Jews.

But what of the radical left, which a minority of highly visible Jews had supported and at times even led in the attempted postwar revolutions? Communist and leftist splinter parties certainly believed in complete Jewish assimilation. Karl Kautsky—the "pope" of prewar socialism—set the tone for the discussion of the Jewish question after the war. He had updated Karl Marx's view of the

Jews without introducing any basic changes. Kautsky's *Race and the Jewish Question (Rasse und Judentum*, 1914) accepted the negative Jewish stereotype in attributing to Jews a fetishistic regard for goods, a love of money, and a devotion to commerce. When capitalism collapsed, he maintained, Jews would vanish. Meanwhile, they must try to shed their religion and join the proletarian fight for the liberation of mankind that would lead to universal peace and brotherhood.

While the German Social Democrats as inheritors of pluralist liberalism never accepted this attitude after the war, because it seemed too dangerous when living under the cloud of a militantly anti-Semitic right,[41] the Communist parties founded after the war adopted Kautsky's reasoning both in Europe and in the Soviet Union. Jews did not constitute a separate nationality but a people victimized by their milieu. Jewish capital must be condemned, together with Aryan capital. However, the stereotype implied in Marx's and Kautsky's view of the Jews now came to haunt communism, especially in Germany, where that party had to compete with the radical right for allegiance. Karl Radek, the emissary of the Comintern to Germany, in 1923 praised the Nazi martyr Albert Leo Schlageter who had fought the French occupation of the Ruhr, and at the same time called for an end to both "circumcised and uncircumcised capital."[42]

The message was plain enough. It was repeated after 1930, when the Communist leader Heinz Neumann called on the Nazi masses to join the Communists in a common struggle and to end the "fratricidal war." At the same time Jews were all but eliminated from the Central Committee of the Communist Party and from most of its press.[43] Soviet policy provided encouragement and leadership to the German Communist Party here as in all other questions. Stalin was winning his fight against Trotsky and anti-Semitism had once again become fashionable in Russia. But racism was not involved here. On the contrary, the objective was that "vanishing of Judaism" for which Karl Marx had called, and which would leave the individual Jew a fully integrated member of the proletariat. The tragedy was that a radical denial of racism was combined with the accusation that the Jews themselves were racist. Ideas of conspiracy again played their part in both Germany and Russia, this time not in a Jewish-Bolshevik conspiracy, but in a "Jewish-Zionist" or "Jewish-cosmopolitan" conspiracy, supposedly directed against Communist ideas of equality and against the German and Russian nations.

On the face of it, the Communist position merely perpetuated the older attitudes which had prevailed in the eighteenth century when the emancipation of the Jews was being advocated: to the individual Jew all rights, to the Jews as a group none. However, in practice the individual Jew in the party tended to be viewed with suspicion as a potential fifth column. After 1918, even the most radical negation of racism could embrace a belief in the Jewish stereotype and in a Jewish conspiracy. The strength of racism in postwar Europe was not solely confined to the radical right, but spread overtly or covertly throughout society and politics.

In 1930 even the German Social Democrats were wary of putting up Jewish candidates for public office in Germany, not only because Jews were thought to be troublesome intellectuals but also because by that time the radical right determined the debate about the national future.[44] Left or center had to argue on the terrain occupied by the racist right, and this may well have been one of the Nazis' principal victories before seizing power. It was in Germany that the right achieved this advantage. Austria and Hungary had undergone similar social and political experiences following the war, but there reactionary régimes had brought at least temporary stability. The Weimar Republic did not get much rest, for political disturbance was followed by the worst inflation any nation in Europe had known. By 1930 even some German Social Democrats were stressing the importance of the "Aryan Engels" rather than the "Jewish Marx."

This condition of the left was not confined to Germany alone, although it was there that it was to have the most momentous consequences. In east central Europe, while the left was usually characterized as "Jewish" by the right, in reality it was nowhere unconditionally sympathetic toward the Jews. For example, it was sadly ironic that during the Hungarian revolution of 1919, led by Jews, anti-Jewish riots and pogroms were instigated by sections of the working class. Anti-Jewish feeling sprang from the grass roots of the party, not only in Hungary but in Rumania as well, where socialist leaders at times made common cause with anti-Semites.[45]

In Poland, the Social Democratic Party was helpful to the Jews, as was its German counterpart, and its relation with the Jewish socialist Bund were good, especially in times of increasing Jewish persecution. However, the Pilsudski dictatorship forced Socialists into alliance with the other Polish parties and the Bund was left isolated.[46]

Although the penetration of racism into the left must not be overplayed, by virtue of this penetration the Jews were further isolated and deprived of effective allies. Most Jews in Europe were living normal and settled lives, deploring racism but thinking that this too would pass. The deeper racist trends of the postwar world were lost on them and on most of their fellow men. Highly visible, yet isolated and deprived of stout and uncompromising allies, Jews were ripe for the picking by a racist policy whose time had apparently come. The position of the assimilated central European Jews was, for all their relative prosperity and security, not unlike the position of their often despised eastern European brothers, described by Leo Pinsker as far back as 1882 when he wrote: "For the living, the Jew is a dead man; for the natives an alien and a vagrant; for property holders a beggar; for the poor and exploited a millionaire; for patriots a man without country; for all classes, a hated rival."[47] The history of racism in Europe had encouraged this state of affairs, though it alone was hardly responsible for its existence. Racism had always exploited every opportunity that came its way, and the biggest of these was just around the corner.

War and revolution were the prelude to the transformation of racist theory into practice. The theory itself had not changed ever since its formulation in the prewar years. Through the eugenics movement, the so-called science of race had forged ahead, but it was the "mystery" of race that became more deeply rooted as a result of the war. Germany and Austria, where such mystique had always found a home, were precisely those nations most directly affected by the aftermath of the war. As we saw, the German Workers Party was born in the Munich revolution and as part of the Thule Bund, the very name of which was meant to evoke the Aryan north. There, Dietrich Eckart of the Thule Bund, the political mentor of Adolf Hitler, expounded his racist anti-Semitism, which blamed all evil upon the Jews. It was in Munich that Alfred Rosenberg, in close touch with the exiled Russian Black Hundreds, began to write his *Myth of the Twentieth Century* (*Der Mythus des 20. Jahrhunderts*, 1930), which saw in the world war the beginning of a world revolution, but hardly that of which Lenin had dreamed. The race-soul was rising up from the blood of the wartime martyrs, breaking through to victory. Racism was the one true "people's Church," which would replace Christianity.

The actual situation after the war encouraged the production and spread of racist theory. Germany, which because of the war and revolution became the center of racist activity, also produced popular handbooks of racism that were widely read. L. Claus in *The Nordic Soul* (*Die Nordische Seele*, 1930), for example, held that the race-soul produced by the Nordic blood was the font of all creativity, regardless of the Aryan's outward appearance.[48] This "idealistic heresy" was attacked by the most prolific writer of popular books on race in postwar Germany, Hans F. K. Günther, whose *Racial Science of the German People* (*Rassenkunde des deutschen Volkes*, 1922) defined and illustrated once more the racial stereotypes of beautiful Aryan and ugly Jew. However, Günther attempted to preserve some ties to scientific observation by contending that no pure racial type existed, only less perfect, less pure types.[49] Yet all Aryans in one way or another shared in their "ideal-type," while Jews possessed the dominant traits of their race.

These books added nothing new to racial thought; they were simply summaries in popular form of previous theory. But it is worth noting that after 1918 such popularizations appeared for the most part in Germany rather than in other European nations, and that they were symptomatic of the fact that this nation was moving to the forefront of racist thought, though as yet Germany was not the only nation girding itself for what Lucy Dawidowicz has called "the war against the Jews."

CHAPTER TWELVE

From Theory to Practice

T HE HURRICANE which had swept through Europe after the
First World War destroyed many a dike that had protected
Jews against terror, defamation, and racism. Governments
proved too weak or too unwilling to restrain the nationalist fury
which followed the abortive revolutions. At the same time, representative government devoted to pluralistic politics was under siege
in central and western Europe, while eastern Europe came under
dictatorship. Everywhere the end of the war ushered in an age of
mass politics and mass movements which advocated a definition of
democracy different from that of parliamentary government. Political participation was defined by acting out a political liturgy in
mass movements or in the streets and by seeking security through
national myths and symbols which left little or no room for those
who were different.[1] The war had transformed politics into a drama
built upon shared emotions. Racism all too easily provided unity to
this drama as it was played out on the European stage.

At first the breakthrough to racist practice was confined to social
and political organizations which did not necessarily reflect government policy. We saw that after 1918 in Germany, for example,
student fraternities, veterans organizations, and certain political
parties closed their doors to Jews. There had always been groups
which had excluded Jews on racial grounds, but now these moved
from the fringe into the center of middle-class life, basing themselves upon "Aryan clauses" of membership. Conservative parties

in central and eastern Europe followed suit, as did various National
Socialist movements which were given a new impetus by the war.
The Great Depression completed the work which had been begun
by war and revolution.

It could well be said that the war against the Jews[2] began after
the First World War as a skirmish and in the 1930's became a full-
fledged offensive. It is this offensive against the Jews with which we
must now be concerned, analyzing the degree to which various European nations participated. Racism provided the dynamic for this
attack, sometimes overtly and other times disguised. The war against
the Jews during the 1930's went least well in western Europe, best
in central Europe, and not badly in eastern Europe; but everywhere
past history determined how well racism was able to penetrate the
nation.

England had lent a hand in the evolution of racism, but her racism
was directed against blacks rather than Jews, and within England
had concentrated on eugenics rather than upon creating an Aryan
nation. Thus England was not receptive to a racial war waged against
Jews. Sir Oswald Mosley was to find it impossible to light the flame
which was burning so brightly in Germany. Indeed, at first the British
Union of Fascists paid little attention to Jews. It was not until 1934,
when the Black Shirts were faltering, that anti-Semitism came to the
fore as a device intended to revive their political fortunes. The example of Nazi success may have played a part in the adoption of this
policy.[3] The Jewish stereotype was now disseminated and violence
against the Jews became more frequent, but the Union was not able
to sustain the momentum.[4]

When parliamentary government drifted into a crisis in 1931, this
was solved by the creation of a national government which kept the
traditional British representative institutions intact. No private armies
were allowed to operate as had been the case in Germany before Hitler became chancellor. The Public Order Act of January 1, 1937, which
forbade the wearing of uniforms and also political demonstrations,
was obeyed even by the Black Shirts (for a satirical comment on the
Act by the British Fascists, see Plate 14). To be sure, there were small
splinter groups such as that of Arnold Leese, who as early as 1935

suggested gassing the Jews.[5] But these counted for nothing in British politics, and neither did the British Union of Fascists at the precise time when German racial policy was moving toward its climax. The war against the Jews in England never had a chance.

Spain was another European nation which proved relatively immune to racist penetration. The Fascist Falange sometimes used anti-Jewish rhetoric, but it generally rejected racism, although in the 1930's a few leading members of the Franco régime were influenced by the Action Française.[6] But anti-Semitism was of no importance in Spain, while neighboring Portugal even offered asylum to some of the persecuted German Jews. Purity of blood may have been a concept, however vague, in the sixteenth-century struggle against the Marranos; but by the twentieth century it was no longer a relevant issue.

There was no breakthrough of racism in France either, though she sailed closer to the wind than any other western nation. The prewar tradition of racism and anti-Semitism was still alive, and it inspired several political movements between the wars; yet France never experienced the cycle of defeat, revolution, counter-revolution, and inflation that was instrumental in transforming racial theory into practice in Germany.

The French political right had been dominated by the Action Française, but even before the First World War members had left the organization of Charles Maurras in order to pursue a more radical course. After the war Fascist organizations were founded which saw themselves competing with the Action Française. Between 1925, when Charles Valois, coming from the Action Française, founded his "Faisceau," and 1936, when Jacques Doriot, the former Communist leader, founded the "Parti Populaire Française" (PPF), a series of Fascist leagues sprang up, none of which assumed great political importance. In 1929 one such league, the "Francistes," revived the title of Drumont's *Libre Parole* for their own newspaper denouncing Jews, Freemasons, and blacks (though in 1943 a colonial affiliate of the Francistes had black members).[7] The Francistes were not alone in attempting to claim the prewar anti-Semitic heritage and to project it into interwar France.

Now Bolshevism was added to the list of "Jewish conspiracies," as everywhere else. For example, the league "Solidarité Française," founded in 1933 by the perfume magnate François Coty, although hostile to Jews, concentrated on the war against Bolshevism. Typically, Coty also gave millions to the Action Française.[8] The leagues were formally opposed to Charles Maurras, but in reality they were not far removed from his ideas and secretly admired the old anti-Dreyfusard.[9] However, this was not true of the only large French Fascist movement, for its leader came from the Communist Party and not from the Action Française.

Jacque Doriot's "Parti Populaire Française" (1936) was the only sizable Fascist movement in France. Even so, it only attracted about 250,000 sympathizers.[10] Two catalysts led to the formation of this party and also seemed to give fascism in France generally a new lease on life. A number of right-wing veterans groups, joined by the Action Française and other conservative movements, marched on the Chamber of Deputies on February 6, 1934. The massive and violent street action failed to overthrow the republic, but it caused Doriot and others to show a heightened concern for national unity and to move toward opposition to the republic at an accelerated pace. The formation of the Popular Front government under Léon Blum in June 1936 strengthened the opposition to the republic by the leagues, who tended to become hysterical and to see in this government the realization of their worst fears: "France is delivered into the hands of the Jews."[11] At the same time, Doriot advocated friendship with Germany,[12] and became an admirer of these National Socialists.[13]

Until 1937, the newspaper of the Parti Populaire, entitled *Émancipation Nationale*, hardly mentioned Jews, but saw Communist conspiracies everywhere. The exceptions were the Jews of Algeria, who were castigated for their supposed disloyalty to France, and the anti-Jewish note struck here may have been a bridge to a more general anti-Semitism.[14] Growing admiration for the Nazis also propelled the movement in that direction. Maurice-Ivan Sicard, editor of the party's paper, at first disclaimed any anti-Semitic intent or racist ideas,[15] but this was to change with the German victory during the Second World War. In 1944 he received the "Prix de la France Aryenne," established by the Parti Populaire, and now he proclaimed his allegiance to "race and soil." At the same time he called for the expulsion of the Jews from France which, given the date, amounted to support for the Nazi final solution.[16]

Yet it is typical of the French situation that neither Sicard's nor Doriot's movement turned racist until the German victory and occupation of Paris where Doriot's party had its headquarters. Once Sicard began to collaborate with the Nazis, he remained consistent even after Germany's defeat in the Second World War. Writing under the pseudonym of Saint-Paulien, he nostalgically recalled the heroic times of Nazi conquest.[17]

The Doriot movement was never a vital political force in France. Instead, French fascism and racism became the province of intellectuals. All over Europe during the 1930's some intellectuals sympathized with ideas of race and soil, but in France they became the chief custodians of such ideas. Here alone racism became a literary fashion rather than a serious political movement.

The group of young writers associated with the newspaper *Je Suis Partout* (founded in 1930) combined admiration for Drumont and Maurras with admiration for war, in which, as they were fond of exclaiming, existing reality could be destroyed at any moment. Though racists themselves, their self-esteem and patriotism required that they distinguish Nazi racism from their own brand. They attempted to do so by stressing that their anti-Jewish racism was more moderate and less irrational. Thus Robert Brasillach, a leader of this group, criticized the Nazis for making race into a metaphysical doctrine (whatever that meant) while he himself considered all Jews as an alien people with undesirable characteristics.[18] Lucien Rebatet, another important young Fascist writer, declared in 1938 that "we are not racists," but at the same time took pride in the fact that France had a powerful anti-Semitic tradition, and called for a clean separation between Frenchmen and Jews.[19]

Apparent moderation was combined with the belief in the "Jewish-Bolshevik rule" of Russia and in the Jewish stereotype which appeared in the cartoons of *Je Suis Partout*.[20] But the admiration of Nazi violence led to a more stringent attitude, which these young writers confused with a Nietzschean *élan*. Thus Lucien Rebatet, in his celebrated *The Rubbish Heap* (*Les Décombres*, 1942), asserted in a kind of ecstasy that thousands of Jews should be killed and the rest deported. Jewish colonies could be established in Russia or in the British Empire.[21] For these young writers, racism in the last resort was the result of a longing to become Nietzschean supermen; to glory in violence. In 1942 also Brasillach compared Georges Sorel to Alfred Rosenberg (the "French master of violence" and the "German master of violence").[22] It was an incredible illusion to characterize the author of the *Myth of the Twentieth Century* in this way and to confuse Sorel's myth of violence with Rosenberg's racial myth. But it was an illusion that these young writers shared with many older men like Sicard, who volunteered to join the French SS Brigade Charlemagne.

More famous than Brasillach and Rebatet, Louis-Ferdinand Céline evolved from a concern with human degeneracy in his *Journey to the End of the Night* (*Voyage au Bout de la Nuit*, 1932) to call for a massacre of the Jews in *Bagatelles pour un Massacre* (1937).[23] Elsewhere in Europe, important literary figures became Fascists in the 1930's usually in support of strong local Fascist or Nazi movements. Thus Gottfried Benn, one of Germany's major poets, found momentary fulfillment in National Socialism. His poetry was replete with the imagery of a decadent and disease-ridden civilization, similar to that Céline had described in *Journey to the End of the Night*. Fascism gave to such men absolute values which they had previously lacked, as well as the thrill of associating with a virile mass movement. Ezra Pound, who found no such fascism at home, came to live in Italy where it existed. The young and politically isolated French Fascist intellectuals had to look abroad for inspiration (though many passed in and out of the Doriot movement).

Neither fascism nor racism made a breakthrough in France because that nation was relatively stable beneath all the apparent turbulence and changes of government. Moreover, for all the French anti-Semitic and racist tradition, a Catholic and largely rural nation was too conservative to accept a racist dynamic easily. Finally, the

Fascists were caught between their own chauvinism and their admiration for the Nazis; exaltation at the Nuremberg party meetings which many of them attended and concern for French power and might were inherently irreconcilable. In short, racism in France became a literary movement, unburdened by political responsibility or the need to attract a mass following.[24]

Racism was rarely openly embraced in eastern Europe either, however much the Jews were persecuted. Here in the 1930's the Jews benefitted from the existence of radical rightist anti-Semitic movements which threatened the established postwar dictatorships. Jews thus found allies in governments bent upon suppressing such rightist parties, which threatened law and order as well as the existing political and social power structures. The dictatorships of nations like Hungary and Rumania were founded upon an alliance with the traditional social and political hierarchies, and therefore had to protect the inherited order against those who wanted to overthrow it. Moreover, in nations where Marxist parties were banned and Soviet subversion considered a constant threat, the danger of revolution came from the radical right and not from the radical left.

When King Carol proclaimed himself dictator of Rumania in 1938, he did so in order to counter the mounting pressure of the Legion of the Archangel Michael.[25] This movement was founded in 1927, and its ambition was to transform Rumania into a dictatorship supported by peasants and workers. The Iron Guard—the Legion's mass organization, created in 1930—had a fanatical hatred of Jews, whom it saw as a symbol of the Rumanian middle class exploiting the people.[26] The Jews did indeed constitute a large part of the middle class of Rumania, while the Iron Guard was largely peasant in composition, led by ex-students under the young leader Corneliu Zelea-Codreanu. Codreanu was a National Socialist, opposed to finance capitalism and corruption (both of which were all-prevalent in Rumania). He advocated a national rebirth, which he defined in terms of blood, soil, and Christianity. Codreanu did not use the usual vocabulary of race, and indeed, according to one of his post-Second World War admirers, he was married by a

priest who was a converted Jew.[27] Nevertheless, he ultimately believed that the Jews wanted to take over much of Rumania in order
to create a new Palestine.[28] More to the point, the Jews had invented Bolshevism; they were both the exploiters and the subverters
of Rumania. Codreanu was a Christian mystic and ascetic, who
talked constantly about Christ's sacrifice and drew parallels between the resurrection of Christ and that of the nation. Still, his
view of the Jews was in fact not easy to distinguish from racism,
just as his admiration for Adolf Hitler was sincere. The Jews were
the absolute evil. Codreanu was a charismatic leader, and after his
assassination in 1938 by order of King Carol, the Iron Guard was
never again able to produce an effective leadership. Horia Sima, its
new chief, counted on Hitler's victories in the Second World War
in order to smooth the Guard's way to power.

The Nazis did force King Carol's abdication in 1940, and General Ion Antonescu, the new dictator, attempted to rule jointly with
the Iron Guard. Yet when a power struggle between them developed, he crushed the Iron Guard with Hitler's support and its leaders were sent into exile. But during the five months in 1941 when
the Iron Guard had been General Antonescu's partner in the
Rumanian dictatorship, some of the most brutal pogroms on record
had slaughtered over 1,000 Jews in Bucharest alone.[29]

In Hungary, also, the conservative dictatorship of Nicolas
Horthy confronted a radical right-wing movement, but this never
gained the strength and the dynamic of the Iron Guard. The Arrow
Cross too wanted to overthrow the Horthy régime and the semi-
feudal social classes on which it was based. But Ferenc Szálasi, its
leader, was a dreamer rather than an activist, and his mystical ideal
of "Hungarism" offered little that was concrete and might bring
about a new order in Hungary. He talked about building an indus-
trialized and highly developed peasant state, but in the last resort it
was the call for Hungarian supremacy, both internally over all
minorities and externally in the Danube Basin, which gave the
movement its dynamic and appeal. Yet the Arrow Cross, like the
Iron Guard, was able to rally masses of workers and peasants to its
banner.[30] The radical right received such support in Rumania and

Hungary because it was the first movement to involve the masses in politics, and it was doing so in nations where no Marxist parties existed to fulfill this function.

Szálasi's nebulous "Hungarism" involved condemnation of the Jewish race, even if this did not occupy as important a place in the thought of the Arrow Cross as in the ideology of the Iron Guard. Indeed, Szálasi refused to support the deportation of Jews from Hungary.[31] Yet, in the end, Szálasi did not matter very much, for he became the Führer of Hungary only from October 1944 to February 1945, at a time when the Soviet armies were already occupying the nation.

The radical right, with its fanatical hatred of the Jews, was not able to overthrow the conservative dictatorships in either Hungary or Rumania during the war. Thus, while Jews suffered some harassment in these nations, no systematic anti-Jewish policy was instituted until German pressure forced the reluctant dictators to act. Racism was no part of the policy pursued by the traditional régimes, which feared all change.

Poland was the exception to this pattern in eastern Europe. There, as we saw in the last chapter, the dictatorship after Pilsudski intermittently pursued a racist policy. Violence against the Jews was even encouraged at times, leading one French newspaper to compare the rule of the colonels to Hitler's Third Reich.[32] A good example of the Polish government's attitude toward the Jews is provided by the fact that whenever the question of German-Jewish refugees was raised in international councils, the Polish government insisted that its "surplus Jews" be considered as well, by which it meant the 3 million Jews in Poland. This gave all nations an easy excuse to prevent the emigration of German Jews, for behind them in line stood millions of Jews from Poland.[33] Yet even Poland, racial attitudes notwithstanding, as a Catholic nation endeavored to avoid using the term "race."[34]

Those Balkan regions under Italian Fascist influence pursued a more moderate course. Thus the "Ustaschi" movement, which, under Anton Pavelic, took over Croatia, did instigate pogroms. However, while they imprisoned some Jews in camps, under Italian pressure they left most of them alive and refused to allow the Nazis to deport them. Moreover, Pavelic attempted to exempt a not inconsiderable number of Jews from such measures, on the Italian model.[35]

II

Italy protected her own Jews whenever she could. In October 1938, Mussolini had proclaimed his racial laws, which forbade mixed marriages and excluded Jews from military service and large landholdings; but he immediately exempted from the law all those Jews who had taken part in the First World War or in the Fascist movement. Moreover, Mussolini himself put out the slogan: "Discrimination and not persecution."[36] The racial laws were designed to give a fascism grown old in power a new dynamic—a task in which they were bound to fail as Italy had no anti-Jewish racist tradition. They were also a gesture of friendship toward Hitler, but this was not very effective either. Indeed, the Nazis marveled at the failure to enforce the laws. Mussolini was no racist. Like Adolf Hitler he was a consummate politician, yet he differed from Hitler in being unencumbered by the weight of much ideological baggage and apocalyptical vision. Hitler viewed every major issue in terms of his eschatology, and for him solutions were to be absolute and "final." For Mussolini the future was open-ended; the vague ideal of the new Fascist man would ensure a positive outcome. This outlook allowed him to maintain a cynically flexible position on the racial question. Thus, he could support Zionism at one time when it suited his anti-English policy and threaten Italian Jews with dire consequences if they held a dual allegiance.

By the mid-1930's the suspicion within Fascism of all internationalism, including Zionism, had won out, and this fact, together with some loose notions of an international Jewish conspiracy, no doubt made it easier for the Duce to press for the promulgation of the racial laws. The prominence of Jews among the Italian anti-Fascists certainly helped him make up his mind. On balance, however, such anti-Jewish feelings were probably not as important as the need for a new *élan* and for a gesture toward National Socialism. Mussolini resolved to use the Jews as pawns in his political game. It was only to the good, as far as he was concerned, that he could in this manner frighten them into loyalty to the Fascist state.

The Abyssinian War of 1935 facilitated his unprincipled racism. Here the concept of race had been applied to the relationship between Italians and Ethiopians. Fraternization with natives was said to show lack of "racial dignity." That war had propelled the concept of race into Italian consciousness, but directed against blacks, not Jews. At first, Mussolini hoped for support from the Zionists in order to break the worldwide sanctions against Italy. When, in spite of some efforts to persuade the British to desert the boycott, the Zionists proved ineffective, Mussolini thought that international Jewish organizations had turned against him. As a result, the Duce felt that the world Jewish conspiracy against fascism had to be destroyed.[37]

Some high Fascist officials, such as Roberto Farinacci, were satisfied with the racial laws because they had been anti-Semites since the 1930's, encouraged by their admiration for the Nazis. But the Fascist-Nazi front against the Jews of which they dreamed never materialized, since generals and state officials collaborated in order to save as many Jews from the Nazis as possible. The few Italian racists were isolated, at least until the Republic of Saló—that part of northern Italy which Mussolini governed after the Italian surrender and his flight from allied custody.

Giovanni Preziosi became the head of a newly established racial office in 1944. He had made his periodical *La Vita Italiana* into a mouthpiece of Italian anti-Semitism. Preziosi had also translated the *Protocols* into Italian in 1921, and clearly believed in the world Jewish conspiracy. But this racial office had no true importance, for the Nazis were calling the tune in the Republic of Saló and Preziosi was merely their collaborator.[38] Julius Evola, the other important Italian theoretician of race, stressed the mystery of race, the "racial soul," and paid scant attention to the biological and anthropological dimensions. Evola believed in a pure Italian race; but as he had to invent it, he simply transposed qualities of the German Aryan to a mythical "mediterranean Aryan race."[39] Evola's dream was the formation of a common European-Aryan front. It is small wonder that he praised the SS as a biological and heroic élite, and compared it to the medieval Ghibelline chivalry.[40] But unlike his peers elsewhere, few Italians took him seriously.

After the Second World War, when he became the elder statesman of the neo-Fascists in Italy, Evola attempted to justify his racism. It had been an attitude of mind, he claimed, at best eugenics. For all that, Evola still believed that the Jews remained subversives waging a secret war against Italy through high finance and Bolshevik revolutions.[41]

III

The future of racism in Europe was largely bound up with the failure or success of Nazi Germany. As that nation seemed to be about to dominate Europe, all racist policy was eventually set within that context.

Racism became the official German government policy on January 30, 1933, when Hitler took over the chancellorship of the Reich. He came to power in a coalition with the conservative German Peoples Party (DNVP). But whatever hope there was that the conservatives might restrain a racist policy, it was misplaced. They were out of the government less than one year later, and furthermore had themselves made full use of racism in order to mobilize the masses.[42] Had they and not Hitler triumphed, German Jews admittedly, though excluded from German life, would not have been driven out of Germany altogether or murdered. As it was, Hitler began his Jewish policy immediately upon accession to power. This policy showed a rhythm of increasingly harsh measures against the Jews, moves that were always preceded by attempts to stir up the masses against them in order to appear the follower of public opinion rather than its instigator.[43]

Mass murder was not yet any part of the Nazi program, which called for the repeal of Jewish citizenship only, however much the S.A. sang about Jewish blood dripping from the knife. On a more respectable level, Joseph Goebbels confined himself to analogies in a Nazi catechism of 1931. Certainly, he wrote, Jews are also human, that has never been doubted. But the flea too is an animal, although an unpleasant one; that is why men do not protect and fatten the flea but seek to render him harmless.[44] We have already seen the important and ominous role that animal analogies played in racism. Moderation in official policy and extremism in the streets were meant to confuse Jews and Germans alike. It seemed at first as if Hitler would simply carry out the official Nazi program, excluding Jews from German life.

Hitler easily found willing collaborators during the first phases of Jewish policy, which involved exclusion and emigration. This would not prove quite so easy during the "final solution." For example, Baldur von Schirach, the leader of the Hitler Youth, and his wife both protested against Jewish deportations after Frau von Schirach had witnessed by accident a Jewish roundup in Holland. Hitler did not react favorably to such interference with his plans.[45] However, those who took part in the initial stages of anti-Jewish policy cannot be absolved of blame for what happened later. Once racism became the official policy of a powerful and dynamic government, the doors were opened to its logical conclusion. Racism was, after all, a total commitment. But for most men, including many Nazis, a policy of mass murder would have been unthinkable in the enlightened twentieth century. One could accept the Nazi propaganda that Jews were aliens in Germany and, assuming this was all that was needed, close one's eyes to any measure which went further than expelling them from the nation. Furthermore, Nazi anti-Jewish policy unfolded very slowly indeed. As late as 1935, many Jews re-emigrated into Germany, having been fooled into security together with many other Jews who had stayed.[46]

Adolf Hitler never acted in a straightforward manner. On the one hand he had his anti-Jewish obsession; on the other, he proceeded slowly, and at times even pulled back too eager collaborators. Thus, for example, of all the versions submitted to him of the famed Nuremberg Laws of 1935, he chose the mildest, as we shall see.[47] Hitler's sense of political timing, which was to prove so superb in foreign policy, was also applied to the evolution of the Jewish question. He always appeared to move under pressure or provocation,

as in the murder of the German diplomat Ernst vom Rath by a
young Jew in Paris in 1938; but in reality everything was planned
to lead up to the final solution.

Hitler linked the "living space" he thought the German people
needed in the east with the extermination of the Jews. In his mind
both formed a single great ambition, for the wide-open spaces and
the presence of a native population enslaved would enable him to
annihilate the Jewish "enemy" without the furor this might cause in
Germany herself. The program of euthanasia which took place in
the midst of the Reich had to be discontinued (at least officially)
when people became aware of what was going on.[48] This experience must have strengthened Hitler's resolve to combine the conquest of Poland with his final solution. Hitler's goal and policy seem
clear in retrospect, but they were not of course so obvious at the
time. The Führer made sure to keep his real feelings and plans to
himself, even if he hinted at them to some of his closest collaborators.

Adolf Hitler himself thus becomes the key to Nazi racist policy
as the true prophet of race, who drove the theory to its logical conclusion. How did Hitler become an adept of race, and what kind of
racism led to his passionate commitment and blind faith? Here we
must pause to discuss the intellectual development of the single
most important figure in the history of European racism.

The young Hitler imbibed his racism in Vienna, where it was so
pervasive, and strengthened it by associations in the years immediately following the First World War. Perhaps he had already
become a radical anti-Semite in Vienna (we shall never know for
certain), but he grew to be a more widely read racist in Munich
after 1918.

The anti-Semitic influences upon Hitler in Vienna must have been
many: the Lueger movement, whose final phase he witnessed; the
more violent Pan-Germans of von Schönerer; and last but not least,
the racist sects who purveyed the "mystery of race." It seems that
the greatest influence upon him derived from the sects of Lanz von
Liebenfels and Guido von List, both of which propagated this mixture of racism and theosophy. He probably read their literature, for

in his conversations many decades later the talk constantly centered upon spiritualism, secret sciences, and the Jew characterized as an "evil principle," not a human creature of flesh and blood.[49] But Hitler adopted none of the cynicism of Lueger, nor his Catholicism, and certainly he himself ignored the theories of the science of race.

After the First World War, similar influences made themselves felt. A list of books which Hitler is purported to have borrowed from the National Sozialistisches Institute—a lending library near Munich founded and supported by an early party member between 1919 and 1921—includes all the staples of racism: Houston Stewart Chamberlain, Richard Wagner, Langbehn, and no less than three books by Max Maurenbrecher, who was a Volkish racist opposed both to Jews and the Christian Church. There are, moreover, several books like *Luther and the Jews* or *Goethe and the Jews* which point out the supposed hatred of Jews by these German cultural heroes. A watered-down version of Rohling's *Talmud Jew* is also on the list, together with books on social democracy as a Jewish movement and Nicostenski's *The Bolshevik's Ecstasy of Blood* (*Der Blutrausch des Bolshevismus*). Interestingly enough, Hitler also glanced at Zola's novel *D'Argent*, which contains the Jewish capitalist stereotype. Treitschke on the Jews is represented in the list as well. Hitler must, therefore, have been familiar with the usual racist literature, except for that with scientific pretensions. It should be added that slightly less than half the books Hitler took out had nothing to do with Jews, but dealt with medieval Austrian and German history, as well as with rightist discussions of contemporary affairs.[50] Hitler was no great reader. He apparently believed that one must read the end of a book first, and claimed that he could get its message by jumping around in its pages.[51] For racist literature, however, this would have been no great matter since its polemical content could be grasped without systematic reading.

Of greater significance than any reading was Hitler's encounter with the playwright and journalist Dietrich Eckart in Munich. For Eckart, the Jew was the evil principle *tout court*. The Jew was responsible for Germany's defeat, for Bolshevism, and for the censorship of Eckart's own writings, which in his opinion lacked the recognition they deserved. Such ideas and paranoia filled Eckart's newssheet *Auf Gut Deutsch* (*In Plain German*) (see Plate 12). Through his friend Alfred Rosenberg, Eckart had become acquainted with the *Protocols of the Elders of Zion*. He must have subsequently passed them on to Hitler. All three men believed the *Protocols* to be basic to an understanding of Jews and their Bolshevist, socialist, or liberal fellow travelers. Yet Eckart did not want to see a violent solution to the Jewish question, and inasmuch as he gave thought to practical measures against the Jews, these involved the reinstitution of ghettos and the total exclusion of Jews from German life.[52] Moreover, for Eckart the Jews were always vital as a foil to the Germans, providing the necessary stimulus to the Aryan "Lichtmensch."[53]

The program of extermination in order to make first Germany and then Europe "Judenrein" seems to have been a conclusion which Adolf Hitler himself drew from his own war against the Jews. Hitler was an outsider at the time when he formulated his racial thought; but what distinguished him from the prophets, private scholars, and poets who elaborated the "mystery of race" was a greater practicality and a superb political instinct. As he wrote in *Mein Kampf*, a world view must become political reality if it is to be taken seriously;[54] and in this cause he was willing to compromise, to use policy and tactics, until the time was ripe. Men like Chamberlain, Langbehn, or Eckart, to mention only a few, despised all compromise and thought that they stood above the hurly burly of politics. Hitler quite rightly, from his point of view, inveighed against such Volkish "wandering scholars," as he called them, who lacked all political sense.[55]

When Hitler became chancellor on January 30, 1933, the way was prepared for an implementation of the Nazi program. He assumed power at a time of near civil war in Germany, and racism, which had allied itself long ago with middle-class morality and the forces of law and order, could point to a better future. The Nazis and the conservatives promised to restore order and to reinvigorate morality and decency in public and private life. But that for a good many people now meant the acceptance of racism as a bulwark of such morality, law, and order, against the negative principles of Bolshevism, communism, and the Jews.

The alliance of racism and middle-class ideals, which we have stressed throughout, meant that even those who were not deeply anti-Semitic could tolerate the initially moderate actions against the Jews and find a new pride and respectability in being Germans. Many must have voted Nazi, as one witness tells us, because it was good to see clean-cut young men march through the streets, a sight that promised order in the midst of chaos and exemplified energy in the midst of despair.[56] After January 1933, official policy at first expressed feelings already long current and from which, as we have shown earlier, even the left was not entirely free. Communists and Nazis had collaborated in the famed Berlin transport workers strike of 1932, but more importantly, the Communist Party even earlier had tried to stop Nazi growth by taking over some of its national appeal. The Social Democrats were reluctant to put up Jews for public office in these last years of the republic, and the Communists all but eliminated them from its Central Committee.[57] Nazi racism came to be in the center of discussion and everyone else had to come to terms with its point of view.

Caution characterized Jewish policy immediately after the take-over. The position of Jews was to be undermined legally or by administrative means.[58] Nevertheless, the S.A. (Sturmabteilung) provoked anti-Jewish riots in towns like Breslau, which caused not only material damage but also an atmosphere of terror. Hitler did not want this kind of individual action unless it was controlled from above, for it would give the troublesome S.A. undue authority, and it was opposed to the rationally constructed system of Jewish exclusion which the Führer had in mind.[59]

In order to capture the terror for his own ends and to set the signposts for his Jewish policy, Hitler approved the boycott against Jewish businesses on April 1, 1933. While many influential Jewish corporations and newspapers were exempt from this action, Hitler took the opportunity to push ahead against the Jews on an apparently unrelated front. Jewish lawyers and judges were removed from German courts.[60] As always, one type of action against a particular segment within the Jewish community was used as a cover to take parallel kinds of action against the entire Jewish community as well. Still more far-reaching, a law was prepared and enacted which excluded Jewish officials from all levels of government. Nevertheless, there was near chaos in matters concerning the treatment of Jews. Every individual German state like Saxony, Prussia, or Bavaria made use of its local prerogatives in order to go its own way, with either harsh or moderate measures.

Yet, for all this confusion, it was clear even to those officials of the Ministry of the Interior who opposed racism that there was nothing they could do on behalf of the Jews themselves, and that at most, they could only protect those living in mixed marriages or of mixed blood.[61] On September 15, 1935, the eve of the "Party Day of Freedom" when the "Laws to Protect German Blood" (to become known as the Nuremberg Laws) were to be proclaimed, all that was certain was that Hitler opposed terrorism against individual Jews,[62] and that he was committed to excluding Jews from German life. It was not at all clear how he wanted to define a Jew, nor whether he intended to go beyond the Nazi Party program in the handling of the Jewish question.

Hitler chose the mildest version of the several drafts submitted to him for these Nuremberg Laws. Jews were forbidden to marry or to have extramarital relations with Aryans, forbidden to keep Aryan servants, or to fly the Nazi flag.[63] Hitler subsequently declared that this law was his final word on the Jewish question.[64] This was the identical assertion he would make after every one of his moves in foreign policy, only to break his word later. The technique, which confused foreign statesmen, also confused both German Jews, who could live with such a law, and many other Germans as well. No definition of Jew was given, and this raised hopes that an eventual definition would be generous and extend the concept of mixed blood to dubious cases which would then be exempt from the law. Hitler, as we now know, intended the very opposite; but for the time being, he basked in the image of a moderate even while gaining flexibility to be used not for, but against the Jews.

The question of who was a Jew was settled by the bureaucracy—

a Jew must have at least three Jewish grandparents. The Jew who had two Jewish grandparents was a Jew only if he belonged to the religious community and had married a Jewess. All others of mixed blood were full citizens of the Reich. Even if a German converted to Judaism, he would remain a citizen.[65] The apparent generosity allowed in this definition seemed to confirm the hopes of those who thought that Jewish policy had now reached its conclusion.

Further, except for the professions, little was done to undermine the economic status of most German Jews. Certainly between 1933 and the autumn of 1937, a few highly visible and powerful Jewish businesses were expropriated, mostly newspapers and department stores; but in spite of the boycott of April 1, 1933, Jewish merchants continued to earn an acceptable living. Yet the portents of the future were there, even if they were generally ignored. For example, in September 1935 a complete list of Jews in Germany, citizens or not, was compiled—an action without which the final solution could never have worked at all. That Himmler and the Gestapo ordered such lists made was ominous in another respect: Jewish policy was passing from the feeble hands of the ministries of interior and justice into the hands of the secret police, the SS, and Heinrich Himmler. Finally, the law for the prevention of hereditary sickness proclaimed on July 14, 1933, was not merely the hoped-for fruition of the agitation for eugenics but would eventually lead to euthanasia. Hitler first mentioned euthanasia privately on the Party Day which proclaimed the Nuremberg Laws.[66]

The end of 1937 and beginning of 1938 saw the sharp turn in Jewish policy which corresponded to a general consolidation of the régime. The remaining conservatives left the government and the army high command. Hitler was getting ready for the showdown on foreign policy and in Jewish policy as well. He revealed his secret war plans in November 1937 to the leaders of the government and the army (the Hossbach Protocol). At the same time, he determined to accelerate the expulsion of Jews from Germany. War was to be waged against foreign nations who were the dupes of the Jews, but inside Germany the "Jewish-Bolshevik conspiracy" maintained a fifth column which must also be destroyed.

At a time when the turn in Jewish policy had not yet begun but was about to take place, Hitler himself signaled the action and gave away the course he was to follow. In a speech on April 29, 1937, he said: "I do not want to force the adversary into battle . . . instead, I tell him . . . I want to annihilate you! And then my cleverness will aid me in maneuvering you into a corner so that you cannot strike me, but I can pierce your heart."[67] This statement on the Jewish question standing at the end of one period of Jewish policy and the beginning of another needs no commentary. It explains the gradual disarming of the enemy and the subsequent actions which rendered him an outlaw. The Jewish conspiracy Hitler feared was being brought under control. From the late autumn of 1937 on, hesitation and ambiguities in Jewish policy were no longer permitted. A veritable flood of legislation now poured out of the ministries, and issues left unsettled before were dealt with in rapid order. Jews were excluded from any tax benefits, and from state aids (which they had previously received if they were in financial need); they were finally expelled from all professions.

But the really important first step of the new policy was the "Aryanization" of the economy, now directed by Hermann Göring with vigor. The concentrated attack on Jewish economic life which took place from the winter of 1937 hit every aspect, from banking to retail stores; it was accompanied by local boycott actions, such as those initiated by Julius Streicher in Nuremberg. The greed of the Nazi state was not the sole cause of this Aryanization. Jews had to be warned that their life in Germany was finished, something not so obvious before that time. The economic measures were not as widely publicized as a law passed on March 28, 1938, which deprived the Jewish religious congregations of legal protection: a clear signal to the Jews of what was in store for them—no longer were they to be "legal personalities," and neither would they be able to retain their security. They were now officially deprived of all rights and removed beyond the law. What had been a fact, however disguised, now became public action.[68]

These measures might not have been necessary had the official policy of encouraging Jewish emigration succeeded. But it had failed by 1937, partly because the Jews themselves were reluctant to leave and partly because of the difficulty of finding asylum. Even so, the Nazis had sought to facilitate emigration through economic transfer agreements with Palestine and certain Latin American nations such as Argentina and Chile. But now, as the Jews were being deprived of their livelihood, forced emigration was attempted. Moreover, Jews could take no possessions with them, were permitted only 10 marks per person, and the transfer agreements were allowed to lapse.

The first to be physically expelled from Germany were those Jews who were stateless because they had never bothered to apply for German citizenship. Polish Jews living in Germany were the next. They were much more numerous, and included many who had lived in Germany for a long time without becoming citizens. On October 28 and 29, 1938, the Gestapo arrested 15,000 Polish Jews and forced them across the border. But the Poles did not want what they called "surplus Jews" either, so these men, women, and children lived for a time in a no-man's land, shuffled back and forth.[69] Poland did receive them eventually, but the plight of this miserable group was a portent of what was to follow. The Jew was not wanted anywhere. He was, in fact, stateless at a time when having no nation meant being an outcast.

Polish Jewish emigrants into Germany had never been accepted, and as early as 1919 and again in 1923 the Republican German government had attempted to harass and expel many of them.[70] For the Nazis, such Jews represented the true face of world Jewry, while the more assimilated Jews constituted simply a fifth column. Hitler had made this point in *Mein Kampf*.[71] On January 5, 1938, he gave it legal form by commanding every Jew to adopt the first names of Israel or Sarah.[72] All Jews were alike, whether poor east European emigrants or old German Jewish families. Thus they were made to live out the stereotype. All Jews now dwelt in a no-man's-land, not merely those who were Polish or stateless.

Two events accelerated these anti-Jewish measures. The *Anschluss* with Austria in March 1938 brought 200,000 additional Jews into the Third Reich. Difficult as it was, emigration could hardly take care of an enemy so increased in number. Secondly, on November 7, 1938, Hershel Grünspan, a young Jew whose parents had been among those Polish Jews expelled to no-man's-land, shot and killed Councillor Ernst vom Rath at the German Embassy in Paris. Hitler now had an opportunity to initiate a wave of terror against the Jews that would never again ebb during his rule.

In Austria, Hitler himself sharpened the anti-Jewish measures. Not only was all the Reich's legislation introduced at once, but he personally eliminated the special status of those of mixed blood who in Austria were deprived of that citizenship they had retained in the Reich after the promulgation of the Nuremberg Laws. Even those Jews who had fought in the First World War were no longer given special consideration.[73] Austria was another rehearsal for the future; all the loopholes were closed from the very moment when Austria rejoined the Reich. Even those who were not truly racists were blinded to its consequences by the opportunity to join the greater German community. The attitude of the cardinal archbishop of Vienna, Theodor Innitzer, was typical. In 1933, he rejoiced that the "voice of the blood of the German Volk" was being heard again, although three years later he condemned racism in public. Nevertheless, he welcomed the *Anschluss* enthusiastically, and only had second thoughts when the Church was being attacked and it was too late for action.[74]

Joseph Goebbels, who had been excluded from the formulation of Jewish policies, took the opportunity offered by the murder of vom Rath to unleash anti-Jewish riots. He chose the night of November 9/10, 1938 (the anniversary of the unsuccessful Hitler putsch of 1923). These officially staged riots came to be known as the "Kristallnacht" (Night of Broken Glass) because virtually every synagogue in Germany had its windows smashed and interior destroyed, and the majority were burned to the ground. After the orgy of destruction, 30,000 Jews were taken to the Dachau or Sachsenhausen concentration camps.[75]

The "Kristallnacht" must be seen in the context of the first large wave of arrests of Jews and their transfer to the camps. Most Jews arrested belonged to the wealthier classes, and if they could show emigration papers they were released. Thus, even though the majority left the camps again this time, a precedent had been set as part of the open war against Jews.[76] Hitler, of course, supported the action and personally ordered Himmler, Goebbels's rival, not to interfere.

Göring and Himmler were distressed by Goebbels's action. Göring saw millions of marks worth of usable property destroyed; Himmler saw his plan for an orderly solution to the Jewish question endangered, and his enemy in the eternal struggle for power among the leadership gain a point. As a matter of fact, their fears were unnecessary. Göring was compensated, as the Jews themselves were made to pay a high tax for the damage. Moreover, haphazard Aryanization was now formalized in a long and inclusive list of economic activities forbidden to Jews once and for all. Jewish bank accounts and investments were confiscated. Himmler did not leave empty-handed either. The Jews definitely became charges of the SS; Reinhold Heydrich assumed full charge of the execution of Jewish policy.[77]

The SS wanted to expel all Jews at once, and Göring, who had the overall direction of Jewish policy as titular head of the secret police, wanted during 1939 to concentrate Jews in ghettos. But Hitler, who once again needed a pause after the measures that had been taken, restrained Himmler, Göring, and Heydrich.[78] It was not that they were wrong, but rather that they were premature. At this point, Hitler revealed still more of his plan for the Jews, indeed his final aim. If on April 29, 1937, he had been (according to his own words) about to maneuver the Jews into a corner in order to finish them off, now in a speech on January 30, 1939, he virtually proclaimed their annihilation. The Jews had defeated Germany in the First World War and thus ideals of mercy and humanity were misplaced as far as they were concerned. "Today I want once again to be a prophet: if international Jewish capitalism in and out of Europe should succeed once more in plunging the nations into war, then the result will not be the bolshevizing of this earth but the destruction of the Jewish race in Europe."[79]

Again Hitler made a self-fulfilling prophecy. He himself was going to plunge Europe into war in order to annihilate the Jews.

The myth of Ahasverus, the wandering Jew who wants to destroy Germany through Bolshevism, and who is waiting to rejoice at the desolation of Europe, was evoked and presented as reality.[80] The war Hitler unleashed would be blamed upon the Jews, who would then be destroyed. As Joseph Goebbels wrote on November 16, 1941, the Jews wanted the war and now they had it.[81] From Hitler's point of view, the enemy had simply been hoist by his own petard. Thus, before the outbreak of such a war, the Jews must be set up for destruction but not yet destroyed. Once Poland had been conquered, the work of annihilation could begin.

CHAPTER THIRTEEN

Racism and Mass Murder

THE TRANSITION from theory to practice in Nazi Jewish policy provided the indispensable background to the "final solution of the Jewish question." Those involved—victims and persecutors alike—could not have envisaged the unprecedented mass murder which lay at the end of this policy, even after the harsh turn of the winter of 1937. When Hitler first in secret issued the verbal order for the practical execution of the final solution sometime during the late spring of 1941 and designated the SS to carry it through,[1] there was some astonishment among the SS leadership. Yet there should have been no doubt that Hitler took racism seriously, even if the will to push it to its logical conclusion was only implicitly evident until the Führer regarded the time as ripe.

The law of July 14, 1933, to prevent the bearing of hereditarily sick offspring was a eugenic measure in which sterilization was defined as voluntary except in certain very precisely described circumstances. But before the law was a year old, sterilizations had become compulsory and it was no longer necessary to obtain the victim's consent.[2] What kind of hereditary sickness would warrant sterilization was discussed in terms of the victim's ability to cope successfully with the exigencies of life and the likelihood of his being able to face the dangers of war. Both these considerations had nothing to do with the usual definitions of sickness, but instead were related to the sick individual's usefulness to society.[3]

The congenitally sick were thought to be unproductive[4] and, as we saw earlier, productivity played a large part in racist thought. The superior race was always considered productive, while the inferior races had nothing tangible to show for their labor. The one book which most impressed Nazi eugenicists centered on this very problem; the congenitally sick and those who had lost their will to work should be killed because the community must be freed from the burden of caring for its useless members. The lawyer Karl Binding and the physician Alfred Hoch wrote their *The Release of Unworthy Life in Order that It Might Be Destroyed* (*Die Freigabe der Vernichtung Lebensunwertes Lebens*, 1920) during the postwar economic crisis. To keep alive those who had lost their usefulness to themselves and society meant wasting the will to work and the fortunes of healthy and productive people. They contrasted the sacrifice of youth in war with the waste of nursing such useless existences. Euthanasia, the book concluded, was based upon respect for "everyone's will to live." [5]

Binding and Hoch were not racists, and no argument based upon racial eugenics can be found in their book. But the concept of usefulness to society, of the ability to work and, last but not least, the thought that some had to be killed so that others could live to the full, were easily assimilated into racial arguments. The qualities Binding and Hoch praised were also those which characterized the "master race." Euthanasia thus became the necessary consequence of attempts to improve the race by doing away with its parasites.

In fact, the killing of those with mental deficiencies and physical peculiarities had already taken place when, on September 1, 1939, Adolf Hitler gave over increased authority to the physicians and laymen chosen to administer the Nazi program. The euthanasia decree was predated by Hitler himself to the first day of the outbreak of the Second World War—a gesture more significant than the administrative decree itself. Hitler saw the victory of the Aryan as the overriding purpose of the conflict; not only was it necessary to put lesser races in their place, but also to free the Aryans of any potential weakness. Euthanasia and the war were interrelated as closely as the war and the final solution. During December 1939, every asylum in Germany was obliged to fill out a questionnaire identifying each patient and the length of time he had been in the asylum. Anyone who had stayed five years or more was closely scrutinized. Was he or she criminally insane, schizophrenic, or senile? They would then have to be transferred to those institutions like Grafeneck or Hadamar that were supposed to be secret, but where in fact everyone knew that euthanasia took place. The list of diseases which led to the transfer was constantly revised, but all of them were illnesses difficult to define accurately. Only one "disease" was precise: all Jewish patients were to be killed, regardless of medical findings. The Jewish mental patients and neurologically ill were the vanguard of the 6 million who were to die. A new questionnaire was devised in 1940, which now openly asked whether patients were able to work. At the same time, physicians not trained in psychiatry were allowed to take part in the selection process.[6]

There was resistance. Some of Germany's most famous institutions for the insane refused to fill out the questionnaire and got away with it. But there were also a few parents who asked that their sick children be killed.[7] Euthanasia could not be kept secret. It took place in institutions near population centers, and parents and relatives were soon suspicious of the all too sudden deaths. The churches took the lead in protesting euthanasia. The Protestant bishop Theophile Wurm was one of the first to protest, and so was Bishop Konrad von Preysing of Berlin. Yet it was Bishop Clemens August Galen of Münster who created the most attention when he publicly exposed the program on August 31, 1941. If so-called unproductive people can be killed like animals, then "woe to us all when we become old and feeble," he exclaimed. Such exposure was only the climax of a feeling of insecurity which euthanasia had spread throughout the population.[8]

The Nazis attempted to popularize euthanasia as a sacrifice that would prove a blessing for the victim. They used the medium of film in order to spread this message, and in *I Accuse* (*Ich klage an*, 1941) tried to demonstrate the innocence of a physician who had killed his incurably sick wife. Reference was made to heroic Roman times when such deaths had been permitted, and to the ancient Germans, who had allowed mercy killings. Only at one point in the film was the killing of the insane obliquely referred to, and then in the context of Hoch and Binding, to point out the supposed absurdity of maintaining a huge staff and many buildings in order to keep "a few miserable creatures" alive.[9] This film did not have a great impact. But the Nazis in their striving for totality whenever possible used film to propagate their policies through visual statements, always so much more important for them than the written word. Thus the roundup of Jews in 1940, wherever it occurred, was accompanied by a showing of an anti-Semitic film, *Jud Süss* (1940), that was highly successful. Süss Oppenheimer was a seventeenth-century court Jew who was executed for his supposed exploitation and corruption of the German state of Württemberg. This was vastly more popular than *I Accuse,* perhaps because its subject did not touch the daily life of the average German and the racial stereotype had been well prepared.

In spite of all propaganda for euthanasia, shortly after Bishop Galen's sermon, Hitler gave the order to halt the program; a combination of ecclesiastical protest and adverse public opinion seemed to convince him that the time was not ripe for such measures. Nevertheless, euthanasia continued in secret.

The opposition which officially ended the program was nowhere to be found when it came to the final solution of the Jewish question. There too the Nazis transgressed the "laws of God and nature" in ignoring the sacrament of baptism by killing converted Jews. But few parishioners were involved, no aunt or uncle was suddenly taken by death, and thus no feeling of insecurity spread within the German population. Euthanasia affected all Germans, while the deportation and death of the Jews affected only a minority that had already been "pushed into a corner," as Hitler put it, and separated from the population as a whole.[10]

The euthanasia program killed some 70,000 people, among them a high percentage of babies and children. At first the victims were shot, but soon they were killed by gas in rooms disguised as showers.[11] The connection between euthanasia and the eventual method of the Jewish mass murder is obvious here, and those who had experience with euthanasia furnished much of the personnel for the final solution. But the link between euthanasia and the destruction of Jews was closer still. Putting euthanasia into practice meant that the Nazis took the idea of "unworthy" life seriously, and a life so defined was characterized by lack of productivity and degenerate outward appearance. Lombrosos's psychology underlay much of the selection process of euthanasia: physical deformity was taken as a sign of mental sickness. While the ideas of unproductivity and physical appearance were both constantly applied to the Jews, euthanasia showed for the first time Hitler's determination to destroy such unworthy life. Ominously, the definition as applied to the mentally sick and to the Jews was very similar.

At the same time, the régime believed, the Aryan race itself must constantly be improved. Even as "unworthy life" was snuffed out, Heinrich Himmler attempted to initiate programs which would transform into reality the utopias of racial breeding that had fascinated racial theoreticians ever since the beginning of the twentieth century. Racial screening in the SS became thorough, demanding not only the presentation of a genealogy but photographs of the applicants as well. The *Lebensborn* (literally, "the source of life") was instituted in 1936 so that mothers bearing pure racial offspring might get the best medical care, even if they happened to be unmarried. All liaisons between racially valuable SS men and racially pure women were encouraged; but the bourgeois values of Himmler restrained such attempts at selective breeding.[12] For him marriage was the answer, and unmarried SS members would never get promotions, while those with many children could count on his goodwill. Eventually, the planned settlements of German peasants in the Slavic lands would serve as Aryan stud farms (among their other duties as outposts of defense), providing the kind of isolated Aryan paradise of which men like Willibald Hentschel had dreamed.[13]

Euthanasia was part of the reciprocal relationship between an unworthy life and one considered especially worthy of continuation. It was built upon the images of inferior and superior races that have filled the pages of this book. But the Jews were not only singled out because of so-called signs of physical degeneration, or their so-called lack of productivity, but also because of their supposed criminality. The Nazis based their concept of criminality on the theories of Cesare Lombroso, for whom the habitual criminal was "an atavistic being who reproduced in his person the ferocious instincts of primitive humanity and the inferior animals."[14] This degeneration (as Lombroso called it) was proved by physical deformities of the skull, though the whole body could be deformed as well. Phrenology had added to this concept not only the assertion (taken from Gall) that "the heads of all thieves resemble each other more or less in shape," but also that criminals, because they are "immoderate," are rootless "and relapse into nomadism."[15] Lombroso had believed that habitual criminals could not be rehabilitated since their very physical appearance was involved in their actions, and that they must therefore suffer the death penalty.[16] The Jews because of their race were regarded as habitual criminals by the Nazis and therefore rightly doomed to destruction.

This concept of criminality has been ignored by scholars of the holocaust, although Nazi literature and films are full of it. There is no doubt that belief in this theory of criminality made it easier to accept the murder of the Jews, because it had sunk so deep into popular consciousness. It was not just a part of Volkish and Nazi writings, but also of the popular literature, with its decisive separation of good and evil, and its criminals who in their very appearance reflected their opposition to the law. In a manner of speaking, such stories perpetuated the evil mental and physical characteristics that earlier writers like Balzac and Eugène Sue had thought typical of the underworld.[17] For some at least, the Jews were similarly degenerate characters; if they did not originate in the sewers of Paris, they were nevertheless compared to rats. Indeed, this was how the Jews had been pictured in the highly successful film *Jud Süss* as they scurried into the city of Stuttgart after the duke of Württemberg had delivered his state into their hands through his minister Süss Oppenheimer. Even as the film was being shown, real-life Jews were being rounded up and deported to the east.

The Jews alone were singled out for extermination. For them the issue of usefulness was not even raised. There were no questionnaires to redeem some Jews and doom others. Even the murder of the gypsies, which came closest in resemblance to the Jewish holocaust, was selective. The gypsies were "primitive nomads" and loved "sweet leisure," said Eva Justin, the Nazi expert in charge of the gypsy question.[18] Once again the work ethic prevailed—the ideal of productivity as a part of those middle-class values which gypsies, the congenitally sick, and the Jews had all violated. But Himmler wanted to settle some of the conquered gypsies, whom he considered descendants of the original Aryan race, on the land. Those gypsies who had bastardized themselves with foreign blood were to be killed.[19] Himmler therefore saved some gypsies, although a majority went to their deaths. This was horrible enough, but no Jew could claim to have Aryan ties in order to be preserved. The story is told that Himmler, watching Jews going to the gas chamber, picked out a blond, blue-eyed boy and asked him if he were a Jew and if both his parents were Jews. When the boy answered in the affirmative, Himmler replied: "What a pity, then I cannot save you."[20]

Even the treatment of Poles under Nazi rule was not intended to lead to their extermination. Instead, they were to become a slave people, and the massacres which took place during the Nazi conquest of Poland in 1939 were, in the main, directed against the Polish intelligentsia. The Poles, deprived of their intellectuals, priests, and educators, would, so the Nazis held, become willing slaves of the superior race. Racism was supposed to lead to the revival of slavery, not merely in the overseas empires, but in Europe itself. Indeed, slavery was put into practice for some Poles, but also for many Jews, who were "given" to Nazi concentration camp leaders and their families to be worked as these saw fit. It could also be claimed, with some justice, that the hundreds of thousands of Jews who worked in armament or textile factories in the ghettos provided slave labor, for they were not paid and instead were given slightly more food than others. Such work in factories or for the private benefit of SS chieftains seemed to give at least some hope for survival. For Jews (but not for Poles) this hope proved illusory. Yet the revival of slavery must not be put on the same plane as the extermination of a whole people. Slavery was a traditional ally and object of racism; the final solution of the Jewish question was something new and quite unprecedented.

The massacre which seemed most closely to foreshadow the final solution was the Turkish attempt in 1915 and 1916 to deport the Armenians to the Syrian Desert and to kill as many as possible. This action was taken during the emergency of war (just like the later massacre of the Jews), and was supposed to rid Turkey once and for all of a troublesome and divisive minority. Statistics differ on how many Armenians lost their lives, but 750,000 seems a fairly accurate figure. This massacre was not racially motivated, for conversion to Islam was a road to survival. The Armenians who lived together in villages and towns (not scattered like many Jews) put up resistance from the beginning and from time to time fought off the Turks. Moreover, the bureaucratic methods and modern techniques of the Nazi murder machine were not yet perfected, though a central planning committee executed the killings.[21]

This massacre helped to accustom Europe to such events, and to deaden the voices of conscience—a process that was accelerated after the Japanese invasion of Manchuria. From 1932, Europeans were assaulted daily by news of inconceivable numbers of dead. But again this was a massacre that took place far away, among people of whom Europeans knew little and cared less. The crucial events which accustomed people both to mass death and to mass violence were the First World War and its consequences. In Germany particularly, as we saw earlier, the war furthered the image of a ruthless hero, dedicated to violence in order to save the race.[22]

The late spring and summer of 1941, when orders to execute the final solution to the Jewish question were passed down first by word of mouth, and then in the written order of July 31, 1941, from Göring to Heydrich, saw racism pass into a new phase.

Anti-Jewish legislation had already turned into practice. Jews had been successfully separated from the population at large and "pushed into a corner."[23] The outbreak of the war was conceived as the first step toward their destruction. If international finance

Jewry were to push Europe once more into war, the result, Hitler proclaimed, would be the destruction of Jewry, not Europe. The argument that the Jews must be exterminated now because they had started the war was one of Himmler's chief justifications for his mass murders.[24] Some Jews had been temporarily imprisoned within the camps after the "Kristallnacht" of November 9/10, 1938. Now Jews entered camps in a more permanent manner as the final step in their isolation and the first step in their destruction. Moreover, in the camps attempts were now made to turn the myths about the Jewish stereotype into reality. Just as Hitler had started the war and then said: "Look at what the Jew did to destroy us," so too in the camps, conditions were reduced to a struggle for naked survival. The Nazis could then claim: "Look at the Jew. We were right all along about his lack of human morality."

Analyses of the conditions in various camps have shown that corruption was furthered by the SS through favoritism, through the manipulation of scarce food supplies, and through a system of constant terror. Men and women were turned into people who had to do anything in order to survive. The SS became masters at setting the inmates against each other. Those prisoners in authority were expected to accomplish a certain amount of daily work dictated by the guards, and had to drive others too hard to help accomplish this end. The "Kapo," as such a prisoner was called, was permitted to beat his fellow inmates at will.[25] The camps, isolated from the outside world, became little kingdoms ruled by terror, corruption, and divisiveness. Thus they were easy for a relatively small number of men to guard. But a psychological factor was also at work. The Jews were supposedly stripped of their humanity and became in the eyes of the SS a people who would steal, rob, curry favor, and betray others. This transformation of myth into reality has no better witness than Rudolf Höss, the commandant of Auschwitz.

Höss contrasted his own moral behavior when imprisoned for a Fehme murder (i.e., murder for political revenge) in the early 1920's with that of the Jews under his rule. He accused them of acting in a "typically Jewish" way, shirking work whenever possible, bribing others do to their work for them, and clawing each other in a wild competition for those privileges and goods that would enable them to live a comfortable, parasitic life.[26] Once again, Jews were accused of lack of productivity, fear of honest work, and of corrupting society. Even in the face of the gallows which awaited him when he wrote his memoirs in Poland after the war, Höss could not bring himself to admit that it was he who was responsible for the behavior of his victims, and that the conditions purposely created in the camps were meant to transform the stereotype into a self-fulfilling prophecy. It is no surprise that Höss believed the Jews, as enemies of the Reich, were responsible for their own destruction.[27] For men like Höss who engaged in the final solution, the myth about Jews actually became reality through the power that the Germans were able to wield. Höss could not admit—perhaps he was not aware of the fact—that tens of thousands of Jews actively resisted the system which the SS created and that hundreds of thousands retained their dignity in the most incredible circumstances.[28]

The way in which the deportations to the east were carried out after 1941 was deliberately designed to strip away any dignity that was left to the Jews, not only in the crowded cattle cars where so many died, but also in what happened on arrival. The victims were stripped nude, inspected, and sorted out according to their supposed ability to work. Those useful for work were sent to labor camps; others were sent to the "showers" to be gassed. For many such men and women, only recently torn from their middle-class respectability and settled life, such humiliation must have been shattering.[29]

After 1941, Jews were deported to the east from all over Europe and there, initially, many were left to their own devices. But such chaos was not allowed to last. They were delivered to work camps like Bergen-Belsen or to the ghettos which were being created. At first Heydrich had opposed the creation of Jewish ghettos for fear that they might become centers of resistance (a fear that later proved partially justified),[30] but such concentration became essential if the final solution was to be carried through. Between the winter of 1939 and the spring of 1940, the Polish Jews already had to create "Jewish Councils" (*Judenräte*), which would govern them in their own localities and would be accountable to the SS for the execution of orders. The Jewish Councils held dictatorial powers, but only as administrative agents of the Germans. As such they controlled all the necessities of life, from the distribution of food to housing and employment. This was an application on a vast scale of that representative body of German Jewry which had been forced into being in 1933.

At the same time that the *Judenräte* were created in Poland, Jews were forced into ghettos. The Warsaw Ghetto was established in November 1939; during 1941, other ghettos in Lodz, Vilna, Lvov, and many smaller towns followed.[31] Whereas in the Middle Ages the ghetto had been closed only at night by gates or a chain, now for the most part walls eventually completely isolated the ghetto from the surrounding population. By the winter of 1941, when almost all the Polish Jews had been imprisoned in ghettos, one of them noted correctly: "We are segregated . . . driven out of the society of the human race."[32] Here too, a self-fulfilling prophecy was to come into play. When the Warsaw Ghetto was stricken by epidemics of typhoid, the slogan "Jews-Lice-Typhoid" was spread by the Germans among a not unreceptive Polish population.[33] The ghettos were soon to become scenes of starvation and death, but the Jews there also provided a slave labor force for the German wartime industries set up in their midst. Until the end of the war, the use of such slave labor in the ghetto industries or in special labor camps persisted side by side with mass murder. Within the SS, a controversy raged over the constant postponement of the deportation of these industrial workers.[34] It was never resolved.

The technique of killing in the death camps once more illustrates the drive to make murder as efficient and impersonal as possible. From 1941 onward, firing squads (*Einsatzgruppen*) operated behind the German front. But the strain on these commandos was great, and one high SS officer feared that the men might become either neurotics or savages.[35] The technicians of the Reich security office then produced the gas van, first tried out in the murder of Jews in November of 1941. But this also required too much effort for too little result, as a van could hold only a limited amount of people and nasty incidents of resistance could not be avoided. Furthermore, the vans could not disguise their functions successfully enough. Finally, the experience of the euthanasia program was utilized. First, in the fall of 1941, makeshift gas chambers were installed in abandoned farmhouses, and by the summer of 1942 the gas chamber disguised as a showerhouse was in full operation. No contact with the victims was now necessary: they entered by themselves and the commandants in the death camps had only to verify death through a peephole. The gas was supplied by prestigious private German firms. Thus an estimated 5,933,900 Jews died by various means as victims of racism in Europe.[36]

The strong technological side of the final solution—the gas van, the skill in mass communication, the bureaucratic efficiency needed to keep track of such an enormous operation—all interacted with the process of dehumanizing the victims. Men involved in the ghastly process of planned human destruction could view themselves as skilled operatives, fulfilling a task which was vital in the national interest. Rudolf Höss as commandant of Auschwitz saw himself at one and the same time as a skilled technician liquidating the treacherous enemy who had started the war, and as the very model of middle-class respectability. Höss tells us without shame how he dreamed about his family, his dog, and the beautiful cherry trees while watching long lines of men, women, and children go to their deaths. For him these nude figures were a homogenized abstract mass of enemies, of degenerate human beings. Thus he could project his middle-class dreams in the midst of mass death.[37] Nothing better illustrates the corruption of middle-class values which racism had so successfully annexed. Höss thought of himself as a decent, moral, and honest person, a good father and husband. All the architects of the final solution saw themselves in the mirror of middle-class respectability, and they liked what they saw.

Racism had taken the ideas about man and his world which we have attempted to analyze and directed them toward the final solution. Such concepts as middle-class virtue, heroic morality, honesty, truthfulness, and love of nation had become involved as over against the Jew; the organs of the efficient state helped to bring about the final solution; and science itself continued its corruption through racism. Above all, anthropology, which had been so deeply involved in the rise of racism, now used racism for its own end through the final solution.

Anthropological studies were undertaken on the helpless inmates of the camps. These experiments were arranged by Himmler's personal assistant Rudolf Brandt and led by August Hirt, professor of anatomy at the University of Strasbourg. They started in 1942 when seventy-nine Jews, fifty Jewesses, two Poles, and four "Asiatics" (i.e., Russian Mongol prisoners) were subjected to anthropological measurements (including the facial angle). They were then killed, and their heads and skeletons became part of the university's anatomical collection. At the same time Bruno Berger, who had been attempting to investigate Aryan origins for the SS, conducted ethnographic studies. Berger chose what he considered interesting skull formations from among the prisoners. He first observed and measured the skulls when his subjects were alive. They were then gassed and the skulls prepared for further investigation in the laboratory. Berger had complained that good skull collections existed for every race except the Jews: "The war in the east gives us the opportunity to rectify matters," he commented.[38] The preoccupations of the eighteenth-century scientists who stood at the beginning of racism with their anthropological measurements and their fascination with the human skull had passed from concern with stereotypes to "murder for the advancement of science." Most anthropologists, in fact, stood aside with horror from experiments with human beings. But just as previously nonracist scientists like Alfred Ploetz and Eugen Fischer became converted by the temptation to aid Nazi eugenic policies[39] (without being involved in the final solution), so others could not resist the temptation to use their power over life and death in order to further their anthropological or ethnographic ambitions.

The practitioners of racial science were joined in their experiments by doctors working for the German armed forces. Jews were used to find out how long downed pilots might live without food or water, how much cold the body could take, and the effect new drugs had on the coagulation of blood. Death was always the end for the objects of a human vivisection unparalleled in history. The Jews in the ghettos and in the camps had become objects of Himmler's fanatical interest in racial science and quack medicine.[40]

II

Hitler intended to destroy all European Jews, as he repeatedly proclaimed during the war. This aim for the most part could be accomplished for those Jews falling directly under the Nazi occupation, but it did not prove so easy to implement elsewhere.

The war led to a basic conflict in Jewish policy. As we saw earlier, Hitler preferred conservative dictators to Fascist chiefs as the heads of his satellite nations.[41] Such dictators, ruling with the support of the army and the traditional social and clerical hierarchies, could guarantee law and order behind the front, while native Fascist régimes might create unrest. For Hitler, winning the war took priority here, while the Iron Guard or the Arrow Cross wanted to seize power at once and destroy their enemies. Indeed, during its short co-rule with Antonescu in Rumania, the Iron Guard unleashed a chaotic and almost uncontrollable pogrom against the Jews. Men like Antonescu, Horthy, or Czar Boris frustrated Hitler's orders on the Jewish question; still, they did collaborate to a degree that prevented open scandal. For Hitler himself, once the war had been won the Jewish question in countries like Rumania or Bulgaria could be solved speedily, and young Fascists could come to power who had felt the rod and spur of the Berlin oligarchs.

Dictators like Antonescu, Horthy, Boris, or Pétain in France were not racists. They disliked Jews but had no desire to endanger the law through violence or to jeopardize the traditional order of things by destroying the Jews. Thus, for example, Horthy collaborated in the partial deportation of Jews only when the Germans had occupied the country and after he had been bullied and blackmailed. Antonescu and Pétain sought another way out: they protected native Jews and threw foreign Jews under their control into the Nazi death machine. Pétain allowed the deportation of stateless Jews from Vichy France, and Antonescu refused to deliver the Rumanian Jews, but did send to their death hundreds of thousands of Jews in his newly acquired territory of Bessarabia.[42] In Bulgaria the pattern was similar. The Bulgarian Orthodox Church protected the Jews in Bulgaria itself where, in any case, a tradition of anti-Semitism had never existed. But in the newly acquired regions of Macedonia, Thrace, and a small part of Serbia, Jews were deported and killed. This in spite of the courageous stand by the Orthodox patriarch and the papal ambassador Angelo Giuseppe Roncalli, the future Pope John XXIII. Indeed, Rome rebuked Roncalli for his strong stand in favor of the Jews.[43]

In Slovakia, the first satellite of the Reich, where a Catholic priest, Josef Tiso, became president in October 1939, matters were different from Bulgaria or the rest of eastern Europe. There severe racial laws were passed in 1941 and the government at first supported the deportation of Jews. But in Slovakia the Church intervened, largely to save Jews who had converted to Christianity. As a result of Church pressure, deportation was only partial and ceased altogether in 1943. Then, after the German occupation of the country in 1944, the government went along with the deportation dictated by the SS. At first Tiso had also fought the radicals in Slovakia, and the Jews benefitted from that struggle. But again after 1944 Tiso treated the Jews without mercy, despite the attempts of his own prime minister to curb the Nazi fury.[44] Clearly, the conditions in each country not under direct German occupation varied; only the outline of what took place has been given here in order to complete the general picture of the Nazis' attempt to bring about the victory of racism in Europe.

Germany's principal ally, Fascist Italy, sabotaged Nazi Jewish policy in the territories under its control. The racial laws which Mussolini had introduced in 1938 on the model of the Nuremberg Laws did deny Jews participation in many occupations, and there was an attempt to gather Jews in forced labor battalions; but whereas in Germany Hitler constantly narrowed the circle of those who could escape the law, in Italy the contrary was the case. The exceptions were legion. Mussolini himself put forward the slogan:

"Discrimination but no persecution," as we saw earlier.[45] However, the Italian army went further, no doubt with Mussolini's tacit consent, as the zone of Italian occupation in France became a refuge for hunted Jews. Everywhere within Nazi-occupied Europe Italian embassies protected Jews who could claim Italian nationality. Jewish deportations only began when the Germans occupied Italy after Mussolini's fall. At that time the active persecution of the Jews also increased in the shadow republic which Mussolini retained, the Republic of Saló; here the small anti-Semitic wing of the Fascist Party got the upper hand. However, the Germans were the real rulers of that republic, and enforced their Jewish policy.[46]

In spite of the difficulties which the SS experienced in trying to deport and kill all the Jews of Europe, they found willing helpers in every nation. The violently anti-Semitic Fascist parties in the Balkan countries were natural allies. But in France the Nazis at first received scant support for the final solution. Xavier Vallat, the first Commissioner for the Jewish Question in Vichy France, was a war veteran leader who hated the Germans more than the Jews. A reactionary, he shared the attitude of men like Pétain or Antonescu, though he did proclaim that the Jews were a foreign race.[47] But in 1942 Louis Darquier de Pellepoix became his successor. Darquier can well be compared to Dietrich Eckart, who had influenced Hitler so much in the early 1920's; and the *L'Anti-Juif* which he edited, similar to Eckart's *Auf Gut Deutsch*, blamed the Jews for all the ills of the world. Darquier had written an introduction to the *Protocols of the Elders of Zion* in which he asserted that it did not matter whether they were true or not; it was the vision that counted.[48] He could not get the Vichy government to deport native Jews, but he pushed vigorously for the expulsion of Jews who did not possess French nationality, and some 60–65,000 were sent to their deaths.[49]

There was no lack of French voices from German-occupied Paris urging Vichy to adopt stronger anti-Jewish measures.[50] But such voices were, in the last resort, less important than those of men and women of nearly every European nation who actively took part in the final solution, who helped to round up Jews, or who worked as guards in the camps. There was never a lack of such collaborators. Not all were racists, but many were Christians who, following medieval ideas that had never died out, saw in the Jews the anti-Christ. At times Christian, medieval, and racist ideals were so mixed that any distinction between them cannot be made. For it turned out that not even the most fervent pleas by the Vatican could get nominally Catholic nations to give refuge to baptized Jews. Latin American states like Argentina or Brazil would make promises to Cardinal Luigi Maglione, the papal Secretary of State, then break them almost immediately. Typical of many replies the cardinal received in his efforts to find refuge for converted Jews was a letter written on June 5, 1939, by the Vatican chargé d'affaires in Bolivia. Popular exasperation against the Jews was so great that little could be done. Jews were accused of cheating, illegal competition, immorality, and disrespect for religion.[51] Apparently it did not matter that the proposed immigrants were, in fact, Catholic. It is significant that in Chile the parish priests were in the forefront of opposition to the immigration of their fellow Catholics. That they were "racially" Jews was all that mattered, and Jews in Chile were accused of ruining agriculture through usury.[52]

The "final solution" of the Jewish problem did not merely represent the triumph of racism in practice, but also its victory as the most widespread ideology of the time. European Jews had become pariahs. People might deny that they were racists. In reality, they used the rhetoric and often characterized their enemies in racial terms. The Nazis did not invent racism; they merely activated it. Yet racism would not end with Adolf Hitler. The Nazi implementation of racial policy was essentially the climax of a long development which we have analyzed from its source in the eighteenth century. The stream flows on into the future.

CHAPTER FOURTEEN

A Conclusion That Does Not Conclude

THE HOLOCAUST transformed racial theory into practice. The racism which Hitler so successfully put into practice exemplified the "mystery of race" at its most extreme, filled with secret life forces and cosmic warfare between Aryan and Jew. The Jews were his enemies, the only people he intended to exterminate. Here was no belief in compromise, charity, or decency. This was the full-scale racial war that men like Houston Stewart Chamberlain had prophesied and that had been propagandized by the small sects in Vienna and Munich where Hitler learned his lessons. In his preparations for the Second World War, the aims of gaining living space for Germany and achieving the "final solution" for the Jews were intimately linked in Hitler's mind. But the extermination of the Jews took precedent, for in them Hitler saw the true enemy of Germany.[1]

The holocaust could not have taken place without the application of modern technology, without the modern centralized state with its card files and communication systems, and without the brutalization of men's minds by the experience of the First World War where, to give just one example, "belief in Germany" was equated with naked force.[2] The Second World War shielded the mass murders which were accompanied by Himmler's and Hitler's repeated litany that the Jews had started it all and were now reaping their just deserts. A self-fulfilling prophecy stood at the center of Hitler's and Himmler's justification for the final solution: the war

the Nazis had started was blamed on the Jews, whom Hitler had
threatened with death if such a war occurred. However, behind all
the attempts at justification stood a fanatical belief in racist ideas.
This was a racism which stemmed from the outer perimeter of the
movement, connected with spiritualism, secret sciences, and cosmic
battles. But such ideas came to dominate the mind of Adolf Hitler,
who was at one and the same time a fanatic and a superb politician.
Hitler always believed that the extermination of the Jews must be
the final aim of his government, yet he was also always ready to
adjust his political timing to the necessities of the moment, and to
learn from his own past mistakes, as in the case of the putsch of
1923.

But racism as a world view was not confined to Hitler's thoughts
and actions. The "mystery of race" which muddled Hitler's mind
never superseded all the other varieties of racism we have discussed
in this book. Hitler, in fact, benefitted from an advantage common
to all practitioners of racism, whether they emphasized spiritual
forces or attempted to annex science. Racist myths not only explained the past and brought hope for the future, but through their
emphasis on stereotypes rendered the abstract concrete. Racist
stereotypes made theory come to life in a simple, direct manner. We
have seen the stereotypes of beauty or ugliness formed at the very
beginning of the history of European racism. They annexed the aesthetic of the time and made the outward appearance of a man symbolic for the working of his inner nature. From the eighteenth century to its use by the Nazis in the holocaust, this stereotype never
changed. The virile, Hellenistic type juxtaposed with the dark and
misshapen villain, the Aryan of Greek proportions versus the ill-
proportioned Jew, made racism a visually centered ideology. And
this stress on the visual, in turn, made it easy for people to understand the thrust of the ideology. Thus, we come back to John
Huizinga's remark about the fifteenth century, that "having once
attributed a real existence to an idea, the mind wants to see it alive
and can effect this only by personalizing it."[3]

The stereotype never varied, whether racism attempted to forge a
tie to science through anthropology or eugenics, to follow scientific

experimentation and observation, or to posit theories of racial "life substances" that had nothing to do with modern science. (Hitler believed that all science must again become a secret, mystical science.)[4] Racism was never at a loss for proofs which would make its stereotypes convincing, whether culled from anthropology, phrenology, or Darwinism, whether citing "life substances" or the "lightening of the blood." The various qualities attached to the stereotype from the very beginning already foreshadowed the Nazi process of turning myth into reality. The stereotype became associated with good or bad qualities, depending upon whether one wrote about an inferior or a superior race.

Racism had no founding father, and that was one of its strengths. It made alliance with all those virtues that the modern age praised so much. Racism picked out such qualities as cleanliness, honesty, moral earnestness, hard work, and family life—virtues which during the nineteenth century came to symbolize the ideals of the middle class.[5] From that class they spread upwards and downwards throughout European society, displacing the frivolous, dishonest, and lazy life style respectable men and women of the nineteenth century saw epitomized by their immediate ancestors. Racism was associated with these virtues rather than with any single philosopher or social theorist of importance. Where racism was associated with figures like Gobineau, de Lapouge, Weininger, or Wagner, they were second-rate thinkers, publicists, and synthesizers. The close connection often made with Darwin is mistaken, for as we have shown, racism was not merely one form of social Darwinism, but instead, a scavenger ideology, which annexed the virtues, morals, and respectability of the age to its stereotypes and attributed them to the inherent qualities of a superior race.

If racism annexed the virtues of the age, it also condemned as degenerate all that was opposed to such respectability. Not to exemplify the ideal-type of "clean-cut American" or "right-living Englishman" was a sign of an inferior race. Though racism was often vague, it clearly embraced all the values of middle-class respectability, and claimed to be their defender. To be sure, few people at first went along with such a claim; to the vast majority of

A Conclusion that Does not Conclude

Europeans, it sufficed to be a Christian gentleman. But even here
racism so infected Christianity that, in the end, no real battle between racism and Christianity ever took place. Both supported the
same middle-class virtues and saw the enemy in the same noncon-
formists—be they Bohemians, Freemasons, or Jews. The support
racism gave to ideals which were opposed to a threatened degeneracy was in practice more important than any differences between
racism and Christianity.

Racism, in its wide penetration, its annexations and infections,
often embraced men and women who were not racists at all, or
whose racism was highly ambivalent; yet their ideas were appropriated in its scavenging. Racism had to take its stereotypes and its
theory of heredity from somewhere. At times only the best would
do, which lent in turn new respectability to the ideology. Darwin,
Gall, Lavater, Lombroso, and Galton stood apart from racism as a
world view. To them I apologize for associating them with such bad
company. But their ideas were so important to racism that they had
to be included in our history of the movement, just as some of the
learned gentlemen of the French Anthropological Society or the
Germans associated with the *Journal for Racial and Social Biology*
contributed to racism even while ambivalent in embracing a racist
world view. The perimeters of racial thought are as elusive and
slippery as the ideology as a whole. And yet, for all that, the myth
was transformed into reality, not just during the holocaust and the
camps, but whenever ordinary people made judgments upon others
based upon the implications of the racial stereotype.

The holocaust has passed. The history of racism which we have
told has helped to explain the final solution. But racism itself has
survived. As many people as ever before think in racial categories.
There is nothing provisional about the lasting world of stereotypes. That is the legacy of racism everywhere. And if, under the
shock of the holocaust, the postwar world proclaimed a temporary
moratorium on anti-Semitism, the black on the whole remained
locked into a racial posture which never varied much from the
eighteenth century to our time. Practically all blacks had been outside Hitler's reach; consequently, there was no rude awakening

from the racial dream in their regard. Moreover, nations which had fought against National Socialism continued to accept black racial inferiority for many years after the end of the war, and did not seem to realize that all racism, whether aimed at blacks or Jews, was cut of the same cloth (see Plate 15).

Unfortunately, this book has to have a conclusion that does not conclude. If through the study of history we can best understand the world man has made for himself, then the history of racism will tell us why this attitude toward life has been so lasting, why it has served for over a century to counter man's fears and to give him hope for the future. Reading the history of racism correctly means also pondering the history of Europe with which it is so closely intertwined. Too often racism has been brushed aside as unworthy of serious study, as a simple and naïve world view that can be laid to rest, a mistaken faith, while historians turn to more sophisticated and fascinating subject matter. Yet to exorcise this evil, no occult powers are required, but merely the attempt to integrate the study of racism within our study of the modern history of Europe. We must never neglect to seek the whereabouts of the scavenger until we have stripped his disguise and found him—even where there seemed to be only virtue, goodness, and truth.

Although practically all the political and cultural systems Europe has produced during the last two centuries have more intellectual substance than racism, that should not keep us from the task of examining racism with the same attention that we have given to socialism, liberalism, or conservatism. Perhaps racism was, in the last resort, so effective just because it was so banal and eclectic, and, more than any other system of the nineteenth century, managed to fuse the visual and the ideological so successfully. It was as if the very commonplaces of a moral and virtuous life, when based on racism and protected by it, came alive to achieve new and horrifying dimensions.

Any book which analyzes one movement over so long a period of time can lose its perspective. To be sure, racism eventually came to dominate Europe; but within the continent it constantly faced opposition. Liberal, socialist, and even Christian anti-racism must not be underestimated. Organizations to combat racism did exist, and were not always condemned to impotence. This is worth recalling because while this book has been concerned with racism and not with the anti-racist tradition in Europe, the troops for a victory over racism did exist, however much beleaguered and defeated, especially between the two world wars. Even now that they are much strengthened the struggle continues, but with greater hope than ever before. The first step toward victory over this scourge of mankind is to understand what brought it about, the longings and hopes that it aroused in the past. This book is meant to contribute toward the diagnosis of the cancer of racism within our nations and even within ourselves.

Notes

CHAPTER ONE

1. Peter Gay, *The Enlightenment: An Interpretation*, vol. I, *The Rise of Modern Paganism* (New York, 1966), 185.

2. Quoted in Arthur O. Lovejoy, *The Great Chain of Being* (New York, 1960), 265.

3. Frank Manuel, *The Eighteenth Century Confronts the Gods* (New York, 1967), 77.

4. Peter Gay, *The Englightenment: An Interpretation*, vol. II, *The Science of Freedom* (New York, 1969), 150.

5. Gay, *The Enlightenment*, I, 171.

6. *Goethes Faust*, ed. Georg Witkowski (Leipzig, 1929), I, 60.

7. See Mircea Eliade, *Myth and Reality* (New York, 1968), 6, 8.

8. Quoted in Gerhard Kaiser, *Pietismus und Patriotismus im Literarischen Deutschland* (Wiesbaden, 1961), 43.

9. Novalis, "Christendom or Europe," in *Hymns to the Night and Other Selected Writings*, tr. Charles E. Passage (New York, 1960), 48.

10. Geoffroy Atkinson, *Les Relations des Voyages du XVIIe Siècle et l'Évolution des Idées* (Paris, n.d.), 41.

11. *Ibid.*, 42.

12. Michael T. Ryan, "New Worlds of Pagan Religion in the Seventeenth Century" (unpublished Ph.D. dissertation, New York University, 1974), 238.

13. Manuel, *op. cit.*, 11, 141.

14. J. J. Winckelmann, *Winckelmanns Werke*, ed. Heinrich Meyer and Johann Schulze (Dresden, 1811), IV, 57.

15. Meiners, *Grundriss der Geschichte der Menschheit* (Lengo, 1785), 43.

16. Johann Friedrich Blumenbach, *Über die Natürlichen Vershiedenheiten im Menschengeschlecht* (Leipzig, 1798), 137.

17. Meiners, *op. cit.*, 76ff.

18. Winthrop D. Jordan, *White over Black: American Attitudes Toward the Negro, 1550–1812* (Chapel Hill, N.C., 1968), 30.

19. William W. Appleton, *A Cycle of Cathay: The Chinese Vogue in England During the Seventeenth and Eighteenth Centuries* (New York, 1951), 123–131.

20. James Walvin, *Black and White: The Negro and English Society 1555–1945* (London, 1973), 46.

21. *Ibid.*, 60.

22. J. F. Blumenbach, "De generis humani varietate nativa," *The Anthropological Treatises of Johann Friedrich Blumenbach* (London, 1865), 305.

23. Alexander Altmann, *Moses Mendelssohn* (University, Alabama, 1973), 465.

24. Gaspard Lavater, *L'Art de Connaître les Hommes par la Physionomie*, ed. M. Moreau (Paris, 1820), 11, 168.

25. Hoxie Neale Fairchild, *The Noble Savage* (New York, 1928), 78.

26. Lovejoy, *op. cit.*, 265.

27. Edward Tyson, *Orang-Outang, Sive Homo Sylvestris Or, the Anatomy of a Pigmie Compared with that of a Monkey, an Ape, and a Man, etc.* (London, 1699), 9, 11, 12.

28. Hester Hastings, *Man and Beast in French Thought of the Eighteenth Century* (Baltimore and London, 1936), 129.

29. See pages 21–24.

30. Meiners, *op. cit.*, 35.

31. Léon Poliakov, *Le Mythe Aryen* (Paris, 1971), 178, 179.

CHAPTER TWO

1. Wilhelm E. Mühlmann, *Geschichte der Anthropologie* (Frankfurt-am-Main, 1968), 13.

2. Jacques Barzun, *Darwin, Marx, Wagner* (Boston, 1946), 49.

3. J. B. Lamarck, *Zoological Philosophy* (London, 1914), xiii.

4. J. L. Buffon, *Buffon's Natural History of Man* (London, 1801), 54.

5. See page 53.

6. Linnaeus, *A General System of Nature Through the Three Grand Kingdoms of Animals, Vegetables and Minerals* (London, 1806), I, "Mammalia."

7. Johann Friedrich Blumenbach, *The Anthropological Treatise of Johann Friedrich Blumenbach* (London, 1865), 306.

8. Johann Friedrich Blumenbach, *Über die Natürlichen Verschiedenheiten im Menschengeschlecht* (Leipzig, 1798), 137, 144.

Notes

9. *Ibid.*, 204, 206.

10. P. Camper, *Dissertation Physique de Mr. Pierre Camper etc.*, ed.
Adrien Gilles Camper (Utrecht, 1791), 11.

11. *Ibid.*, 97; Camper, *Discours Prononcés par Feû Mr. Pierre Camper
en l'Académie de Dessein d'Amsterdam* (Utrecht, 1792), 35.

12. Camper, *Dissertation . . .* , 97, 98.

13. Camper, *Discours Prononcés . . .* , 94–96.

14. *Ibid.*, 3.

15. Camper, *Dissertation . . .* , 21.

16. *Physiognomie: Complexion und Art eins jeden Menschen aus Gestalt und Form des Angesichts, Glieder und allen Geberden zu Erlernen etc.*
(n.p., 1541), n.p.

17. Alexander Altmann, *Moses Mendelssohn* (University, Alabama,
1973), 261 and *passim*.

18. J. K. Lavater, *Johann Kasper Lavaters ausgewählte Schriften*, ed.
Johann Kaspar Orelli, III (Zurich, 1844), 52.

19. Gaspard Lavater, *L'Art de Connaître les Hommes par la Physionomie*, ed. M. Moreau (Paris, 1820), 141.

20. Lavater, *Johann Kaspar Lavaters ausgewählte Schriften*, IV, 55.

21. *Ibid.*, III, 138.

22. *Ibid.*, IV, 60, 61.

23. Ruth Zust, *Die Grundzüge der Physiognomik Johann Kaspar
Lavaters* (Zürich, 1948), 74.

24. Lavater, *Johann Kaspar Lavaters ausgewählte Schriften*, IV, 49.

25. *Ibid.*, 16, 33.

26. *Ibid.*, III, 115.

27. Gotthold Ephraim Lessing, *Nathan the Wise*, Act 1, Scene 2.

28. Altmann, *op. cit.*, 733.

29. Baptista Porta quoted in *The Phrenological Magazine*, IV (1883),
495.

30. Sir Walter Scott, *Ivanhoe* (New York, New American Library,
1962), 205, 229, 466.

31. *The Phrenological Magazine*, I (1880), 214.

32. D. Gall, *D. Gall's Vorlesungen über die Verrichtung des Gehirns*
(Berlin, 1805), 119; *The Phrenological Review*, I (1880), 73.

33. D. Gall, *D. Gall's Vorlesungen. . .* , 126.

34. A. C. Haddon, *History of Anthropology* (London, 1949), 33.

35. Artur Krewald, *Carl Gustav Caro seine Philosophischen, Psycho-
logischen und Charakterologischen Grundgedanken* (Berlin, 1939), 57.

36. Carl Gustav Carus, *Symbolik der Menschlichen Gestalt*, ed.
Theodor Lessing (Celle, 1925), 140.

37. *Ibid.*, 251, 277, 278, 323; Krewald, *op. cit.*, 63, 65.

38. Carus, *Symbolik der Menschlichen Gestalt*, 265.

39. This discussion on the origin of the "Jewish nose" is based on the work of Isaiah Shachar, especially his essay "The Emergence of the Modern Pictorial Stereotype of 'The Jews' in England," *Studies in the Cultural Life of the Jews in England; Folklore Research Center Studies*, IV (1975), 331–365. His forthcoming book, *The Jew by His Looks*, will add a new dimension to our discussions of race and stereotypes. See also Johann Winckelmann's *Sämtliche Werke*, ed. Joseph Eiselein, III (Donaueschingen, 1825), 132; recently, Bernard Glassman, *Anti-Semitic Stereotypes Without Jews: Images of the Jews in England 1290–1700* (Detroit, 1975), 71, has described the hooked or large nose as part of the Elizabethan Jewish stereotype used by some dramatists. Still, such a physical stereotype was far from consistent even on the evidence in this important book, and its real significance before the eighteenth century may yet be doubted. Supposed hostility to Christianity defined the anti-Jewish stereotype during this period and looks played a minor role. Thomas W. Perry, *Public Opinion, Propaganda, and Politics in Eighteenth Century England: A Study of the Jew Bill of 1753* (Cambridge, Eng., 1962), though informative on the written polemics, virtually ignores iconography, except for the mention of the supposed "malignant blackness" underneath a Jew's eyes, a lasting legend, and the dirtiness of his skin, another deep-rooted prejudice (p. 93). As late as 1925 a German handbook for lay actors stressed that the makeup of a "Jewish usurer" must include a pale and unhealthy coloration of skin and empty, deep-set eyes; George L. Mosse, "Die NS Kampfbühne," *Geschichte im Gegenwartsdrama*, ed. Reinhold Grimm and Jost Hermand (Stuttgart, 1976), 35.

40. Lavater cited in *The Phrenological Magazine*, II (1881), 13.

41. *Ibid.*, 15, 16.

42. David de Giustino, *Conquest of Mind: Phrenology and Victorian Social Thought* (London, 1975), 70, 74.

43. *Berliner Illustrierte Nachtausgabe*, 16 and 17, August 1935 (Wiener Library Clipping Collection, Tel Aviv).

44. See Plate 8 and page 177.

45. Quoted in Mühlmann, *op. cit.*, 57.

46. Immanuel Kant, "Von den Verschiedenen Racen der Menschen," *Kants Werke, Akademie-Textausgabe*, vol. II, *Vorkritische Schriften* (Berlin, 1968), 11, 431, 432.

47. Walter Clyde Curry, *The Middle English Ideal of Personal Beauty, as Found in the Metrical Romances, Chronicles and Legends of the XIII, XIV, and XV Centuries* (Baltimore, 1916), 3, 6, 7.

48. Johann Gottfried von Herder, "Stimmen der Völker in Liedern,"

Johann Gottfried von Herder's Sämmtliche Werke zur Schönen Literatur und Kunst, ed. Johann von Müller, I (Stuttgart and Tübingen, 1828), 15.

49. Winthrop D. Jordan, *White over Black: American Attitudes Toward the Negro, 1550–1812* (Chapel Hill, N.C., 1968), 17.

50. Mühlmann, *op. cit.*, 59.

51. Philip D. Curtin, *The Image of Africa, British Ideas and Action, 1780–1850* (Madison, 1964), 368.

52. *Ibid.*, 369.

CHAPTER THREE

1. Gerhard Kaiser, *Pietismus und Patriotismus im Literarischen Deutschland* (Wiesbaden, 1961), 143.

2. *Ibid.*, 79.

3. *Ibid.*, 76.

4. *Ibid.*, 164.

5. Johann Gottfried Herder, "Zur Philosophie und Geschichte," *Johann Gottfried von Herder's Sämmtliche Werke zur Schönen Literatur und Kunst*, ed. Johann von Müller, VII (Stuttgart and Tübingen, 1838), 30, 23.

6. Herder, "Ideen zur Geschichte der Menschheit," *op. cit.*, V, 64; *ibid.*, VII, 43.

7. Johann Gottfried Herder, "Abhandlung Über den Ursprung der Sprache," *Werke in Zwei Bänden*, I (Munich, 1953), *passim.*

8. Eugen Lemberg, *Nationalismus*, I (Hamburg, 1964), 138ff.

9. George L. Mosse, *The Nationalization of the Masses* (New York, 1975), 77.

10. Ludwig Volkmann, *Egypten-Romantik in der Europäischen Kunst* (Leipzig, 1942), 128.

11. W. Jones, *The Works of Sir William Jones*, I (London, 1794), 11, 21, 273.

12. Friedrich Schlegel, "Über die Sprache und Weisheit der Inder," *Friedrich Schlegel's Sämmtliche Werke*, VII (Vienna, 1846), 278, 294, 298.

13. *Ibid.*, 302.

14. *Ibid.*, 308, 309, 369.

15. Christian Lassen, *Indische Altertumskunde*, I, Part 2 (Leipzig, 1877), viiff., 11.

16. F. Max Müller, *Three Lectures on the Science of Language* (Chicago, 1895), 54.

17. Léon Poliakov, *Le Mythe Aryen* (Paris, 1971), 204.

18. Salomon Reinach, *L'Origine des Aryens* (Paris, 1892), 16ff.

19. Michael H. Kater, *Das 'Ahnenerbe' der SS, 1935–1945* (Stuttgart, 1974), 79; for the students, see *The Times* (London), August 5, 1943 (Wiener Library Clipping Collection, Tel Aviv).

20. Müller, *op. cit.*, 45, 49.

21. *Ibid.*, 55, 65.

22. James Walvin, *Black and White: The Negro and English Society 1555–1945* (London, 1973), 63.

23. John R. Barker, *Race* (London, 1974), 204.

24. Reinhard Bollmus, *Das Amt Rosenberg und Seine Gegner* (Stuttgart, 1970), 154–162.

25. Eugene Lunn, *Prophet of Community: The Romantic Socialism of Gustav Landauer* (Berkeley, 1973), 6ff.

26. Alfred Rosenberg, *Der Mythus des 20. Jahrhunderts* (Munich, 1935), 28, 662.

27. W. H. Riehl, *Land und Leute* (Stuttgart, 1867), 17.

28. Ernst Weymar, *Das Selbstverständnis der Deutschen* (Stuttgart, 1961), 30, 33, 73.

29. Wolfgang Emmerich, *Zur Kritik der Volkstumsideologie* (Frankfurt-am-Main, 1971), 41.

30. Fustel de Coulanges, *Questions Contemporaines* (Paris, 1917), 24.

31. Thomas Nipperdey, "Zum Jubiläum des Hermannsdenkmals," *Ein Jahrhundert Hermannsdenkmal 1875–1975* (Detmold, 1975), 15.

32. Arthur Hertzberg, *The French Enlightenment and the Jews* (New York and London, 1968), 302.

33. This aspect of Herder has been stressed by Isaiah Berlin, *Vico and Herder* (London, 1976).

CHAPTER FOUR

1. A. de Gobineau, *L'Essai sur l'Inégalité des Races Humaines* (Paris, 1967), 121.

2. I am following the interpretation of the *Essay* given by Robert Edward Dreher, "Arthur de Gobineau: An Intellectual Portrait" (unpublished Ph.D. dissertation, University of Wisconsin, 1970). For the quotation in text, see 84.

3. Quoted in Michael D. Biddiss, *Father of Racist Ideology: The Social and Political Thought of Count Gobineau* (London, 1970), 114.

4. Gobineau, *op. cit.*, 658.

5. *Ibid.*, 58, 59; Biddiss, *op. cit.*, 125.

6. Winfred Schuler, *Der Bayreuther Kreis* (Münster, 1971), 104; George L. Mosse, *The Crisis of German Ideology* (New York, 1964), 91.

7. Mosse, *op. cit.*, 91.

8. *Ibid.*, 220–221.

9. Schuler, *op. cit.*, 243.

10. Pierre-Marie Dioudonnat, *Je Suis Partout, 1930–1944* (Paris, 1973), 220.

11. Alphonse de Candolle, *Histoire des Sciences et des Savants Depuis Deux Siècles* (Geneva-Basle, 1885; first published in 1873), 172–182, 186–195, 199; I owe this reference to Seymour Drescher. "Alphonse de Candolle über die Judenfrage," *Mitteilungen des Vereins zur Abwehr des Antisemitismus* (July 25, 1893), 294.

12. G. Vacher de Lapouge, *Der Arier und Seine Bedeutung für die Gemeinschaft* (Frankfurt-am-Main, 1939), 224ff, 188ff.

13. *Ibid.*, 228.

14. *Ibid.*, 234, 242, 254, 260.

15. *Ibid.*, 306–316, 240, 242.

16. *Ibid.*, 307.

17. G. Vacher de Lapouge, *Les Séléctions Sociales* (Paris, 1896), 488.

18. *Ibid.*, 488. Revolution for Lapouge was the transmission of power from one race to another, *ibid.*, 251.

19. See pages 78–79.

20. J. M. Winter, "The Webbs and the Non-White World: A Case of Socialist Racialism," *Journal of Contemporary History*, IX (January 1974), 190–191.

21. Hubert Thomas-Chevalier, *Le Racisme Français* (Nancy, 1943), xi.

22. *Ibid.*, xix.

CHAPTER FIVE

1. Quoted in Peter Viereck, *Metapolitics from the Romantics to Hitler* (New York, 1941), 4.

2. See *Moritz Lazarus und Hermann Steinthal*, ed. Ingrid Belke (Tübingen, 1971), 139, 450.

3. See Reginald Horsman, "Origins of Racial Anglo-Saxonism in Great Britain Before 1850," *Journal of the History of Ideas*, XXXVII (July–September 1976), 387–410.

4. Edward A. Freeman, *Lectures to American Audiences* (Philadelphia, 1882), 15, 33.

5. Robert Knox, *The Races of Men* (London, 1862), v, 57.

6. *Ibid.*, 50.

7. *Ibid.*, 404, 287.

8. *Ibid.*, 447.

9. *Ibid.*, 194.

10. *Ibid.*, 4, 196, 445.

11. Robert Blake, *Disraeli* (London, 1966), 203.

12. T. Carlyle, *Occasional Discourse on the Nigger Question* (London, 1853), 19, 33.

13. James Hunt, "On the Study of Anthropology," *Anthropological Review*, I (1863), 4.

14. James Hunt, *Dr. Hunt's Farewell Address as President of the Anthropological Society* (London, 1867), 21.

15. *Ibid.*, 17.

16. *Ibid.*, 19.

17. James Hunt, *On the Negro's Place in Nature* (London, 1863), 26, 37, 52, 58.

18. *Ibid.*, 58; Christine Bolt, *Victorian Attitudes to Race* (London, 1971), 21–22.

19. Charles C. Gillispie, "The Darwinian Heritage," in *The Making of the Modern World*, ed. Norman F. Cantor and Michael S. Wertham (New York, 1967), 125 and *passim*.

20. Karl Pearson, "Charles Darwin, 1809–1882," reprinted in *The Making of Modern Europe*, ed. Herman Ausubel (New York, 1951), 760.

21. *Ibid.*, 761.

22. Quoted in C. P. Blacker, *Eugenics, Galton and After* (London, 1952), 108.

23. Karl Pearson, *The Relative Strength of Nurture and Nature* (Cambridge, Eng., 1915), 48ff.

24. Blacker, *op. cit.*, 108.

25. Willibald Hentschel, *Varuna* (Leipzig, 1907), 274.

26. See page 219.

27. *Speeches Delivered at a Dinner Held in University College, London, in Honour of Professor Karl Pearson, 23 April, 1934* (Cambridge, Eng., 1934), 23.

CHAPTER SIX

1. Eugen Fischer, "Begriff, Abgrenzung und Geschichte der Anthropologie," *Anthropologie*, ed. G. Schwalbe and E. Fischer (Leipzig, 1923), 10.

2. *Archiv für Rassen- und Gesellschafts Biologie*, I (1904), iv, vi. (Cited hereafter as *Archiv*.)

3. Karl Pearson, "Über den Zweck und die Bedeutung den National-Eugenik für den Staat," *Archiv*, V (1908), 91.

4. Karl Pearson, *The Moral Basis of Socialism* (London, n.d.), 5.

5. Ludwig Woltmann, *Politische Anthropologie*, ed. Otto Reche (Berlin, 1936), 388, 392.

6. A. Nordenholz in *Archiv*, VI (1909), 131.

7. See M. von Gruber, "Wilhelm Schallmayer," *Archiv*, XIV (1922 and 1923), 52–55; Wilhelm Schallmayer, "Der Krieg als Züchter," *Archiv*, V (1908), 388–399; Fritz Bölle, "Darwinismus und Zeitgeist," *Zeitschrift für Religion und Geistesgeschichte*, XIV (1962), 167.

8. Alfred Ploetz in *Archiv*, I (1904), 892, 893.

9. Alfred Ploetz, *Die Tüchtigkeit unserer Rasse und der Schutz der Schwachen* (Berlin, 1895), 138–140; see also pages 91–92.

10. Arnold Dodel, *Moses oder Darwin? Eine Schulfrage* (Stuttgart, 1895), 114, 116; G. Beck, *Antidodel*, accused Dodel of Darwinianism; Dodel, *op. cit.*, 132.

11. P. Näcke, "Zur Angeblichen Rasse der Romanischen Völker, Speziell Frankreich," *Archiv*, III (1906), 380.

12. Alfred Ploetz in *Archiv*, VI (1909), 139.

13. *Archiv*, VI (1909), 280.

14. Alfred Ploetz in *Archiv*, XXVII (1933), 423. As a matter of fact the anti-Semitic Volkish publishing house, J. F. Lehmann of Munich, was the official publisher for the Society for Racial Hygiene, as well as Eugen Fischer's publisher in the 1920's.

15. But even so, together with praise for Zionism, *Archiv*, XXIX (1935), 457.

16. Erwin Bauer, Eugen Fischer, Fritz Lenz, *Menschliche Erblichkeitslehre* (Munich, 1923), 147, 148.

17. Quoted in Erwin H. Ackerknecht, *Kurze Geschichte der Psychiatrie* (Stuttgart, 1957), 51.

18. *Ibid.*, 52.

19. There is only one modern biography of Lombroso, Gina Lombroso de Ferrero, *Vida de Lombroso* (Mexico, 1940); cf. C. Lombroso and R. Laschi, *Der Politische Verbrecher und die Revolutionen* (Hamburg, 1891); C. Lombroso, *Der Antisemitismus und die Juden* (Leipzig, 1854), 84.

20. Cesare Lombroso, *Entartung und Genie*, ed. Hans Kurella (Leipzig, 1894), 91 ff.

21. *Ibid.*, 94.

22. Cesare Lombroso, "Introduction" to Gina Lombroso Ferrero, *Criminal Man According to the Classification of Cesare Lombroso* (New York and London, 1911), xv.

23. *Ibid.*, xviii.

24. See pages 219, 220.

25. Max Nordau, *Degeneration* (New York, 1968), 541.

26. *Ibid.*, 560.

27. *Ibid.*, 269.

28. Daniel Gasman, *The Scientific Origins of National Socialism* (London and New York, 1971), on the link between Haeckel and racism, 40ff.

29. *Ibid.*, 95.

30. *Ibid.*, 10.

31. Ernst Haeckel, *Die Welträthsel* (Stuttgart, n.d.), 126, 132, 174.

32. Alfred Kelly, "Wilhelm Bölsche and the Popularization of Science in Germany" (unpublished Ph.D. dissertation, University of Wisconsin, Madison, 1975), 195ff.

33. M. Paul Broca, "Histoire des Travaux de la Société d'Anthropologie (1859–1863)," *Mémoirs de la Société d'Anthropologie de Paris*, II (Paris, 1865), ix.

34. *Ibid.*, xxvii.

35. M. Paul Broca, "Recherches sur l'Ethnologie de la France," *ibid.*, I (Paris, 1860–1863), 3, 53.

36. François Pruner, *ibid.*, I (Paris, 1860), 333.

37. J. A. H. Périer, "Les Croisements Ethniques," *ibid.*, II (Paris, 1865), 371.

38. J. Deniker, *Les Races de l'Europe*, I (Paris, 1899), 99; *ibid.*, II (Paris, 1908), 123, 124.

39. Jean-Louis Armand de Quatrefages, *Rapport sur Les Progrès de l'Anthropologie* (Paris, 1867), 115, 151, 315.

40. Jean-Louis Armand de Quatrefages, *The Prussian Race, Ethnographically Considered* (London, 1872), *passim*.

41. Erwin H. Ackerknecht, *Rudolf Virchow* (Madison, Wis., 1953), 209–210.

42. *Ibid.*, 213, 214. Only one Jewish school cooperated. See the detailed description of the project in *Archiv für Anthropologie*, XVI (January 1886), 285–367.

43. See page 172.

44. Statistics from Ackerknecht, *Rudolf Virchow*, 214, and also in G. Sergi, *The Mediterranean Race* (Oosterhout, 1967), 14 (first published in 1895).

45. Arthur Ruppin, *The Jewish Fate and Future* (London, 1940), 20.

46. *Ibid.*, 20.

47. *Archiv für Anthropologie*, XVI (January 1886), 367.

48. For example, in Carl Paasch, *Geheimrath Professor Dr. Rudolph Virchow aus Schievelbein, Unser Grosser Gelahrter* (Leipzig, 1892), *passim*.

49. Rudolf Virchow, "Rassenbildung und Erblichkeit," *Adolf Bastian als Festgruss* (n.p., 1896), 17, 43.

CHAPTER SEVEN

1. G. Trobridge, *Swedenborg Life and Teaching* (London, 1945), 186.
2. For all this and what follows, see George L. Mosse, "The Mystical Origins of National Socialism," *Journal of the History of Ideas*, XXII, no. I (January–March 1961), 81–96.
3. George L. Mosse, "Changes in Religious Thought," *The New Cambridge Modern History*, IV (Cambridge, Eng., 1970), 173–175.
4. For Langbehn, see George L. Mosse, *The Crisis of German Ideology* (New York, 1964), 39–46.
5. Johannes Baltzli, *Guido von List* (Vienna, 1917), 26, 27.
6. Mosse, *Crisis of German Ideology*, 75, 76, 306.
7. *Ibid.*, 295; Wilfred Daim, *Der Mann der Hitler die Ideen Gab* (Munich, 1958), *passim*; Andrew G. Whiteside, *The Socialism of Fools* (Berkeley, 1975), 248, 253 254.
8. Mosse, *Crisis of German Ideology*, 31–39.
9. Cosima Wagner, *Die Tagebücher*, vol. I, *1869–1877*, ed. Martin Gregor-Dellin and Dietrich Mack (Munich, 1976), 378.
10. *See ibid.*, 569.
11. This discussion follows George L. Mosse, *The Nationalization of the Masses* (New York, 1975), 101–108.
12. Wagner, *op. cit.*, 627, 744.
13. See page 113.
14. Hans Kohn, *Martin Buber Sein Werk und Seine Zeit* (Cologne, 1961), 93.
15. Franziska Gräfin Zu Reventlow, *Der Geldcomplex, Herrn Dames Aufzeichnungen, von Paul Zu Pedro* (Munich, 1958), 138. This book contains one of the best accounts of the cosmic philosophers in Munich, including Schuler and Stefan George.
16. See page 56.
17. Mosse, *Nationalization of the Masses*, 106.
18. Quoted in *ibid.*, 105.
19. See, for instance, Karl Kupisch, "The 'Luther Renaissance,' " *Journal of Contemporary History*, II (October 1967), 39–49.
20. Houston Stewart Chamberlain, *Auswahl aus seinen Werken* (Breslau, 1934), 65, 66, 68.
21. Otto Weininger, *Geschlecht und Charakter* (Vienna and Leipzig, 1920), inside title page.
22. See Jeannine Verdes-Leroux, *Scandale Financier et Antisémitique: Le Krach de l'Union Générale* (Paris, 1969), 113–116.
23. Colette Guillaumin, *L'Idéologie Raciste Genèse et Langue Actuel* (The Hague, 1972), 37.

24. Zeev Sternhell, *Maurice Barrès et le Nationalisme Français* (Paris, 1972), 264.

25. See *Judenkenner*, Folge 32 (September 25, 1935), *passim.*

26. Weininger, *op. cit.*, 438–439.

27. Friedrich Heer, *Der Glaube des Adolf Hitler* (Munich, 1968), 271.

28. Adolf Hitler, *Mein Kampf* (Munich, 1934), 59–65.

29. The seminal work on the history of sex and smell which provides a new perspective on the history of European culture is Stephen Kern, *Anatomy and Destiny: A Cultural History of the Human Body* (Indianapolis, 1975).

30. *Ibid.*, 50–51.

31. Albert Hagen (Iwan Bloch), *Die Sexuelle Osphresiologie* (Berlin, 1906), 179, 12. I owe this reference to Stephen Kern.

32. Jacob Toury, *Der Eintritt der Juden ins Deutsche Bürgertum. Eine Dokumentation* (Tel Aviv, 1972), 184.

CHAPTER EIGHT

1. *The Jews of Czechoslovakia*, The Society for the History of Czechoslovak Jews (Philadelphia-New York, 1968), 152.

2. See, for example, Jeannine Verdes-Leroux, *Scandale Financier et Antisémitique: Le Krach de l'Union Générale* (Paris, 1969), 223.

3. George K. Anderson, *The Legend of the Wandering Jew* (Providence, 1965), 21, 22.

4. *Raemaekers Cartoons* (n.d., n.p.), Part 3, p. 69.

5. Josef Müller, *Die Entwicklung des Rassenantisemitismus in den letzten Jahrzehnten des 19. Jahrhunderts* (Berlin, 1940), 25, 67; Müller analyzes the *Antisemitische Correspondenz* from, roughly, 1887 until 1892.

6. Quoted in Herman Bernstein, *The History of a Lie* (New York, 1921), 23.

7. *Ibid.*, 32.

8. *Ibid.*

9. *Ibid.*, 33.

10. See page 26.

11. Norman Cohn, *Warrant for Genocide* (New York, 1966), 43. I have followed this classic work in my discussion of the *Protocols.*

12. *Protocols of the Learned Elders of Zion* (Union, N.J., n.d.), 25. This is a modern version of the English edition of 1922.

13. *Ibid.*, 33; *Arbeiterzeitung* (Vienna), December 3, 1933 (Wiener Library Clipping Collection, Tel Aviv).

14. H. Lutostanski, *The Talmud and the Jew* (n.p., 1876), *passim.*

15. *Actes du Premier Congrès Antimaçonnique Internationale*, Sep-

tember 24 to 30, 1894, at Trente (Fournay, 1897), 119, 124.

16. Paul W. Massing, *Rehearsal for Destruction* (New York, 1967), 94.

17. The Paris police called it "anti-Jewish confetti," Archives de la Préfecture de Police, Paris, B. a/1341.

18. *Schmeitzner's Internationale Monatsschrift*, II (January 1883), *passim*; *ibid.*, II (May 1883), *passim*. Schmeitzner was the secretary of the congress.

19. Mosche Zimmermann, "Gabriel Riesser und Wilhelm Marr im Meinungsstreit," *Zeitschrift des Vereins für Hamburgische Geschichte*, vol. 61 (1975), 59–84.

20. Michael D. Biddiss, "The Universal Races Congress of 1911," *Race*, XIII (July 1971), 43.

21. Max Jungmann, "Ist das Jüdische Volk degeneriert?", *Die Welt*, 6. Jahrg., Nr. 24 (June 13, 1902).

22. Elias Auerbach, "Die Jüdische Rassenfrage," *Archiv für Rassen- und Gesellschafts Biologie*, IV (1907), 333.

23. J. M. Judt, *Die Juden als Rasse: Eine Analyse aus dem Gebiet der Anthropologie* (Berlin, 1903), 213. This was published by the Jewish publishing house, Jüdischer Verlag.

24. Richard Andree, *Zur Volkskunde der Juden* (Bielefeld and Leipzig, 1881), 3, 10, 25.

25. Ignaz Zollschan, *Das Rassenproblem unter Besonderer Berücksichtigung der Theoretischen Grundlagen der Jüdischen Rassenfrage* (Vienna and Leipzig, 1910), 8, 235, 260ff., 427.

26. Ignaz Zollschan, *The Jewish Question* (New York, 1914), 14.

27. Adolf Böhm, *Die Zionistische Bewegung*, II (Tel Aviv, 1937), 84.

28. No study of this problem exists. I am grateful to Miss Deborah Hershmann and Mr. Warren Green for the information upon which this discussion of orthodox Jewry is based. See also the reliance on Noahic law as a code of morals for non-Jews in Germany in Sidney M. Bolkosky, *The Distorted Image: German Jewish Perceptions of Germans and Germany, 1918–1935* (New York, 1975), 80.

29. Theodor Herzl quoted in *Die Welt*, XVIII (July 3, 1914).

30. Amos Elon, *Herzl* (New York, 1975), 171, 251.

31. Moses Calvary in *Die Welt*, XVII (November 7, 1913), 540.

32. Robert Weltsch in *Die Welt*, XVII (March 21, 1913), 366.

33. Maurice Fishberg, *Die Rassenmerkmale der Juden* (Munich, 1913), 49, 51; see also Maurice Fishberg, "Zur Frage der Herkunft des blonden Elementes in Judentum," *Zeitschrift für Demographie und Statistik der Juden* (1907).

34. Felix von Luschan, *Völker, Rassen, Sprachen* (Berlin, 1922), 25, 169.

252

Notes

35. Gustav Krojanker, *Zum Problem des Neuen Deutschen Nationalismus* (Berlin, 1932), 17, 19.

CHAPTER NINE

1. Ursula Henriques, *Religious Toleration in England, 1787–1833* (London, 1961), 181.
2. Edward L. Schaub, "J. G. Fichte and Antisemitism," *Philosophical Review*, XLIX (January 1, 1940), 49. Yet even when Jews were considered as part of the divine plan, their supposed malicious behavior toward Christ and Christianity was deemed inexcusable. For example, it was principally a Christian tradition which kept anti-Semitism alive during those centuries when hardly any Jews at all lived in England; Bernard Glassman, *Anti-Semitic Stereotypes Without Jews: Images of the Jews in England 1290–1700* (Detroit, 1975), 12, 144, and *passim*.
3. Ernest Renan, *Das Leben Jesu* (Leipzig, n.d.), 24, 29, 244, 293.
4. D. Karl Hase, *Das Leben Jesu* (Leipzig, 1835), 151, 152; Karl von Hase, *Ideale und Irrtümer* (Leipzig, 1917), 170.
5. See pages 105–106.
6. Wolfgang Tilgner, *Volksnomostheologie und Schöpfungsglaube* (Göttingen, 1966), 30.
7. *Ibid.*, 67.
8. Pauline Relyea Anderson, *The Background of Anti-English Feeling in Germany, 1890–1902* (Washington, D.C., 1939), 151.
9. *Ibid.*, 360.
10. See pages 97, 98, 100, and 101.
11. See, for example, Hans Liebeschütz, *Das Judentum im deutschen Geschichtsbild von Hegel bis Max Weber* (Tübingen, 1967), 99.
12. See Karl Kupisch, "The 'Luther Renaissance,' " *Journal of Contemporary History*, II (October 1967), 39–49.
13. George L. Mosse, *The Nationalization of the Masses* (New York, 1975), 77, 78.
14. Cited in Jacob Toury, *Der Eintritt der Juden ins Deutsche Bürgertum. Eine Dokumentation* (Tel Aviv, 1972), 309.
15. Eleanor Sterling, *Judenhass* (Frankfurt-am-Main, 1969), 162–163.
16. Jeannine Verdes-Leroux, *Scandale Financier et Antisémitique: Le Krach de l'Union Générale* (Paris, 1969), 214.
17. Bishof Alois Hudal, *Die Grundlagen des Nationalsozialismus* (Leipzig and Vienna, 1937), 86.
18. W. Feldman, *Geschichte der politischen Ideen in Polen seit dessen Teilung* (Osnabrück, 1964), 423.

19. Norman Cohn, *Europe's Inner Demons: An Enquiry Inspired by the Great Witch-Hunt* (New York, 1975), 69.

20. Verdes-Leroux, *op. cit.*, 214.

21. Uriel Tal, *Christians and Jews in Germany* (Ithaca, N.Y., 1975), 89.

22. *Ibid.*, 88; Verdes-Leroux, *op. cit.*, 226–227.

23. Verdes-Leroux, *op. cit.*, 227.

24. Jürgen Puhle, *Agrarische Interressenpolitik und Preussischer Konservatismus im Wilhelminischen Reich* (Hannover, 1967), 123.

25. For a discussion of these unions, see Adrien Toussaint, *L'Union Centrale des Syndicats Agricoles, Ses Idées Directrices* (Paris, 1920), but especially H. de Gailhard-Bancel, *Quinze Années d'Action Syndicale* (Paris, 1900).

26. Robert O. Paxton, *La France de Vichy* (Paris, 1973), 175–177; Xavier Vallat, *La Croix les Lys et la Peine des Hommes* (Paris, 1960), 184, 295.

27. *Le Sang Chrétien dans les Rites de la Synagogue Moderne*, Archives de L'Alliance Israélite, Allemagne: I. c. 2, Paris.

28. Archives de L'Alliance Israélite, Allemagne: I. c. 2, Paris, Report of November 2, 1885.

29. Friedrich Heer, *Der Glaube des Adolf Hitler* (Munich, 1968), 66; Werner Jochmann, "Struktur und Funktion des deutschen Antisemitismus," *Juden im Wilhelminischen Deutschland 1890–1914*, ed. Werner Mosse and Arnold Paucker (Tübingen, 1976), 398.

30. *Die Socialen Lehren des Freiherrn Karl von Vogelsang*, ed. Wiard Klopp (St. Polten, 1894), 184; Wiard Klopp, *Leben und Wirken des Sozialpolitikers Karl Freiherr von Vogelsang* (Vienna, 1930), 70; Andrew G. Whiteside, *The Socialism of Fools* (Berkeley, 1975), 87.

31. *Die Socialen Lehren der Freiherrn Karl von Vogelsang*, 194.

32. Ignaz Seipel, *Nation und Staat* (Vienna and Leipzig, 1916), 3, 6.

33. *Balthasar Schmids Verfasste und Ausgefürrte Reise-Beschreibung etc.*, edited and corrected by P. Magnus Schleyer (Babenhausen, 1723), 413, 414.

34. Report of Proceeding of the Berlin Jewish Community Council, September 9, 1881, M/16 (Jewish National Archives, Jerusalem).

35. Pierre Sorin, *La Croix et les Juifs* (Paris, 1967), 141. The *Talmud Jew* went through 17 editions until 1922; one Catholic group in Westphalia distributed 38,000 copies. I. A. Hellwing, *Der konfessionelle Antisemitismus im 19. Jahrhundert in Österreich* (Vienna, 1967), 90. This is the best and most thorough analysis of the Rohling affair.

36. Hellwing, *op. cit.*, 107.

37. *Ibid.*, 79–81, 87, 111–112.

38. See Michael Marrus, *The Politics of Assimilation: A Study of the French Jewish Community at the Time of the Dreyfus Affair* (Oxford, 1971), *passim.*

39. Houston Stewart Chamberlain, *Die Grundlagen des 19. Jahrhunderts*, I (Munich, 1932), 486; Alfred Rosenberg, *Der Mythus des 20. Jahrhunderts* (Munich, 1935), 463; Catalogue of the *Exposition le Juif et la France au Palais Berlitz* (September 1941–January 1942), 15.

40. Sorin, *op. cit.*, 7.

41. "Liberal" was said to be synonymous with "Judenliberal," *Mitteilungen des Vereins zur Abwehr des Antisemitismus* (October 26, 1895), 339.

42. Felix Czeike, *Liberale, Christlichsoziale und Sozialdemokratische Kommunalpolitik* (Vienna, 1962), *passim.*

43. Franz Stauracz, *Dr. Karl Lueger, Zehn Jahre Bürgermeister* (Vienna and Leipzig, 1907), 151ff.

44. Stauracz, *op. cit.*, 230; Adolf Hitler, *Mein Kampf* (Munich, 1934), 131.

45. Eugen Weber, *Action Française* (Stanford, Calif., 1962), 198.

46. Charles Maurras, *Political and Critical Dictionary* (n.p., n.d.), 303–305.

47. Maurice Pujo, *Les Camelots du Roi* (Paris, n.d.), *passim.*

48. *Ibid.*, 25.

49. Theodor I. Armon, "La Guardia di Ferro," *Storia Contemporanea*, VII (September 1976), 513.

50. *Cahiers du Cercle Proudhon*, I (January–February 1912), 41; *ibid.* (May–August 1912), 158, 160; *ibid.* (n.d.), 248. Zeev Sternhell, "Anatomie d'un Mouvement Fasciste: Le Faisceau de George Valois," *Revue Française de Science Politique*, no. I, vol. 26 (February 1976), 7.

51. *Cahiers du Cercle Proudhon*, I (March–April 1912), 80; Sternhell, *op. cit.*, 8.

52. Hudal, *op. cit.*, 244.

53. *Ibid.*, 90.

54. Friedrich Engel-Janosi, *Vom Chaos zur Katastrophe, Vatikanische Gespräche 1918 bis 1938* (Vienna and Munich, 1971), 188.

55. The Vatican disavowed Hudal's book. See *ibid.*, 186.

56. Guenter Lewy, *The Catholic Church and Nazi Germany* (New York, 1964), 301.

57. Paul W. Massing, *Rehearsal for Destruction* (New York, 1967), 28; Karl Kupisch, *Adolf Stoecker, Hofprediger und Volkstribün* (Berlin, 1970), 36ff.

58. Massing, *op. cit.*, 31.

59. *Ibid.*, 64ff.

60. *Der Berliner Antisemitismusstreit*, ed. Walter Boehlich (Frankfurt-am-Main, 1965), 9. All the relevant documents are reprinted here.

CHAPTER TEN

1. Jeannine Verdez-Leroux, *Scandale Financier et Antisémitique: Le Krach de l'Union Générale* (Paris, 1969), 12.

2. *Édouard Drumont ou L'Anticapitalisme Nationale*, ed. E. Beau de Loménie (Paris, 1968), 80.

3. For these ideas at mid-century, see George Lichtheim, "Socialism and the Jews," *Dissent* (July–August 1968).

4. Alphonse Toussenel, *Les Juifs, Rois de l'Époque, Histoire de la Féodalité Financière*, I (Paris, 1947), 320.

5. Quoted by Lichtheim, *op. cit.*, 322.

6. *Ibid.*, 322.

7. Karl Marx, *A World Without Jews*, ed. Dagobert D. Runes (New York, 1959), 41.

8. *Ibid.*, 37.

9. For the consequences of Marx's view of the Jews, see George L. Mosse, "German Socialists and the Jewish Question in the Weimar Republic," *Year Book of the Leo Baeck Institute*, XVI (London, 1971), 123–151.

10. *Édouard Drumont ou L'Anticapitalisme Nationale*, ed. de Loménie, 108.

11. *Ibid.*, 357.

12. Léon Furiette, *Drumont* (Puteaux, 1902), 61.

13. *Ibid.*, xxi. This is from the preface which Drumont wrote for this book and which was first published in 1862.

14. *Ibid.*, iii.

15. Édouard Drumont, "Preface," Henri Desportes, *Le Mystère du Sang* (Paris, 1889).

16. The argument here is taken from George L. Mosse, "The French Right and the Working Classes: Les Jaunes," *Journal of Contemporary History*, VII (July–October 1972), 185–208.

17. Georges Bernanos, *La Grande Peur des Bien-Pensants* (Paris, 1931), 16, 405. Bernanos repeated this praise in 1939 in his *Scandale de la Vérité*; see also Frank Field, *Three French Writers and the Great War* (Cambridge, Eng., 1975), 168ff.

18. Pierre-Marie Dioudonnat, *Je Suis Partout, 1930–1944* (Paris, 1973), 224.

19. Mosse, "Les Jaunes," 191.

20. Henri de Bruchard, "Un Héros de l'Antisémitisme: Le Marquis de Morès," *Revue Critique des Idées et des Livres*, XIII (April–June 1911), 274.

21. Report of the Police, Archives de la Préfecture de Police, Paris, B. a/1107.

22. Charles da Costa, *Les Blanquistes* (Paris, 1912), 59ff.

23. Mosse, "Les Jaunes," 192.

24. The most useful source for what follows is Michel Ansky, *Les Juifs d'Algérie, du Décret Crémieux à la Libération* (Paris, 1950).

25. Louis Durieu, *Les Juifs Algériennes (1870–1901)* (Paris, 1902), 87.

26. Ansky, *op. cit.*, 59.

27. Gustave Rouanet, *Discours Prononcé à la Chambre des Députés, Les 19. et 24. Mai 1899* (Paris, n.d.), 82–83.

28. See Report of the Police, Archives de la Préfecture de Police, Paris, B. a/1107.

29. See pages 141ff. for another grass roots anti-Semitic movement led by Karl Lueger in Vienna.

30. Peter G. J. Pulzer, *The Rise of Political Anti-Semitism in Germany and Austria* (New York, 1964), 207–209.

31. Viktor Bibl, *Georg von Schönerer ein Vorkämpfer des Grossdeutschen Reichs* (Leipzig, 1942), 23; Erwin Mayer-Löwenschwerdt, *Schönerer der Vorkämpfer* (Vienna and Leipzig, 1939), 87, 240. The best book on Schönerer is Andrew G. Whiteside, *The Socialism of Fools* (Berkeley, 1975) to which I am greatly indebted.

32. Andrew G. Whiteside, *Austrian National Socialism Before 1913* (The Hague, 1962), 91.

33. *Ibid.*, 105.

34. *Ibid.*, 96, 100.

35. *Ibid.*, 102; Pulzer, *op. cit.*, 207.

36. Dühring condemned Drumont, as he did all possible rivals: E. Dühring, *Die Judenfrage als Frage der Rassenschädlichkeit* (Berlin, 1892), 110–111.

37. Gerhard Albrecht, *Eugen Dühring. Ein Beitrag zur Geschichte der Sozialwissenschaft* (Jena, 1927), 247.

38. Gustav Mayer, *Friedrich Engels* (New York, 1969), 238.

39. Albrecht, *op. cit.*, 258, 265.

40. Rüdiger Mack, "Antisemitische Bauernbewegung in Hessen (1887–1894)," *Wetterauer Geschichtsblätter*, XVI (1967), 19.

41. *Ibid.*, 17 n. 49.

42. Eugen Schmahl, *Die Antisemitische Bauernbewegung in Hessen von der Boeckelzeit bis zum Nationalsozialismus*; Wilhelm Seipel, *Entwicklung*

Notes   257

der Nationalsozialistischen Bauernbewegung in Hessen (Giessen, 1933), 99–100.

43. *Mitteilungen des Vereins zur Abwehr des Antisemitismus*, vol. II, no. 26 (June 26, 1892), 221; Schmahl, *op. cit.*, 106.

44. Richard S. Levy, *The Downfall of the Anti-Semitic Political Parties in Imperial Germany* (New Haven, Conn., 1977), 90, 105, 106.

45. Schmahl, *op. cit.*, 98.

46. Mack, *op. cit.*, 35.

CHAPTER ELEVEN

1. Egmont Zechlin, *Die deutsche Politik und die Juden im Ersten Weltkrieg* (Göttingen, 1969), 527.

2. *Ibid.*, 531, n. 74.

3. Philippe Rudaux, *Les Croix de Feu et le P.S.F.* (Paris, 1967), 31; George L. Mosse, "The Genesis of Fascism," *Journal of Contemporary History*, I (1966), 14–27; George L. Mosse, "The Poet and the Exercise of Political Power: Gabriele d'Annunzio," *Yearbook of Comparative and General Literature* (Bloomington, Ind., 1973), 24.

4. Frances Cornford quoted in Bernard Bergonzi, *Heroes' Twilight, A Study of the Literature of the Great War* (London, 1965), 36; Otto Braun, *Aus Nachgelassenen Schriften Eines Frühvollendeten*, ed. Julie Vogelstein (Berlin, 1921), 120; Paul Fussell, *The Great War and Modern Memory* (New York and London, 1975), 275ff.

5. Ernst Jünger, *Der Kampf als inneres Erlebnis* (Berlin, 1922), 33.

6. George L. Mosse, "Tod, Zeit und Geschichte. Die völkische Utopie der Überwindung," *Deutsches utopisches Denken im 20. Jahrhundert*, ed. Reinhold Grimm and Jost Hermand (Stuttgart, 1974), 55.

7. *Ibid.*, 56.

8. Michael Ledeen, *The First Duce, D'Annunzio at Fiume* (Baltimore, 1977), is now the best work on his rule over Fiume.

9. Karl Hammer, *Deutsche Kriegstheologie 1870–1918* (Munich, 1974), 157.

10. I have relied here upon Keith L. Nelson, "The 'Black Horror on the Rhine': Race as a Factor in Post-War I Diplomacy," *Journal of Modern History* (December 1970), 606–628; see also Alfred Brie, *Geschändete deutsche Frauen. Wie die farbigen Franzosen in den besetzten Gebieten wüten* (Leipzig, 1921), n.p.

11. Manfred Sell, *Die Schwarze Völkerwanderung; Der Einbruch des Negers in die Kulturwelt* (Vienna, 1940), 301.

12. Letter of Dr. Engel, Hamburg (January 22, 1914), N. 223, Akte

1889 (Hamburg), Jewish National Archives, Jerusalem; N. 310, Akte 1889 (Hamburg), Jewish National Archives.

13. George L. Mosse, "Die deutsche Rechte und die Juden," *Entscheidungsjahr 1932*, ed. Werner Mosse (Tübingen, 1966), 184.

14. Bradley F. Smith, *Heinrich Himmler: A Nazi in the Making, 1900–1926* (Stanford, Calif., 1971), 123.

15. Walter Laqueur, *Russia and Germany* (London, 1965), 5off.

16. Norman Cohn, *Warrant for Genocide* (London, 1966), 151.

17. Norman Davies, "Great Britain and the Polish Jews 1918–1920," *Journal of Contemporary History*, VIII (April 1973), 126; Gina M. Mitchell, "John Buchan's Popular Fiction, A Hierarchy of Race," *Patterns of Prejudice*, VII (November–December 1973), 24–30.

18. Louis Fischer, *The Soviets in World Affairs* (New York, 1960), 427; interview with Churchill's biographer Martin Gilbert, *The Times* (January 10, 1977), 9.

19. Cohn, *op. cit.*, 165.

20. Alan Bullock, *Hitler, A Study in Tyranny* (New York, n.d.), 589; *Hitler's Secret Conversations, 1941–1944*, ed. H. R. Trevor-Roper (New York, 1953), 65.

21. George L. Mosse, *The Crisis of German Ideology* (New York, 1964), 190ff; *Native Fascism in the Successor States 1918–1945*, ed. Peter F. Sugar (Santa Barbara, Calif., 1971), 97.

22. Uwe Dietrich Adam, *Judenpolitik im Dritten Reich* (Düsseldorf, 1972), 68.

23. S. Ettinger, "Jews and Non-Jews in Eastern and Central Europe between the Wars: An Outline," *Jews and Non-Jews in Eastern Europe, 1918–1945*, ed. Bela Vago and George L. Mosse (Jerusalem and New York, 1974), 10ff.

24. George Barany, "Magyar Jew or Jewish Magyar? Reflections on the Question of Assimilation," *ibid.*, 56ff.

25. Harry M. Rabinowicz, *The Legacy of Polish Jewry* (New York and London, 1965), *passim*.

26. Adam, *op. cit.*, 200.

27. Edward D. Wynot, Jr., " 'A Necessary Cruelty': The Emergence of Official Anti-Semitism in Poland, 1936–1939," *American Historical Review*, LXXVI (October 1971), 1042, 1047, 1051; Rabinowicz, *op. cit.*, 58.

28. Lucy S. Dawidowicz, *The War Against the Jews, 1933–1945* (New York, 1975), 189.

29. Werner Jochmann, "Die Ausbreitung des Antisemitismus," *Deutsches Judentum in Krieg und Revolution 1916–1923*, ed. Werner E. Mosse and Arnold Paucker (Tübingen, 1971), 457.

30. On this society, see *Mitteilungen des Vereins zur Abwehr des Antisemitismus* (January 12, 1922), 4.

31. Ernst von Salomon, *Die Geächteten* (Gütersloh, 1930), 71.

32. E. J. Gumbel, *Vier Jahre Politischer Mord* (Berlin, 1922), *passim*; Donald L. Niewyk, "Jews and the Courts in Weimar Germany," *Jewish Social Studies*, XXXVII (Spring, 1975), 111.

33. Jochmann, *op. cit.*, 464, 465.

34. E. J. Gumbel, *Vom Femenmord zur Reichskanzelei* (Heidelberg, 1962), 50.

35. Jochmann, *op. cit.*, 467.

36. Mosse, *Crisis of German Ideology*, 239–241.

37. Jochmann, *op. cit.*, 471.

38. Francis L. Carsten, *Reichswehr und Politik 1918–1933* (Cologne, 1964), 223.

39. For an excellent discussion of this issue, see Francis L. Carsten, *Revolution in Central Europe: 1918–1919* (Berkeley and Los Angeles, 1967), Chapter 10.

40. Arnold Paucker, *Der jüdische Abwehrkampf* (Hamburg, 1968), 96, 97.

41. George L. Mosse, "German Socialists and the Jewish Question in the Weimar Republic," *Year Book XVI of the Leo Baeck Institute* (London, 1971), 123–134.

42. *Ibid.*, 136.

43. *Ibid.*, 134–143.

44. *Ibid.*, 131–132.

45. Bela Vago, "The Attitude Toward the Jews as a Criterion of the Left-Right Concept," *Jews and Non-Jews in Eastern Europe*, 33.

46. Bernard K. Johnpol, *The Politics of Futility, the General Jewish Workers Bund of Poland, 1917–1943* (Ithaca, N.Y., 1967), 193.

47. Leo Pinsker, *Auto-Emancipation: An Appeal to His People by a Russian Jew* (1882), quoted by Walter Laqueur, *A History of Zionism* (New York, 1972), 72.

48. Mosse, *Crisis of German Ideology*, 303, 304; L. F. Clauss, *Rasse und Seele, Eine Einführung in den Sinn der Leiblichen Gestalt* (Berlin, 1933), *passim*.

49. Mosse, *Crisis of German Ideology*, 302, 303.

CHAPTER TWELVE

1. See George L. Mosse, *The Nationalization of the Masses* (New York, 1975), *passim*.

2. Lucy Dawidowicz, *The War Against the Jews, 1933–1945* (New York, 1975).

3. W. F. Mandle, *Anti-Semitism and the British Union of Fascists* (London, 1968), 23.

4. *Ibid.*, 37, n. 6.

5. *Ibid.*, 44, n. 4.

6. Stanley G. Payne, *Falange. A History of Spanish Fascism* (Stanford, Calif., 1961), 126; Juan J. Linz, *An Authoritarian Regime: Spain* (n.p., mimeographed, 1963), 25.

7. Cf. *X. Congrès Francisme, Paris 1, 2, 3, 4 Juillet 1943* (Paris, 1943), *passim*.

8. Eugen Weber, *Action Française* (Stanford, Calif., 1962), 190.

9. Robert J. Soucy, "The Nature of Fascism in France," *Journal of Contemporary History*, I (1966), 33–34.

10. Dieter Wolf, *Die Doriot-Bewegung* (Stuttgart, 1967), 158–159, 162.

11. Marcel Bucard, *L'Emprise Juive* (Paris, 1938), 12.

12. Gilbert D. Allardyce, "The Political Transition of Jacques Doriot," *Journal of Contemporary History*, I (1966), 69–70.

13. *Ibid.*, 72.

14. *L'Émancipation Nationale* (November 14, 1936), 11.

15. Adolf Hitler, Dr. Goebbels, A. Rosenberg, J. von Ribbentrop, *L'Avenir de l'Allemagne, précédé d'une Étude par Y.-M. Sicard* (Paris, 1937), 18.

16. *L'Émancipation Nationale* (March 11, 1944), 2; *ibid.* (January 29, 1944), 2. Sicard claimed to have called for the expulsion of the Jews as far back as 1936, but I find no warrant for this statement.

17. Saint-Paulien, *Les Maudits* (Paris, 1958), 12, 14.

18. "Les Juifs," special issue of *Je Suis Partout* (April 18, 1938), 2.

19. *Ibid.*, 9.

20. *Ibid.*, 3.

21. Lucien Rebatet, *Les Décombres* (Paris, 1942), 32, 566.

22. *Je Suis Partout* (December 11, 1942), 6.

23. George L. Mosse, "Fascism and the Intellectuals," *The Nature of Fascism*, ed. S. J. Woolf (London, 1968), 212ff.

24. *Ibid.*, *passim*.

25. Stephen Fischer-Galati, "Fascism, Communism and the Jewish Question in Romania," *Jews and Non-Jews in Eastern Europe, 1918–1945*, ed. Bela Vago and George L. Mosse (New York and Jerusalem, 1974), 167–168.

26. Nicholas M. Nagy-Talavera, *The Green Shirts and the Others. A History of Fascism in Hungary and Rumania* (Stanford, Calif., 1970), 260.

27. Carlo Sburlati, *Codreanu Il Capitano* (Rome, 1970), 200.
28. Nagy-Talavera, *op. cit.*, 261, 254; Theodor I. Armon, "La Guardia di Ferro," *Storia Contemporanea*, VII (September 1976), 507.
29. Raul Hilberg, *The Destruction of the European Jews* (Chicago, 1961), 489.
30. Nagy-Talavera, *op. cit.*, 114, 118.
31. *Ibid.*, 184.
32. *Paix et Droit* (January 1937), 4.
33. See, for example, A. J. Sherman, *Island Refuge: Britain and Refugees from the Third Reich* (Berkeley and Los Angeles, 1973).
34. *Paix et Droit* (July 1938), 7.
35. Ladislaus Hory and Martin Broszat, *Der Kroatische Ustascha-Staat 1941–1945* (Stuttgart, 1964), 92.
36. Renzo de Felice, *Storia degli ebrei Italiani sotto il fascismo* (Milan, 1961), 347–350, 296.
37. Luigi Preti, *Impero fascista e ebrei* (Milan, 1968), 87; Michael Ledeen, "The Evolution of Italian Fascist Antisemitism," *Jewish Social Studies*, XXXVII (January 1975), 3–17.
38. De Felice, *op. cit.*, 510.
39. Julius Evola, *Grundrisse der faschistischen Rassenlehre* (Berlin, n.d.), see, for example, 67.
40. *Ibid.*, 219; *La Vita Italiana* (August 1938), 172.
41. J. Evola, *Il Cammino del Cinabro* (Milan, 1963), 172–174. Still later, he accused Mussolini of having confused the idea of race with mere nationalism: Julius Evola, *Il Fascismo* (Rome, 1964), 89.
42. George L. Mosse, *The Crisis of German Ideology* (New York, 1964), 237ff.
43. See, for instance, Uwe Dietrich Adam, *Judenpolitik im Dritten Reich* (Düsseldorf, 1972), 61, 115.
44. Joseph Goebbels, *Der Nazi-Sozi, Fragen und Antworten für den Nationalsozialisten* (Munich, 1931), 12.
45. The incident is referred to in Albert Speer, *Spandauer Tagebücher* (Frankfurt-am-Main, 1975), 463.
46. Adam, *op. cit.*, 114, n. 2.
47. *Ibid.*, 128.
48. See pages 217–218.
49. I have given my views on Hitler's aims in *Crisis of German Ideology*. For the sectarianism of his racism, see 74ff., 294ff.; and Chapter 8 in my *The Nationalization of the Masses* (New York, 1975).
50. Memorandum by Friedrich Krohn, Zs. nr. 69 (Archive of the Institut für Zeitgeschichte, Munich), 5–11; I owe the reference to Professor Rudolph Binion, to whom much thanks. Krohn was the editor of the

Starnberger Seebote, which carried articles sympathetic to National Socialism and anti-Semitism. George Franz-Willing, *Krisen-Jahr der Hitlerbewegung, 1923* (Preussisch Oldendorf, 1975), 132.

51. Speer, *Spandauer Tagebücher*, 174.
52. Margarete Plewnia, *Auf dem Weg zu Hitler, der "Völkische" Publizist Dietrich Eckart* (Bremen, 1970), 56.
53. *Ibid.*, 47.
54. Adolf Hitler, *Mein Kampf* (Munich, 1934), 418.
55. *Ibid.*, 395.
56. Albert Speer, *Erinnerungen* (Frankfurt-am-Main, 1969), 34. The witness was Speer's mother.
57. George L. Mosse, "German Socialists and the Jewish Question in the Weimar Republic," *Year Book XVI of the Leo Baeck Institute* (London, 1971), 123–150.
58. Karl A. Schleunes, *The Twisted Road to Auschwitz, 1933–1939* (Urbana, Ill., 1970), 70.
59. Adam, *op. cit.*, 125.
60. *Ibid.*, 50.
61. "Das Reichsministerium des Inneren und die Judengesetzgebung. Aufzeichnungen von Dr. Bernhard Lösner," *Vierteljahrshefte für Zeitgeschichte*, IX (1961), 266, 268.
62. Adam, *op. cit.*, 125.
63. I have followed Adam, *op. cit.*, 114ff., in the discussion of the Nuremberg Laws.
64. *Ibid.*, 130.
65. *Ibid.*, 143.
66. *Ibid.*, 130, 155.
67. Quoted in *ibid.*, 125, n. 63.
68. Schleunes, *op. cit.*, 226.
69. Adam, *op. cit.*, 200.
70. S. Adler-Rudel, *Ostjuden in Deutschland 1880–1940* (Tübingen, 1959), 112ff.
71. Hitler, *op. cit.*, 54–61.
72. Adam, *op. cit.*, 170–171.
73. *Ibid.*, 196–197.
74. Viktor Reimann, *Innitzer, Kardinal zwischen Hitler und Rom* (Vienna and Munich, 1967), 59, 236.
75. Lionel Kochan, *Pogrom 10 November 1939* (London, 1957), 11, 76.
76. Helmut Krausnick, Hans Buchheim, Martin Broszat, and Hans-Adolf Jacobsen, *Anatomy of the SS State* (New York, 1968), 458.
77. Adam, *op. cit.*, 207ff.

78. *Ibid.*, 210, 219.
79. *Ibid.*, 235.
80. That is, in Hitler's speech of January 30, 1944, at a moment when the Jews of Europe were actually being destroyed, where he asserts that the Jews are ready to celebrate the desolation of Europe with a second Purim. *Ursachen und Folgen vom deutschen Zusammenbruch 1918 und 1945*, XIX, ed. Herbert Michaelis, Ernst Schraepler, and Günter Scheel (Berlin, n.d.), 275.
81. *Ibid.*, 417.

CHAPTER THIRTEEN

1. Lucy Dawidowicz, *The War Against the Jews, 1933–1945* (New York, 1975), 129.
2. *Gesetz zur Verhütung erbkranken Nachwuchs vom 14. Juli 1933, nebst Ausführungsverordnungen*, ed. Arthur Gutt, Ernst Rudin, and Falk Tuttke (Munich, 1936), iii, 176.
3. Gerhard Schmidt, *Selektion in der Heilanstalt 1939–1945* (Stuttgart, 1965), 42–43.
4. W. V. Bayer, "Die Bestätigung der NS—Ideologie in der Medizin unter besonderer berücksichtigung der Euthanasie," *Nationalsozialismus und Universität* (Berlin, 1966), 64.
5. Karl Binding and Alfred Hoch, *Die Freigabe der Vernichtung Lebensunwertes Lebens; ihr Mass und ihre Form* (Leipzig, 1920), 29.
6. Schmidt, *op. cit.*, 42–43.
7. *Ibid.*, 124–125.
8. Quoted in *Ursachen und Folgen vom deutschen Zusammenbruch 1918 und 1945*, XIX, ed. Herbert Michaelis, Ernst Schraepler, and Günter Scheel (Berlin, n.d.), 518, 520.
9. Erwin Leiser, *Nazi Cinema* (New York, 1974), 91ff, 145.
10. See, for example, Uwe Dietrich Adam, *Judenpolitik im Dritten Reich* (Düsseldorf, 1972), 125.
11. Dawidowicz, *op. cit.*, 133.
12. Larry V. Thompson, "Lebensborn and the Eugenics Policy of the Reichsführer SS," *Central European History*, IV (1971), 57–71.
13. Robert L. Koehl, *RKFDV: German Resettlement and Population Policy, 1939–1945* (Cambridge, Mass., 1957), *passim*.
14. Cesare Lombroso, introduction to Gina Lombroso Ferrero, *Criminal Man According to the Classification of Cesare Lombroso* (New York and London, 1911), xvi.
15. *Illustrations of Phrenology, Being a Selection of Articles from the Edinburgh Phrenological Journal and the Transactions of the Edinburgh*

Phrenological Society (Baltimore, 1832), 179; Moritz Benedict, "The Psychology of Crime and Criminals," *The Phrenological Review*, vol. I, no. 3 (October 1905), 38.

16. See pages 83 ff.

17. Louis Chevalier, *Laboring Classes and Dangerous Classes* (New York, 1973), 411.

18. Eva Justin, *Lebensschicksale artfremd erzogener Zigeunerkinder und ihrer Nachkommen* (Berlin, 1944), 3, 7.

19. Michael H. Kater, *Das 'Ahnenerbe' der SS 1935–1945* (Stuttgart, 1974), 206, 207.

20. Raul Hilberg, *The Destruction of the European Jews* (Chicago, 1961), 218.

21. Dickran H. Boyajian, *Armenia, the Case for a Forgotten Genocide* (Westwood, N.J., 1972), 127; Yves Ternon, *Les Arméniens, Histoire d'un Genocide* (Paris, 1977), 201 ff.

22. Adolf Hitler, *Mein Kampf* (Munich, 1934), 197; Karl Prümm, *Die Literatur des Soldatischen Nationalismus der 20er Jahre*, I (Kronberg, 1974), 38 ff.

23. Quoted in Dawidowicz, *op. cit.*, 106.

24. Heinrich Himmler, *Geheimreden 1333 Bis 1945*, ed. Bradley F. Smith and Agnes F. Petersen (Frankfurt-am-Main, 1974), 202.

25. Eberhard Kolb, *Bergen-Belsen* (Hannover, 1962), 273.

26. Rudolf Höss, *Kommandant in Auschwitz*, ed. Martin Broszat (Munich, 1963), 111–112.

27. *Ibid.*, 133.

28. See, for instance, Yehuda Bauer, *Flight and Rescue: Bricha* (New York, 1970).

29. Interrogation of Rudolf Höss, in *Ursachen und Folgen vom deutschen Zusammenbruch. . .* , XIX, 504.

30. Adam, *op. cit.*, 310ff; Dawidowicz, *op. cit.*, 117.

31. The authoritative work on this subject is now Isaiah Trunk, *Judenrat* (New York, 1972).

32. Dawidowicz, *op. cit.*, 206.

33. Hilberg, *op. cit.*, 151.

34. Adam, *op. cit.*, 291–292.

35. Hilberg, *op. cit.*, 218.

36. Dawidowicz, *op. cit.*, 403.

37. Höss, *op. cit.*, 18.

38. Kater, *op. cit.*, 245, 246ff.

39. See page 82.

40. *Ursachen und Folgen vom deutschen Zusammenbruch. . .* , XIX, 538–544.

41. See page 198.

42. See, for example, Bela Vago and George L. Mosse, eds., *Jews and Non-Jews in Eastern Europe, 1918–1945* (Jerusalem and New York, 1974), 171.

43. Frederic B. Chary, *The Bulgarian Jews and the Final Solution* (Pittsburgh, 1972), 141, 189.

44. Y. Jelinek, "The Vatican, the Catholic Church, the Catholics and the Persecution of the Jew During World War II: The Case of Slovakia," in *Jews and Non-Jews in Eastern Europe*, 221–257.

45. See pages 200ff.

46. See pages 201, 202.

47. Xavier Vallat, *Le Problème Juif* (Paris, n.d.), 8. But he is quite unclear about the concept of race and confuses it with the idea of nationality —see, for example, 11.

48. *Le Complot Juif, les Protocols des Sages de Sion*, preface by Darquier de Pellepoix (Paris, ?1939), *passim*.

49. Robert O. Paxton, *La France de Vichy* (Paris, 1973), 180. This included a small number of French Jews.

50. See pages 193ff.

51. *Le Saint Siège et les Victimes de la Guerre, Mars 1939–Décembre 1940; Actes et Documents du Saint Siège Relatifs à la Seconde Guerre Mondiale*, edited by Pierre Blet, et al., VI (Rome, 1972), 94.

52. *Ibid.*, 222.

CHAPTER FOURTEEN

1. For this argument, see Rudolph Binion, *Hitler Among the Germans* (New York, 1976).

2. Hans Zöberlein, quoted in Karl Prümm, "Das Erbe der Front," *Die Deutsche Literatur im Dritten Reich*, ed. Horst Denkler and Karl Prümm (Stuttgart, 1976), 149.

3. J. Huizinga, *The Waning of the Middle Ages* (London, 1924), 186.

4. Hermann Rauschning, *Gespräche mit Hitler* (New York, 1940), 40.

5. W. E. Mosse, *Liberal Europe* (London, 1974), 54; George L. Mosse, *The Culture of Western Europe* (Chicago, 1974), 94ff.

Index

Rodin, Auguste, 85
Rohling, August, 138–41, 156, 182, 205
Rome, 133
Rome, Ancient, 40, 44, 55
Roncalli, Angelo Giuseppe, 229
Rosenberg, Alfred, 45, 46, 140–1, 146, 189, 196, 206
Rothschild, House of, 151, 152
Rousseau, Jean-Jacques, 8, 9, 32
Rowlandson, 29
Rubinstein, Anton, 102
Ruhr occupation, 176, 186
Ruppin, Arthur, 92, 124

S.A. (*Sturmabteilung*), 207
Sachsenhausen concentration camp, 212
St. Paul, 100, 131
Saint-Paulien (Maurice-Ivan Sicard), 195
Salo, Republic of, 201, 230
Sanskrit, 39–41
Savonarola, 55
Saxons, 66–9
Schallmayer, Wilhelm, 79–80
Scheemann, Ludwig, 56
Scheidemann, Philip, 183
Schirach, Baldur von, 203
Schirach, Frau Baldur von, 203
Schlageter, Leo, 186
Schlegel, August Wilhelm, 41
Schlegel, Friedrich, 40–1, 55
Schleyer, Magnus, 138
schoolchildren, survey of German, 91–2
Schönerer, Georg R. von, 99, 161, 168, 204
Schröder, Leopold, 105
Schudt, Johann, 29
Schuler, Alfred, 98–9
Scott, Sir Walter, 26–7, 66
Seipel, Ignaz, 138, 182
Senegalese, 175–6
Serbia, 137, 229
Serpaille, Clement, 57
Sessa, Karl B. A., 44
sex, 85, 101, 108–11, 176

Shakespeare, William, 107
Sicard, Maurice-Ivan, 194–6
Sima, Horia, 198
Simon of Trent, 114
slavery: blacks, 54, 68, 70, 71; Jews, 221–2, 225; Roles, 221–2
Slavs, 37, 42, 68, 161–2
Slovakia, 229
smell, as stereotype, 111–12
social Catholicism, 137–8, 141–2, 146, 147
social Darwinism, 31, 60, 81; *see also* Darwinism
Social Democrats (Germany), 182, 185–7, 207
Social Democrats (Poland), 188
socialism, 61–2, 79; *see also* names, subjects
Socialists (France), 155, 185
Society Against Jewish Arrogance, 183
Society for Racial Hygiene, 81
soldiers, glorification of, 172–5
Solidarité Française, 194
Sorel, Georges, 144, 196
soul: aesthetic of, 10, 23, 25; Aryan, 105–7; Jewish, 106; materialism and, 18; racial, 3, 11, 105–7, 189, 201; smell and, 111
Spain, 193
Spartans, 59, 61
spiritualism, 95–7, 100, 205
SS, 202, 209, 213, 215, 219, 223–5, 230
SS Brigade Charlemagne, 196
Stahl, Julius, 147
Steiner, Rudolf, 96
Stalin, Josef, 186
stereotypes, 67, 233–4; aesthetics, *see* Aesthetics; animal analogies, 14, 22, 26, 28, 68, 117, 139; Aryan, 28, 34, 42, 105–6, 108–10; atavistic, 9–10; blacks, 10, 14, 15, 20, 53, 68, 71, 112, 128ff., 176; cephalic index, 28, 59; classicism, 2; criminality, 84, 177, 219–20; degeneration, racial, 83–4; Hitler's, 110–11; immutability, 31;